Universality and Utopia

Universality and Utopia: The 20th Century *Indigenista* Peruvian Tradition

by Daniel Sacilotto

ANTHEM PRESS

Anthem Press
An imprint of Wimbledon Publishing Company
www.anthempress.com

This edition first published in UK and USA 2026
by ANTHEM PRESS
75–76 Blackfriars Road, London SE1 8HA, UK
or PO Box 9779, London SW19 7ZG, UK
and
244 Madison Ave #116, New York, NY 10016, USA

First published in the UK and USA by Anthem Press in 2023

© 2026 Daniel Sacilotto

The author asserts the moral right to be identified as the author of this work.

All rights reserved. Without limiting the rights under copyright reserved above, no part of this publication may be reproduced, stored or introduced into a retrieval system, or transmitted, in any form or by any means (electronic, mechanical, photocopying, recording or otherwise), without the prior written permission of both the copyright owner and the above publisher of this book.

British Library Cataloguing-in-Publication Data
A catalogue record for this book is available from the British Library.

Library of Congress Control Number: Submitted
A catalog record for this book has been requested.

ISBN-13: 978-1-83999-838-6 (Pbk)
ISBN-10: 1-83999-838-5 (Pbk)

Cover image: Daniel Sacilotto

This title is also available as an eBook.

CONTENTS

List of Figures   vii

Introduction: The Question of *Indigenismo* and the Socialist Imaginary   1
   The Dream of Social Restoration   1
   The Liberal Precursor to Socialist *Indigenismo* in the Late Nineteenth Century   7
   José Carlos Mariátegui's Critique of Liberalism: From Acculturation to Revolution   12
   A Roadmap: From Creative Antagonism to Democratic Crisis   17

1. José Carlos Mariátegui: The Dialectics of Andean Socialism   23
   Introduction: *Indigenismo*, Socialism and Philosophy   23
   Between Representation and Revolution: On Creative Antagonism   24
      Indigenismo as a literary category in Mariátegui's dialectics   24
      An active philosophy: Creative antagonism, myth and faith   37
   Toward a Peruvian Socialism: The Indian Proletariat Subject and the Coming Nation   49

2. From Existential Despair to Collective Jubilation: César Vallejo's Materialist Poetics   67
   Introduction: Vallejo's Universalist Poetics and the Question of *Indigenismo*   67
   Vallejo's Cry of Protest: Nostalgia, Temporality and the Subject of Loss   71
      The nostalgia of absence   71
      The nostalgia for what is to come   78
   A Materialist Reduction of the Subject: Hermetism, Sexuality and Temporality in *Trilce*   80
      The material bases of experience   81
      The collective subject to come: Materiality, animality and history   85

The Paris Years—Vallejo's Aesthetics of Transmutation in *El Arte y la Revolución*	87
The National and the Global: El *Tungsteno* and the Militant Indian Proletariat Subject	96
The Time of Harvest: The Global Proletariat Subject in *Poemas humanos*	101
Nostalgia for the Future: The World of Justice and the Generic Human Subject	106
3. The Light within the World: José María Arguedas and the Limits of Transculturation	113
Introduction: The Limits of the Integrative Dream	113
The Tasks of the Intellectual: Between Regionalism and Universalism	114
The Rehabilitation of Culture against Economism	118
Transculturation and Heterogeneity: Synthesis and Difference	122
Form and Content: Literary Transculturation and the Search for a New Language	126
The Revolutionary Indian Subject in the Narratives of the Village: *Agua*	130
The Collective Indigenous Subject in the Narratives of the "Big Towns": *Yawar Fiesta*	134
The Post-Indian Transcultural Subject: *Todas las sangres*	141
The Limits of Transculturation and the Post-Cultural Subject: *The Foxes*	152
4. The Contemporary Scene: The Future of *Indigenismo* and the Collapse of the Integrative Dream after Arguedas	163
Introduction: A Brief Retrospective—*Indigenismo* after Arguedas	163
The Collapse of the Revolutionary Ideal in Literary *Indigenismo* after Arguedas	166
The Ethical Turn and Democratic Materialism	173
Beyond the Ethical Turn: The Critique of Violence and the Politics of Creation	177
The Collapse of Socialist Productivism and the Proletariat Subject	184
The Crisis of Democracy and the Peruvian Situation Today	187
Bibliography/Cited Works	197
Index	203

LIST OF FIGURES

Diagram 0.1	Figures of the Revolutionary Subject in Socialist *Indigenista* Literature	21
Diagram 1.1	Mariátegui's Dialectics of Peruvian History	37
Diagram 1.2	Mariátegui's System	65
Diagram 3.1	Acculturation, Deculturation, Transculturation	123
Diagram 3.2	Strata in The Foxes	158
Diagram 3.3	Figures of the Subject in Arguedas' Works	161
Diagram 4.1	The Post-Revolutionary Subject	171

INTRODUCTION: THE QUESTION OF *INDIGENISMO* AND THE SOCIALIST IMAGINARY

The Dream of Social Restoration

In a broad sense, *indigenismo* is a literature about the rural *indio* written by the urban mestizo, describing the particularities of their native traditions and critically addressing the history of their subjugation since colonial times.[1] In this general sense, *indigenismo* is an urban production written with an urban audience in mind, shaped by and responding to the political debates that transpired among city intellectuals and activists.[2] Its origins can be dated back,[3] at least, to Narciso Aréstegui's 1848 novel *El padre Horán*, which narrates the abuses of religious and state authorities in the Peruvian republic since the mid-nineteenth century, tracing back the origins of the social division between the rural Indian and the mestizo to the cultural clash unleashed by the colonial experience.[4] Toward the turn of the twentieth century, however, *indigenismo* was more commonly dated to the publication of Clorinda Matto de Turner's *Aves sin nido* in 1889. In this sense, the incipient *indigenista*

---

1 Even more broadly, the term *indigenismo* is used to designate not only a literary tradition(s), but to refer to all representations of the rural Indian, regardless of genre or medium. In this sense, *indigenismo* encompasses all kinds of cultural production and domains of practice and can be dated back to the chronicles of the conquest written by Fray Bartolomé de las Casas (1474–1566).
2 Efraín Kristal traces back the relations between the literary and political ambience within which *indigenismo* is configured since Aréstegui's novel, situating the movement in a wider spectrum of intellectual debates and political circumstances. See Kristal, Efraín. *The Andes Viewed from the City: Literary and Political Discourse on the Indian in Peru, 1848–1930*, P. Lang, 1987.
3 Castro Arenas, Mario, *La novela peruana y la evolución social*, J. Godard, 1967; Tord, Luis Enrique, *El indio en los ensayistas Peruanos 1848–1948*, Editoriales Unidas, 1978.
4 Aréstegui in fact traces the rift between the rural Indian and the mestizo to the fateful encounter between the Inca Atahualpa and the fray Valverde in 1532.

literature formed part of a new social realist aesthetic that moved away from the tenets of Ricardo Palma's *costumbrismo*, inspired by Manuel González Prada's endorsement of urban modernization and education to overcome the exploitation of the Indian by coastal and rural oligarchies.

In its more narrow and technical uses, the term *"indigenismo"* designates different periodizations and genealogies through which intellectuals, artists and activists thematized the situation of the rural Indian in the nation, guided by different philosophical ideals, aesthetic styles and political orientations. Since its definition by José Carlos Mariátegui (1928),[5] *indigenismo* has been understood thus in various ways: as the "cosmopolitan" period in Peruvian literary history in which the representations of the Indian by the mestizo break with colonial forms and sterile idealizations, acquiring a higher degree of authenticity (Mariátegui); as a literature that depicts processes of "transculturation" between Western and pre-Hispanic forms of cultural production (Ángel Rama[6]); as a utopian provincialist archaism guided by a dangerous tendency to fetishize the precolonial Amerindian past, confusing fiction and reality (Vargas Llosa[7]); as a process in which irreducibly heterogeneous social, economic and cultural contexts interact (Cornejo Polar[8]), and so on.[9] This rich polysemy suggests to us that any assessment of *indigenismo* must

---

5 Unless noted, all references to Mariátegui (1928) are cited from: *Seven Interpretative Essays on Peruvian Reality*, translated by Jorge Basadre U. of Texas Press, Austin. Copyright 1971, available in full at https://www.marxists.org/archive/mariateg/works/7-interpretive-essays.htm
6 Rama, Ángel. *Transculturación narrativa en América Latina*, Siglo XXI, 1982.
7 Cornejo Polar, Antonio. "El indigenismo y las literaturas heterogéneas," *Revista de Crítica Literaria Latinoamericana*, no. 7–8, Latinoamericana Editores, 1978, pp. 6–21.
8 Vargas Llosa, Mario. *La utopía arcaica*, Fondo de Lectura Económica, 1997.
9 In his book *Los narradores andinos, herederos de Arguedas*, Nieto Degregori subsumes the history of representations of the Indian world under the term "Andean narratives" (*"narrativa andina"*) rather than "indigenismo," in contrast to so-called creole narratives whose representational matrix is centered in the urban and coastal space. In contrast, in *La narrativa indigenista*, Tomás G. Escajadillo distinguishes between two historical moments: *indigenismo* proper, which evinces a gulf between representing agent and represented Indian—dating back to the 1920s, and to the work of López Albújar—and *neo-indigenismo*, in which the Indigenous world seeks to be represented from within, as in the works of Ciro Alegría and José María Arguedas. A more comprehensive assessment of these variegated conceptual frameworks would demand a separate study. See Degregori, Nieto. "Los narradores andinos herederos de Arguedas," in Arguedas y el Perú de Hoy, edited by Carmen María Pinilla, Gonzalo Portocarrero Maisch, Cecilia Rivera, Carla Sagástegui, SUR Casa de Estudios del Socialismo, 2005; Escajadillo, Tomás. *La narrativa indigenista peruana*, Amaru Editores, 1994.

be understood relative to the scope and aims that each author assigns to the term, and to its place within a specific methodological and narrative frameworks guided by both theoretical principles and political ideals.

Across its divergent manifestations and definitions, what is clear is that in the late nineteenth century literary *indigenismo* emerges as an attempt to narrativize the historic reality and destiny of a nation born under the conditions of social fissure, confronting the lingering effects of the colonial experience after the independence.[10] Accordingly, since its inception *indigenista* literature evinces at once an ambition toward descriptive realism and utopian projection: it confronts social reality in its inherent disarticulation and contradictions, but it also imagines and anticipates the conditions necessary to overcome such disarticulation, giving rise to a genuine, integral national identity. In the terms of Reinhart Koselleck (2004), we can therefore say that *indigenista* narratives have fulfilled a double function: first, to construct a "space of experience" through which one interprets the past from the perspective of the present; second, to construct a "horizon of expectation" in which alternative futures are conceived.[11] To describe the articulation and fulfillment of these two functions, *indigenista* narratives envisaged new forms of individual and collective agency, whose role would be to mediate the passage from the inarticulate present, marked by the shadow of colonialism, to the national future: new forms of subjectivity that anticipate *the nation to come*.

The following study proposes to examine the different forms of revolutionary subjectivity developed in the twentieth-century Peruvian *indigenista* socialist tradition and their articulation of aesthetic, philosophical and political ideals, following from the works of José Carlos Mariátegui in the 1920s, and tracing their development in the literary works of César Vallejo and José María Arguedas. As I aim to show, the articulation of theoretical and political ideals in *indigenista* works comprises the attempt by intellectuals, writers and activists to think of the conditions of an alternative modernity for Peruvian society, not only representing the historic oppression of the rural Indian since colonial

---

10 Marquez characterizes *indigenismo* as a movement of "ideological and aesthetic projections," encompassing not only literary or aesthetic works, but also the theoretical or philosophical accounts used to assess the place of such works, their authors and traditions. See Marquez, Ismael. "The Andean Novel," in *The Cambridge Companion to the Latin American Novel* , edited by Efraín Kristal, Cambridge University Press. 2005 pp. 143.
11 Koselleck, Reinhart. *Futures Past—On the Semantics of Historical Time*, translated by Keith Trible. Columbia University press, 2004. pp 32.

times, but conceiving new forms of subjectivity as integral to an emancipatory process leading to the construction of a Peruvian nation. To realize this vision, socialist *indigenista* writers resisted the liberal view, championed among others by Manuel González Prada, according to which the destiny of the emerging republics in the Andean region was that of capitalist modernization, through which the rural Indian would become assimilated to the norms of Western culture in the growing city. Instead, they proposed to think of processes of constructive mediation between the Western and Indigenous productive modalities and cultural norms, while imagining a new emerging consciousness that traversed the tensions between the rural Indian and the urban mestizo.

Studying the ambition of the *indigenista* socialist project to think of a possible reconciliation between modernity and tradition has two principal aims. First, to engage in a more nuanced critical appraisal of the aspirations and theoretical foundations guiding *indigenista* writers, in their attempts to coordinate the tasks of literature and politics by adapting the principles of socialist philosophy to the Peruvian socioeconomic and cultural context. Second, to challenge readings of *indigenismo* as a kind of "regionalist," "culturalist" or "telluric literature," restricted to describing its local traditions (often to point of fetishism).[12] Rather, I will argue that the emphasis on forging constructive mediations between the Western and pre-Hispanic worlds reveals the complementarity that *indigenista* writers attempted to find between the aims of regionalism and those of universalism, resolving the perceived contradiction between them.[13] For socialist *indigenista* writers conceived of socialist philosophy and emancipatory politics as a self-correcting descriptive and

---

12 Just to take three paradigmatic exemplars, in *Journeys Through the Labyrinth* Gerald Martin categorizes the *indigenista* works of Ciro Alegría and José María Arguedas under the rubric of the "social realist" narrative in Latin American literature, characterized by a "telluric" tendency, and predating the modernist experimentation of the so-called (Joycean moment, Juan Rulfo, Miguel Ángel Asturias, Jorge Luis Borges, etc.). In a more critical tone, Rafael Gutierrez Girardot places *indigenismo* alongside other variants of "Americanisms" and "tropicalisms," defined by fetishistic isolationism. Finally, Mario Vargas Llosa characterizes *indigenista* narrative as part of what he names "the archaic utopia" which confuses reality and fiction as it idealizes a bygone past (cf. Chapter IV).

13 In his recent study about the "Latin American universalist tradition," and following Rafael Gutierrez Girardot's verdict, Fernando Zalamea contrasts the universalist vector following downstream from the works of Bello, Henriquez Ureña and Rodó, to the "Americanist," "tropicalist" and "indigenista" regionalisms of the continent. See Zalamea, Fernando. *Ariel y Arisbe: evolución y evaluación del concepto de América Latina en el siglo XX*, convenio Andrés Bello, 2000, pp. 5.

prescriptive enterprise, where its central concepts, methods and aspirations had to be measured against ever-changing historical circumstances.[14] As we shall see, it is in anticipating a "national literature" that coincides with the prospects of social integration that the term *indigenismo* is formally introduced in Mariátegui's *Seven Essays*, as part of a three-stage historical dialectic leading from the colonial past to the socialist future.[15] Mariátegui identifies *indigenismo* as a transitory moment in Peruvian literature, characterized by an unprecedented degree of authenticity in its representation of the Andean world and paving the way for an "Indigenous literature" written by the *indio* themselves. The Indian was thus to join urban revolutionary intellectuals and workers in the formation of a new "national consciousness" that would obviate the need for a liberal capitalist model of social development.

In this regard, it is clear that, despite its *relative realism* in relation to the *Indianista* representations that preceded the "cosmopolitan" social realist moment in Peruvian literature in the nineteenth century, Mariátegui believed that *indigenismo* was necessarily still an idealization of the rural Indian, insofar as it remained a literature written by mestizos. At the same time, Mariátegui's own characterization of the problem of the Indian as an "economic problem" and his ideal for a "Peruvian socialism" would become subsequently interrogated. Socialist *indigenista* writers would thereby retrospectively assess the theoretical and practical limitations of the emancipatory and integrative ideal as forecast by Mariátegui's dialectical narrative, modifying the figurations of the revolutionary subject and the historical process to come. In tracing this historical unfolding, I propose to place the Peruvian socialist *indigenista* search for a collective future in the context of a wider problematic concerning the ensuing legacy of socialism and the crises of democracy in the twenty-first century. My study thus serves the purposes of what Bruno Bosteels (2012) has

---

14 Terra Rodrigues, Cassiano, and Daniel Campos. "Originality and Resistance in Latin American Culture," in *Inter-American Journal of Philosophy*, Vol. I, No. I, 2016, pp. 61–62.

15 As Efraín Kristal shows, however, the "pretension to realism" is by no means the prerogative of the socialist approach to *indigenismo*, but more generally characterizes the circular logic by virtue of which critics evaluate the value of literary tradition on the basis of a conception of "authenticity" which coincides with and presupposes in advance the author's political–theoretical proclivities: "Critics use the same norms to evaluate the degree to which characters and situations are realistic that writers use to create fictional characters and situations. [...] Once a particular critic has chosen a writer with an 'appropriate' view of the Indian to set the stage, he or she then describes who to include and exclude from a history of 'imperfect' literary works which lead to the 'satisfactory' indigenista novel [or narrative]" (Kristal 1987: 7–8).

named the historical work of "genealogical counter-memory" incumbent upon any contemporary historical and literary assessment of the legacy of Marxism in Latin America: not a mere historiographical retrieval or apology of exhausted political ideals, but an attempt to excavate latent possibilities so as to critically and constructively address the prospects of emancipatory politics and the crisis of democracy in the contemporary world:

> [T]he point of the exercises of genealogical counter-memory [...] is not to retrieve such subjective elements by inserting them into a nostalgic re-objectification of the past, but rather to reactivate their silent and still untapped resources for the sake of a critique of the present. (Bosteels 2012: 7)

Extending this coordinated critical-constructive and retrospective-prescriptive task, this work examines how socialist *indigenista* writers interrogated the priority accorded to the moment of insurrectionary violence inherent to the revolutionary process, as well as the nationalist and economic emphasis given by Mariátegui's incipient coordination of emancipatory politics with a new kind of literary production. Instead, they proposed to emphasize the role of *creation* and *integration* across autonomous but communicating domains of human practice: scientific-philosophical theories, artistic-literary experiments and political–social programs.[16] It is in this wider context that I assess the ambitions of *indigenista* writers, departing from a consideration of what Mariátegui names "creative antagonism," and elaborated in different ways in the works of Vallejo and Arguedas.

---

16 In the first part of *Logics of Worlds*, Alain Badiou outlines his rejection to three predominant philosophical and critical approaches to the theorization of the subject, which prevent a thinking of human agency outside contemporary ideology: (1) The phenomenological conception of the subject: as the conscious pole which registers experiences through a schema of reflexivity (separating conscious from non-conscious apprehension, for instance). This conception attempts an impossible approximation toward conceptually unmediated presence. (2) The moralist conception of the subject, assigned to the "bioethical" imperative of recognizing and respecting the Other as subject for life; finally flattening the subject "onto the empirical manifestness of the living body." This conception is insensitive to the possibility of a constructive vision of the subject, since it remains a priori circumscribed to specific or empirical normative registers. (3) The Althusserian conception of the subject as an *ideological* construct: directly interpolated by statist designations, reducing the subject to being the effect of discourse and rhetoric and leaving no room for its material being in the form of a body (Ibid.). This position eradicates the possibility of situating the subject outside the representational protocols of state legislation, thus blocking a thinking of the transformative (material) power of subjective agency (Badiou 2009: 48).

INTRODUCTION

In the following section, by way of introduction, I briefly situate the nascent Peruvian socialist project developed by Mariátegui in relation to "problem of the Indian" at the turn of the twentieth century, establishing an approach to the development of *indigenismo* since and after Mariátegui.

The Liberal Precursor to Socialist *Indigenismo* in the Late Nineteenth Century

As Antonio Cornejo Polar remarks in his preface to Clorinda Matto de Turner's 1989 novel *Torn From the Nest* (*Aves sin nido*), the demand for a social realist perspective addressing the fragmentation of the Peruvian nation was exacerbated in the aftermath of War of the Pacific in 1979. The war had traumatically revealed the "fragile constitution of Peruvian society, its unqualified disintegration, and the substantial failure of the different [...] national projects assumed until then by the diverse parts of the ruling class"[17] (Cornejo Polar 1994: 3, my translation). Speaking to this shift in the collective consciousness of the nation in general, and of urban intellectuals in particular, on 29 July 1888, Manuel González Prada had given his *Discurso en el Politeama*, diagnosing the fundamental reason behind the lingering disarticulation of the Peruvian nation: it stemmed from a generalized premodern backwardness and ignorance persisting from the colonial period, which generated a complicity between state authorities and the feudal oligarchic system that kept the Indian under servitude:

> Chile's brutal hand tore our flesh and battered our bones; but the true victors, the enemies' arms, were our ignorance and our spirit of servitude. [...] If of the Indian we made a servant, what country will he defend? As the serf from the middle-ages, it will only fight for the feudal lord.[18] (González Prada 1998, my translation)

---

17 Cornejo Polar, Antonio. "Aves sin Nido como alegoría nacional," in Matto de Turner, Clorinda. *Aves sin Nido*, Biblioteca Ayacucho, 1994.

> "La derrota fue la casi inevitable culminación de un proceso de deterioro económico, social, político y ético, y mostró—más que la obvia debilidad militar- la muy endeble constitución de la sociedad peruana, su desintegración sin atenuantes y el fracaso sustancial de los distintos (pero muy parecidos) proyectos nacionales que habían sido asumidos hasta entonces por las diversas (aunque también muy parecidas) fracciones de la clase-casta dirigente."

18 González Prada, Manuel, "Discurso en el Politeama," in *Pájinas libres*, edited by Thomas Ward, 1998, http://evergreen.loyola.edu/tward/www/gp/libros/paginas/pajinas6.html)

For González Prada, to overcome the spirit of servitude meant to inculcate a "just hatred" (*odio justo*) capable of confronting the wound of the colonial past, at the same time projecting a vision of the future through a process of modernization, guided by educational reform and professionalization of the Indian. In overcoming the inarticulacy of the nation, such a reformist agenda would progressively integrate the rural Indian into the life of the city and assimilate them to Western cultural norms. González Prada anticipates the triumph of science and industrial technology, giving birth to a new epistemic regime, continuous with the pedagogical and professional urban milieu, rendering obsolete the theological and metaphysical knowledge that was still hegemonic in the Peruvian university.[19] Paving the transition away from the premodern "barbarism" of the colonial world toward a true cultural independence emblemized by modern "civilization," the figure of *the enlightened mestizo* appears as the privileged mediating agent of historical change, an exceptional subjective type enjoying not only greater knowledge in relation to the oligarchic class, but crucially a superior *moral* character. In short, the enlightened mestizo was to become the emblem of an *atheological humanist ethics* "towering over and above scientific specialization or humanistic culture."

> Now let us see what is understood by civilization. Over industry and art, over science and learning, morality gleams like a shining light on the apex of a great pyramid. Not theological morality based on punishment after death, but humane morality which seeks no sanction far removed from the world. The essence of morality, for individuals as well as for societies, consists in transforming the struggle of man against man into a mutual accord for living. Where there is no justice, pity, or benevolence, there is no civilization; where the struggle for life is made the law of society, barbarism reigns. What does it avail to acquire the wisdom of an Aristotle if one's heart is that of a tiger? What is there worthwhile in having the talent of a Michelangelo if

---

"La mano brutal de Chile despedazó nuestra carne i machacó nuestros huesos; pero los verdaderos vencedores, las armas del enemigo, fueron nuestra ignorancia i nuestro espíritu de servidumbre. [...] Si del indio hicimos un siervo ¿qué patria defenderá? Como el siervo de la Edad media, sólo combatirá por el señor feudal."

19 González Prada had written: "No hablo, señores, de la ciencia momificada que va reduciéndose a polvo en nuestras universidades retrógradas: hablo de la Ciencia robustecida con la sangre del siglo, de la Ciencia con ideas de radio jigantesco, de la Ciencia que trasciende a juventud i sabe a miel de panales griegos, de la Ciencia positiva que en sólo un siglo de aplicaciones industriales produjo más bienes a la Humanidad que milenios enteros de Teolojía i Metafísica."

one has the soul of a pig? It is better to go through the world distilling the honey of goodness than shedding the light of art and science. The societies that deserve to be called highly civilized are those in which the practice of the good has become a habitual obligation and the beneficent act instinctive. Have they any right to consider the Indian incapable of civilization? (Ibid.)

A new literary aesthetic orientation would assist in articulating the idealized modernizing process coordinating cultural assimilation, scientific-humanistic education and professionalization. This vision informs the liberal *indigenista* narratives of the late nineteenth century and becomes clearly expressed in Clorinda Matto de Turner's preface to her novel Torn From the Nest. She describes the inextricability of the *realist* and *utopian* impetus of a rising cosmopolitan spirit, whose historical locus is the modern city, arguing that "the flexibility of the aerial Limeñan forms that carry thought to the blue of the skies has come with all the realism of the epoch in which it was conceived" (Matto de Turner 1895: 2).[20] At the same time, Matto de Turner's pronouncement also marks a decisive shift in the dominant mode of literary prose and the representations of the rural Indian envisaged by mestizo intellectuals. Such a movement coincides with an ideological and stylistic shift away from the ornamental qualities and satirical kernel associated with Ricardo Palma's *costumbrismo*, and toward a new kind of social realist aesthetic in concert with liberal modern ideals. Accordingly, while her 1884 collection *Tradiciones Cuzqueñas* had already attempted an approximation to the rural world, it remained within the descriptivist tenets of *costumbrismo*, depicting the life and customs of the Indian without thereby conceiving of a solution or path toward social change; indeed, it was only under the influence of González Prada's atheological ethics and modernizing vision that Matto de Turner conceives of the emancipation of the Indian within the horizon of an integral future for the Peruvian nation.[21] Literary creation was thus to assume the historic

---

20 Matto de Turner, Clorinda. *Herencia*, Impresa Masías- Baquijano, 1895.
21 Matto de Turner situates González Prada's liberal ideas and social typology to allegorize Peruvian society in the fictional setting of the town of Killac, modeled on the southern sierra of the Cuzco region. The characterological frame which structures these texts thus closely mirror González Prada's typology of Peruvian society, in which three basic subjective positions were discerned: the joint ignorance of abusive and corrupt institutional powers, the uneducated Indian victims and finally the educated Enlightened mestizo who realize the prospect of modernization. In *Aves sin*

responsibility of intellectuals to provide the moral ground for a new collective consciousness, producing "a photograph that stereotypes the vices and virtues of a people, with the corresponding moral corrective for the former and homage of admiration for the latter" (Matto de Turner 1994: 3).[22]

Despite its realist impetus, a lingering debt to the aesthetics of *costumbrismo* remains clearly visible in Matto de Turner's novel trilogy. For the imperative to faithfully represent Peruvian social reality and its divisions turned out to require, in her own words, a *stereotypical* characterization of "the vices and virtues" of a society. Accordingly, the characterological frame that structures the novel closely mirrors González Prada's idealized typology of Peruvian society, in which three basic positions are defined in terms of their educational status: (i) the integral complicity between ignorant institutional powers, representing the colonial remnants in the present; (ii) the innocent but uneducated Indian victims, representing the agonic rabble of the pre-Columbian past and (iii) the enlightened mestizo, who represents the project of the emancipation of the Indian within the collective future of urban modernization. In *Aves sin Nido*, Matto de Turner accordingly focuses on the portrayal of the uneducated rural authorities, the *notables*, conforming to what González Prada named in *Pájinas libres* "the stupefying trinity against the Indian" ("*la trinidad embrutecedora del indio*"): the priests (*curas*), the policing governors (*governadores*) and the local mayors (*caciques-alcaldes*). In relation to the three morally corrupt figures of the notables, the uneducated but morally pure rural Indian appears destined to a shadow of its ancestral imperial grandeur, with no hope for self-vindication.

> Three hundred years since the Indian ruminates in the inferior layers of civilization, having become a hybrid of the vices of the barbarian without the virtues of the European: teach it to read and write, and you shall see whether in a quarter of a century the dignity of Man may rise or not. You, school teachers, ought to vindicate a race that falls asleep under the tyranny of the peace judge, the governor and priest, that stupefying trinity of the Indian. (González Prada 2009)

Nido, Matto de Turner focuses on the portrayal of the uneducated rural authorities, the notables, as they conform to what Prada called a "stupefying trinity" of domination against the rural Indian ("*la Trinidad embrutecedora del indio*"): the priests ("*curas*"), the policing governors ("*gobernadores*") and the local "majors" ("*caciques-alcaldes*.") The Marin couple, Lucía and Fernando, in turn assumes the role of the enlightened mestizo, facilitating the emancipation of the Indian from subjugation under the rule of the notables, delivering the promise of migration and education in the city.

22 Matto de Turner, Clorinda, *Aves sin Nido*, Biblioteca Ayacucho, 1994.

Framing this social topology into a subjective typology, Matto de Turner allegorizes Peruvian society by a "stereotypical" depiction of characteristic ethical qualities, its "vices and virtues." The story is set in the fictional setting of the town of Kilac, modeled in the Cuzco region. The Marin couple, Lucía and Don Fernando, assumes the role of the enlightened creoles, facilitating the transition of the Indian into the city space and away from the abusive rule of the *notables*. Acting as a cultural and social mediator, Lucía is at once characterized by her humanistic curiosity and her desire to learn about the culture of the rural Indian, as she bears witness to the abuses of the notables directed against the Yupanqui family, victims to economic extortion and sexual predation. At once victimized and idealized, Matto de Turner thereby represents the rural Indian as an illiterate and helpless creature shorn of any agency, torn from without yet in itself morally pure, so that "when the unhappy Peruvian Indian does evil, it is because he is either forced by oppression, or desperate from abuse" (Kristal 1987: 131). As such, they depend on the empathic guidance of the educated mestizo, who facilitates their transition to the life of the city and literate-professional Western norms of sociality and production. It is finally the task of morally righteous mestizo pedagogues to assist the "vindication" of the rural Indian, integrating them to the liberal dream of a modern nation to come.

Lack of education not only defines the impotence of the Indian victim against their oligarchic rulers; however, it also contrasts with the power of the notables. Indeed, both the notables and the oligarchic rulers jointly compose the barbaric vortex of the rural world and its relative backwardness in relation to the nascent enlightenment of the city. The narrative depicts the false spirituality of corrupt religious authorities, exemplified by the sexual abuses of Father Vargas, who "inspired from the first moment serious doubts that, in the Seminar, he had been instructed and learned Theology or Latin." In turn, Governor don Sebastian Pancorbo reveals a complementary perversion, rooted not only in a lack of education, but also of tact and even of spiritual vitality: his bloodless expression conceals an irremediable intellectual mediocrity, as we learn that "he received elementary school education as basic as the three years in which he was in a city school allowed."

Conspicuously, within González Prada's typology and Matto de Turner's characterology, the figure of *the educated Indian* remains absent, not only because it does not exist in the present, but in an important sense because it *cannot* exist. For the rural Indian must depend on the enlightened mestizo to transform themselves into something altogether other, subjected to geographical migration, ethnic miscegenation, educational professionalization and social acculturation.[23]

José Carlos Mariátegui's Critique of Liberalism: From Acculturation to Revolution

It is precisely in response to the liberal modernizing vision of the coming nation, and the role of the Indian within it, that the socialist *indigenista* tradition takes shape during the first decades of the twentieth century. Developing a three-stage dialectic of Peruvian history in his *Seven Interpretative Essays on Peruvian Reality*, José Carlos Mariátegui notably criticizes Manuel González Prada's liberal views and the concomitant fate of assimilation prescribed to the rural Indian. His critique is ridden with ambivalence; he celebrates the experimental and "cosmopolitan" cultural liberation from the colonial age toward a social realist and thoroughly modern vision, supporting González Prada's call for the eradication of the landlord oligarchy. At the same time, he sharply dissociates the aspiration toward social integration from the liberal solution of capitalist modernization and Westernizing urbanization, which would transform the acculturated Indians into small-property owners as the country transitioned into an industrial economy. Adhering to the Marxist priority of economic determinations in the name of a materialist and realist view that would stand against the lingering romanticism of the liberal imaginary, Mariátegui above all takes issue with González Prada's focus on morality and the role of a pedagogical program centered on humanistic-professional formation when confronting the "problem of the Indian." For Mariátegui, the realism required by a true emancipatory and modern vision coeval with socialist principles begins by going beyond the negation of the latifundio and its moral condemnation, to positively affirm of the Indian's *right to land*.

> First, we protest against the instinctive attempt of the criollo or mestizo to reduce it to an exclusively administrative, pedagogical, ethnic, or moral problem in order to avoid at all cost recognizing its economic aspect.

---

23 Matto de Turner avows the role of immigration as potentially serving to resolve the ethnic division which underlies the social fragmentation of the nation in the country. In her 1889 essay *El Perú Ilustrado*, she claims, "We call for foreign immigration that can mend our country through the mixture of blood. In our country, the majority of the population is composed of feeble people and tubercular sufferers both physically and morally speaking" (Matto de Turner 2017: my translation). See Matto de Turner, *El Perú ilustrado: 23 de Noviembre de 1889*, Forgotten Books, 2017.

Therefore, it would be absurd to accuse us of being romantic or literary. By identifying it as primarily a socio-economic problem, we are taking the least romantic and literary position possible. We are not satisfied to assert the Indian's right to education, culture, progress, love, and heaven. We begin by categorically asserting his right to land.[24] (Mariátegui 1928)

The hope that education—promoted through the slogan "science and freedom" (*ciencia y libertad*)—would suffice to eradicate the landlord oligarchy and resolve the alienation and exploitation of the rural Indian was for Mariátegui hopelessly naïve. For the prescient colonial heritage and its intellectual backwardness permeated not only the rural economy but also the urban educational institutions which were supposed to mediate the transition of the Indian into the urban space.

In particular, Mariátegui argues that the Peruvian schooling system had remained under the control of bourgeois culture, breeding an elitist consciousness in which liberal and religious conservatism unwittingly converged, reiterating the colonial heritage rather than assisting in the process of national cultural independence:

> The republic feels and declares its loyalty to the viceroyalty and, like the viceroyalty, it belongs more to the colonizers than to the rulers. The feelings and interests of four-fifths of the population play almost no role in the formation of the national identity and institutions. Peruvian education, therefore, has a colonial rather than a national character. (Ibid.)

> The problem of Indian illiteracy goes beyond the pedagogical sphere. It becomes increasingly evident that to teach a man to read and write is not to educate him. Primary school does not redeem the Indian morally and socially. The first real step toward his redemption must be to free him from serfdom.[25] (Mariátegui, 1971, my translation)

In tracing the continuity between the emerging "bourgeois consciousness" and the liberal call for modernization emblemized by the views of González Prada, Mariátegui diagnoses a deeper complicity between the colonial

---

24 Mariátegui 1928. https://www.marxists.org/archive/mariateg/works/7-interpretive-essays/essay03.htm
25 Mariátegui, José Carlos, *Seven Interpretative Essays on Peruvian Reality*, translated by Jorge Basadre, University of Texas Press, 1971. Available at: https://www.marxists.org/archive/mariateg/works/7-interpretive-essays/essay04.htm

remnants in the economy, and the rise of an urban middle class and mestizo intellectuals, jointly protecting their class privilege. Prioritizing morality and scientific-humanistic education encouraged the formation of "writers and lawyers," whose abstract knowledge was indifferent to a democratic reorientation of the pedagogical ideal of making culture accessible to all:

> The liberals, the old landholding aristocracy, and the new urban middle class all studied together in the humanities. They liked to think of universities and colleges as factories producing writers and lawyers. The liberals enjoyed rhetoric as much as the conservatives. No one was interested in a practical orientation encouraging work in commerce or industry, still less in a democratic orientation making culture accessible to all. (Ibid.)

For Mariátegui, the complicity between bourgeois intellectuals and educational institutions would only be aggravated with the counter-reformism of the *civilista* movement between 1924 and 1927 in the capital, even though he applauded the thriving reform movement in the University of Cuzco during the same years.

This reorientation away from the professionalism and intellectualism fostered by liberals in the city implied a definitive change of emphasis in the conception of *education*: its primary role was not to disseminate knowledge, but to function as a vehicle for social change. As we shall see below, this is precisely the role of *socialism* conceived as what Mariátegui names *an active philosophy*, that is, a philosophical *realist* program that, in strict Marxian terms, does not merely aim to represent the world, but to transform it. Subtracting the ideal of modernization from the urban capitalist destiny prescribed by the cosmopolitan imaginary, Mariátegui thereby argues that socialism constitutes "the antithesis of liberalism," pointing to the latter's failure to lay the foundations for civilizational and technological progress, despite its intellectual advances.

> Socialist thought proclaims itself anti-liberal as a result of dialectical necessity, so that socialism appears in History as the antithesis of liberalism, concretely defined as the doctrine of capitalist society. But it does not represent the liberal patrimony, in its civilizing value, at the same time as it doesn't renounce the capitalist heritage, in what concerns its technical progress.[26] (Mariátegui 1929)

---

26 Mariátegui, José Carlos, "Breve Epílogo," in *Variedades*, March 13, 1929. https://www.marxists.org/espanol/mariateg/oc/historia_de_la_crisis_mundial/paginas/breve%20epilogo.htm

Contemporary socialism—other historical periods have had other kinds of socialism under different names—is the antithesis of liberalism; but it is born from its womb and is nourished on its experiences. It does not disdain the intellectual achievements of liberalism, only its limitations. It appreciates and understands everything that is positive in the liberal ideal; it condemns and attacks what is negative and selfish in it. (Mariátegui 1928)[27]

As Juan Carlos Ubilluz (2017) has argued, this ideological shift toward socialism in the pursuit for an alternative modern national horizon was not only inspired by the international socialist movement but also responded to local Indigenous insurrections at the turn of the century: Atusparia (1885), Rumi Maqui (1915) and above all The Great Uprising of the South ("*La Gran Sublevación del Sur*," 1920–23.[28]

For Mariátegui, socialist thinkers had organized this insurrectionary furor to reconceive the relation between the Indian and the mestizo, as well as the kind of socioeconomic productive model for a future Peruvian society. In his 1929 *Ideological Theses*, he will argue that educating the masses and the awakening of "class consciousness," for the rural Indian could only be achieved through the syndical and political construction of a "worker's avant-garde," rather than from academic centers oriented toward legal and professional training. Laying out what would become a recurrent motif throughout *indigenista* literary narratives, this pedagogical program implied that the urban and rural Indian worker was to progressively attain independence from the tutelage of revolutionary mestizo intellectuals, returning to their communities to become the agents of their own emancipation:

In sight of the progressive ideological education of the Indigenous masses, the worker's avant-garde lays at its disposal those militants of the Indian race, in the mines or urban centers, particularly in the latter, coming into contact with the syndical and political movement. They assimilate principles and train themselves to play a role in the education of their race. It is common that workers who come from the Indian

---

27 Mariátegui 1928. https://www.marxists.org/archive/mariateg/works/7-interpretive-essays/essay03.htm
28 Ubilluz, Juan Carlos. *La Venganza del Indio: Ensayos de interpretación por lo real en la narrativa indigenista*, Fondo de Cultura Económica, 2017.

context return temporarily or definitively to it.[29] (Mariátegui 1929, my translation)

This line of criticism against the liberal modern and in favor of socialism becomes reflected in Mariátegui's assessment of the cosmopolitan literature to which *indigenista* writers belonged. For just as González Prada elided the need for class consciousness by emphasizing moral and pedagogical factors, so the literary representation of the rural Indian as a "pure" and wretched victim in early *indigenista* literature failed to conceive of a revolutionary destiny for the rural Indian facing the persistence of the latifundio. The imagined journey of the rural Indian from its exploitation under the landlord oligarchy into the modern city was premised on a reductive idealization that deprived them from all active potentials and submitted them to the passive destiny of cultural assimilation.

For Mariátegui, the emergence of the *indigenista* socialist tradition within the cosmopolitan period of Peruvian literary history—legible above all in Valcárcel's *Tempest in the Andes* (1927) as well as César Vallejo's *The Black Heralds* (1919) and *Trilce* (1922)—coincides with the progressive realization of a realist aesthetics and nationalist vision beyond the liberal capitalist model. To the righteous enlightened mestizo that facilitates the acculturation of the Indian, Mariátegui opposes the figure of the *socialist mestizo revolutionary*, integrating the efforts of intellectuals and workers, and the urban and social productive worlds. Nevertheless, this figure is but a "vanishing mediator" in Peruvian history, preparing and anticipating the rise of an *Indian revolutionary subject* that no longer depends on the mestizo for its liberation and representation. The continuity between the emerging socialist movement and *indigenista* literature was then bound to the search for a new realist disposition as much as a new utopian vision, articulating a reciprocal relation binding theoretical and practical imperatives: *from the local to the universal*—understanding the dynamics of Peruvian history within the internationalist and collectivist principles

---

29 Mariátegui, José Carlos. "El problema de las razas en la América Latina," in *Tesis ideológicas*, 1929, https://www.marxists.org/espanol/mariateg/oc/ideologia_y_politica/paginas/tesis%20ideologicas.htm

"Para la progresiva educación ideológica de las masas indígenas, la vanguardia obrera dispone de aquellos elementos militantes de raza india que, en las minas o los centros urbanos, particularmente en los últimos, entran en contacto con el movimiento sindical y político. Se asimilan sus principios y se capacitan para jugar un rol en la emancipación de su raza. Es frecuente que obreros procedentes del medio indígena, regresen temporal o definitivamente a éste."

of socialist philosophy and the "proletariat revolution"; *from the universal to the local*—adapting and revising the tenets of socialism in light of Peru's economic, social and historical reality. As I hope to show in the chapters to follow, the literary works of Vallejo and Arguedas would adhere to this realist and utopian horizon, while problematizing the conditions for a new emancipatory practice beyond Mariátegui's incipient socialist program. In particular, these thinkers would question the *nationalist* and *economicist* emphasis inherent to Mariátegui's vision, while also leading to a more nuanced conception of the conditions under which a "Peruvian socialism" could take place.

A Roadmap: From Creative Antagonism to Democratic Crisis

In the first chapter, I explore the ways in which José Carlos Mariátegui's revisionary and heterodox understanding of socialism articulates the principles of what he calls an "active philosophy," binding revolutionary politics to a new social realist aesthetic orientation. I show how it is within such an integrative conception of socialism, binding intellectuals and workers, that *indigenismo* is first defined within a dialectical narrative conception of Peruvian history and its future. My central wager is that, for Mariátegui, dialectical materialism did not merely provide a theoretical lever to interpret Peruvian reality in its socioeconomic, political and literary aspects. Rather, it was essential to a conception of philosophy as a self-revising, historically grounded integrative practice that unifies the labor of intellectual production, avant-garde artistic creation and revolutionary political action. This "synthetic-integrative" conception of socialism implied both that philosophy had to be responsive to historical circumstances in not only describing but also assisting the process of social change, while becoming itself subject to historical development in relation to contingent circumstances.

In the first chapter, I explain how Mariátegui conceives of *indigenismo* within a dialectical framework informed not only by Marxist orthodoxy, but drawing from various theoretical and practical domains outside of socialism proper. This interdisciplinary labor encapsulates the synthetic practice of what Mariátegui calls "creative antagonism," through which the adaptation and revision of dialectical materialism within the context of the Andean world takes place. I then show how Mariátegui anticipates the figure of a *proletariat Indian subject*, who enters in coalition with urban workers and intellectuals, while also achieving independence from the guidance and representations of the mestizo. Drawing from insights formulated by, among others, Alberto Flores Galindo, Juan Carlos Ubilluz and Bruno Bosteels, I show how Mariátegui's project appears in this light as largely continuous with contemporary philosophical attempts think of the conditions for a *materialist dialectical* philosophy that emphasizes the role of affirmation-creation through the interdisciplinary integration of theoretical domains, political agencies, and social classes. In the last instance, for Mariátegui, the ideal of a "Peruvian socialism" gives way to a more capacious concept of the "working class," adapted to a socialist political organization and intellectual collective effort apposite to the Peruvian context.

In the second chapter, I explore the way in which César Vallejo's works attempt at once to speak for the rural Indian sentiment, while situating the destiny of the Indian within a universal horizon, so that, as Mariátegui put it, "the poet of his race" is also "the poet of his era." In doing so, I argue, Vallejo elaborates upon the delicate task of negotiating between the demands of a socialist vision that captures the uniqueness of the Andean world and the internationalist vision implicit in socialist thought. In clarifying this dynamic, I periodize the development of the link between Vallejo's local and universal address across four stages, passing from an existential to a political register. In the first section, I examine the heretical "cry of protest" and domestic nostalgia of the subject of loss, which Mariátegui recognized also as the paradigmatic exemplar of nascent *indigenista* literature in its more authentic expression of the Indigenous sentiment. In the second section, I explore Vallejo's "materialist poetics," which obeys the poetic "duty to be free" in *Trilce* (1922), and through which he pulverizes the integrity of the self in a libidinal reduction of the human subject to its "material bases." In the third section, I trace Vallejo's critical relation to European socialist philosophy and aesthetics, following his conflicted relation with the Bolshevik revolutionary sequence. Drawing from his schematic theoretical forays into aesthetic theory in the 1930s, I argue that what Vallejo names an "aesthetics of transmutation" follows the integrative spirit that guided Mariátegui's alignment of the tasks of literary experimentalism with those of a revisionary Marxism, while at the same time distinguishing between the tasks of revolutionary arts and politics. I then briefly follow the critique of capitalist imperialism within the Peruvian rural context elaborated in his 1931 novel, *Tungsten*. Through the transvaluation of the nostalgic sentiment of his earlier poetry and a transmutation of the lyric poetic voice, I go on to show how Vallejo's Paris poems embrace the possibility of overcoming individual finitude in collective existence, focusing on some exemplars from his posthumous *Poemas humanos* (1923–38). Finally, I follow the apotheosis of internationalist universalism elaborated in *Spain, Take Away from Me This Cup* (1937). I argue that Vallejo's solemn affirmation of humanity does not negate the alienation of the individual or the time of the flesh, but incorporates the militant voice of the socialist revolutionary into an impersonal, universal human subject, unbound from national, cultural, economic or even biological determinations, transfixed only by the desire for justice. For Vallejo, the mortal destiny which binds all individuals is thus traversed by sublimating the body in an integrative movement beyond the limits of corporeality, collapsing the contingent order of differences which separate humans from one another. Rather than simply tracing Vallejo's intellectual trajectory as a passage from the individual-existential-domestic to the universal-political, I emphasize that Vallejo never relinquishes the nostalgic sentiment which grounds the poetic and human voice in his domestic setting, so that the shattered rapport with the rural setting and the curse of loss find resolution in the construction of a new generic humanity.

In the third chapter, I explore how the work of José María Arguedas extends the inextricability between regionalism and universalism, thinking the conditions by which to reconcile what he calls the "magical and rational conceptions of the world." Placing culture at the center of the integrative ambition, Arguedas reconceives the conditions for a literary approximation and appropriation of the Indigenous world. Above all, Arguedas rejects the occidentalist simplification of the regional in the name of the global, while also rejecting Mariátegui's economicist isolation of productive dynamics from a cultural, existential matrix. Correcting rather than disavowing the ideal of a productive mediation between the Indigenous and Western worlds, I show how Arguedas resists the reduction of culture to an object of sentimentalist, fetishistic contemplation or even vindication. As Ángel Rama has insisted, Arguedas's anthropological work must therefore be seen as inextricable from his literary vocation as inherent to a process of *transculturation*, since "both dimensions unfold as parallel paths, mutually complimented and intercommunicated, born from the same creative impulse that makes itself adequate to disparate expressive forms without losing their unitary source" (Rama 1982, 276).

Dismantling the artificial disjunction between readings of Arguedas as a thinker of "transculturation" and the reading which interprets him as a reader of "heterogeneity," I show how the literary arc which organizes the narratives of the "small and large towns" aspires to what he explicitly names a "superior universalism." Within such a process, the invention of a new language that would reflect existing but also unforeseen mediations between Quechua and Spanish gives way to successive figurations of the revolutionary subject, in which the contradiction between the Indian and the mestizo is definitively overcome. In Arguedas's literary works, the ideal of economic appropriation woven by Mariátegui becomes extended through the transcultural imaginary, passing through different subjective figures: the fiery Indian militant who returns from the city in his 1935 short story *Agua*; the impersonal subject of integrated Indigenous communities in his 1941 novel *Yawar Fiesta* and finally a *post-Indigenous revolutionary subject* that, in his 1964 novel *Todas las sangres*, emerges as the strategic mediator between the waning landlord oligarchy, the rising capitalist urban class and the Indigenous community. In this stage, the appropriative-economicist ideal becomes complemented through a threefold cultural appropriation: a collectivist ethics of *work-for-itself* from the rural Indigenous ayllu; the sacrificial logic of martyrdom from the Christian, Western tradition; and a pragmatic, secular intelligence, which separates the rationalist kernel of capitalist modernity from the cannibalistic logic of competition and accumulation. The figure of Rendón Willka is thus defined by its synthetic potency, tracing a diagonal across Peruvian society in endorsing at once a collectivist, sacrificial and rationalist ethics, and traversing both ancestralist fetishism and occidentalist violence.

Nevertheless, I also argue that Arguedas's late, unfinished work provides a definitive testament to the failure of the appropriative revolutionary dream. Witnessing the mass migration of the Indian into the city wherein the cultural bond becomes dissolved after the 1968 agrarian reform, Arguedas's late prose testifies to a thwarted modernity in which individuals become subject to a new regime of exploitation under wage labor and hedonist surrender in the urban milieu. In sight of such a progressively uncertain future, however, Arguedas timidly insinuates a new subjectivity, no longer woven from divergent cultural foundations, but rather from the inconstancy of the rabble of culture.

In the fourth and final chapter I survey some of the major developments in *indigenista* literature in the decades after Arguedas, following the collapse of the appropriative revolutionary dream inaugurated by Mariátegui. In particular, I show how a new sequence of "postrevolutionary" *indigenista* literature proposed a pacifist, humanist answer to the utopian furor of the socialist imaginary. Focusing in particular on Edgardo Rivera Martinez's 1993 novel *País de Jauja* and Manuel Scorza's 1983 novel *La danza inmóvil*, I show how *indigenista* narrative fiction pulled apart the ideal of transculturation from the revolutionary and socialist imaginary, adapting it to a new version of the "liberal" figure of the educated mestizo that was at the center of the pre-socialist *indigenista* novel of the nineteenth century. No longer endorsing a base process of acculturation for the rural Indian, the enlightened mestizo now appears as the promise for a new hybrid subjectivity that mediates a peaceful generational change and cultural exchange, at once aesthetic and affective, without the necessity of violent struggle. In assessing this sequence, I show how this literary moment belongs to an epochal and ideological shift which follows the collapse of the internationalist revolutionary dream, and with it the figure of the proletarian subject, a process which Alain Badiou,

Jacques Rancière and Slavoj Žižek, among others, have titled "the ethical turn." This shift gives way to a critique of emancipatory struggle and violence in the name of a democratic politics guided by a nonnegotiable "respect for the Other." In assessing this constellation of thought within the Peruvian context, I address Mario Vargas Llosa's extension of the critique of revolutionary politics to the socialist *indigenista* tradition in his 1993 work *La utopia arcaica*. In this work, Vargas Llosa follows the general tenets of the ethical turn, diagnosing a tendency in *indigenista* socialist thinkers to conflate the freedom of imagination in the speculative tasks of fiction with the ambition to direct historical and social reality. I then diagnose the limits of such critical approaches, showing how they distort the integrative vision of the *indigenista* socialist tradition, which aimed to think an emancipatory politics without relapsing into a vindication of authoritarian politics.

In the concluding sections, I analyze the lingering limitations of the project to rekindle the ideals of a revolutionary subjectivity in the contemporary Peruvian social context, after the collapse of the figure of the proletarian and the failure of the productivist ambition to succeed capitalism with a superior mode of production, an ideal which animated the integrative spirit from Mariátegui to Arguedas. Having sedated the utopian and universalist aspirations from philosophy and literature, and having scaled down the ambitions of socialism from the revolutionary spirit to the conditions of democratic politics, I provide a brief assessment of the contemporary Peruvian left in its social democratic configuration, tracing its economic and political reformist agenda, as well as its relation to the problematic of rural Indigenous communities, serving as a prolegomena to any future assessment concerning the contemporary relevance of *indigenismo* in the present.

The following diagram provides a schematic representation of the path to be followed:

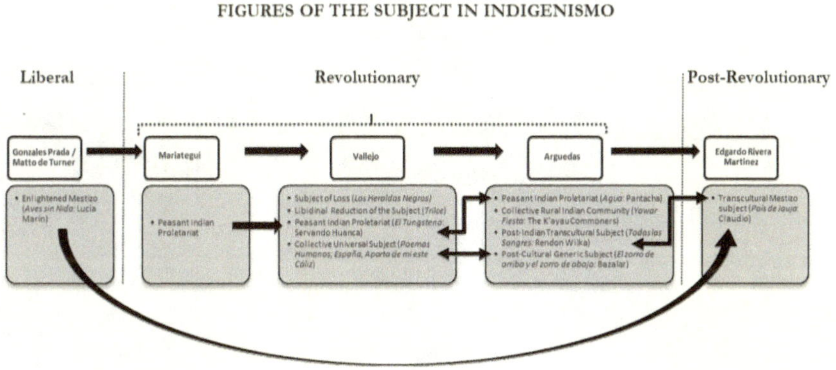

FIGURES OF THE SUBJECT IN INDIGENISMO

Diagram 0.1 Figures of the Revolutionary Subject in Socialist *Indigenista* Literature.

Chapter 1
JOSÉ CARLOS MARIÁTEGUI: THE DIALECTICS OF ANDEAN SOCIALISM

Introduction: *Indigenismo*, **Socialism and Philosophy**

In this chapter I explore how José Carlos Mariátegui's understanding of socialism as an "active philosophy" conceives of a new kind of literary and artistic practice adequate to a heterodox vision of revolutionary politics, within which *indigenismo* becomes first defined and situated historically. In this context, socialism does not merely provide Mariátegui with a theoretical lever to interpret Peruvian reality; it becomes part of an integrative *practice of theory* and *theory of practice* that articulates the labor of intellectual production, avant-garde artistic creation and emancipatory political action.

In the first section, I explain how Mariátegui conceives of *indigenismo* within a dialectical narrative informed not only by Marxist and Leninist tenets but also by various theoretical registers and disciplines. I show how *indigenismo* emerges within a unique periodization of Peruvian history, coordinating the literary and political process. I explain how Mariátegui's understanding of socialism as an "active" philosophy prefigures a revolutionary praxis that forges a cooperation between intellectuals and the working class, giving rise to a "national consciousness" through which Peruvian history also enters the internationalist horizon of the proletariat revolution.

In the second section, I explore the different ways in which, for Mariátegui, attending to Peruvian social reality also enjoins an amendment of Marxist theory and practice. Drawing from insights formulated, among others, by Alberto Flores Galindo, Bruno Bosteels and Alain Badiou, I show how Mariátegui reconceptualizes the figure of the proletariat subject, inspired by the principles of European syndicalism and the perceived latent potentials of rural Indigenous cooperativism. In particular, I focus on how Mariátegui's dialectical history of the development of Peruvian society and of the place of the rural Indian within it is of a piece with a re-elaboration of the Marxist dynamics of class struggle, conducive to a more capacious concept of the working class. Adapting socialist philosophy to the Peruvian sociohistorical context implied an unprecedented coalition between intellectuals and workers, that is, the organizational tasks of the socialist party and syndicate union had to operate alongside the doctrinal and theoretical practice proposed through the periodical *Labor* and the multidisciplinary work of the journal *Amauta*. For Mariátegui, the complication of the central contradiction between proletariat and bourgeoisie within capitalist societies by divisions in the Peruvian economy's modalities of production and forms of organization transformed the envisaged path toward a socialist future, obviating the necessity of a capitalist stage in the modernization of the nation. As we shall see, the vision of a "Peruvian socialism" that would give rise to a national consciousness, nurtured by rural Indigenous collectivist modalities of labor and production, informed the subsequent history of the *indigenista* literary tradition and its figurations of the revolutionary subject.

Between Representation and Revolution: On Creative Antagonism

Indigenismo as a literary category in Mariátegui's dialectics

In Mariátegui's 1928 *Seven Interpretative Essays on Peruvian Reality*, the term *indigenismo* is defined as a distinctive moment in the historical development of Peruvian literature. Freeing itself from the mimetic mediocrity of an artistic creation beholden to Spanish colonial forms, and radicalizing experimentation with new European influences transpiring in the "cosmopolitanized" life of the city, Mariátegui characterizes indigenismo as part of an ongoing historical process of liberation. As such, *indigenismo* emerges as a movement initiated by urban intellectuals, artists and activists, through which spiritual emancipation from the colonial age was to be realized in the domain of cultural production, anticipating an authentic "national consciousness." In this trajectory, artistic creation is oriented toward both a *realist* and *utopian* disposition, describing the disjointed present of Peruvian socioeconomic reality which follows from the colonial past, but also anticipating a conciliatory and ideal future for the nation beyond social and economic divisions.[1]

---

1 Mariátegui 1928. The periodization of *indigenismo* which appears in the *Seven Essays* was originally published between January and February in 1927 as a three-part piece

More precisely, *indigenismo* is the second term in a proposed three-stage periodization forming what Mariátegui names "the literary process" of Peruvian history, where the reality and destiny of the rural Indian becomes conceived in different ways. In this dialectical narrative, *indigenismo* appears as a transitory stage, succeeding the representations of the rural Indian derived since colonial times (*Indianismo*) and preceding the authentic self-portrayal of a literature written by the Indians themselves: no longer *indigenista*, but rather an *Indigenous literature*.[2] These three stages in the representation of the Indian correspond to a broader periodization of Peruvian literary history that distinguishes between three successive phases: *colonial, cosmopolitan* and *national*:

> A modern literary, not sociological, theory divides the literature of a country into three periods: colonial, cosmopolitan, and national [corresponding to the *Indianista, indigenista,* and Indigenous-literary phases in the Peruvian representations of the Indian]. In the first period, the country, in a literary sense, is a colony dependent on its metropolis. In the second period, it simultaneously assimilates elements of various foreign literatures. In the third period, it shapes and expresses its own personality and feelings. Although this theory of literature does not go any farther, it is broad enough for our purposes.[3]

It is within this "modern literary" genealogy that Mariátegui conceives of a teleological development, within which the consolidation of socialism coincides with the rise of an Indigenous literature.[4] It expresses the ideal of achieving a spiritual and not only political emancipation from the colonial past, shattering not only the mimetic dependency on Spanish aesthetic forms, but the idealizations of cosmopolitan writers. Still beholden to an urban context of production, the *indigenista* moment in the cosmopolitan phase of Peruvian literary history therefore was to mediate the passage from the colonial to the national phase. In this transition, Mariátegui shows how utopian imagination and social realism coincide with the creative spirit of the revolutionary socialist practice: if *Indianista* literature remained necessarily an idealization

---

in the newspaper *Mundial*. https://www.marxists.org/archive/mariateg/works/7-interpretive-essays/essay07.htm

2　Ibid.

3　Ibid.

4　Mariátegui's dialectic is transfixed within the teleological impetus that, as Angel Rama argues, drives Latin American writers to free themselves from the European imaginary: that of capturing the "spirit" of its own people by forging an authentic style and scientifically attuned representation.

of the Indian derived from the colonial consciousness, then the prospect for an Indigenous literature to come, after *indigenismo*, expressed the *ideal to overcome idealization* altogether.[5]

This genealogical and conceptual periodization invites a certain hermeneutic, however; when using the term *indigenismo* to designate Mariátegui's own position or production, we are already using the term in a different sense than his own. With this said, it is important to distinguish *indigenismo* as a *literary* phenomenon from *socialism* as an integrative practice binding emancipatory processes in science, politics and the arts, including literature. As can be read in his fierce polemic with Luis Alberto Sánchez, in a letter dating from February 1927, Mariátegui speaks of the synergy between socialism and the nascent *indigenista* literature, but localizes his own thinking as an expression of the former rather than the latter:

> The *indigenismo* of the avant-garde does not seem sincere to Luis Alberto Sánchez. [...] In Peru, the masses—the working class—are four-fifths Indian. Our socialism would not be Peruvian—nor would it be socialism—if it did not establish its solidarity principally with the Indian's vindications. [...] Do not call me, Luis Alberto Sánchez, "nationalist," "*indigenista*," nor—"pseudo-*indigenista*," for these terms are not necessary to classify me. Call me simply, Socialist. (Mariátegui 1927)[6]

According to Mariátegui, and despite its emancipatory force, indigenismo was still limited within the horizon envisaged by socialism in two ways: (1) it could not produce a wholly faithful representation of the *objective* socio-economic reality of the Indigenous world, and (2) it could not authentically express the *subjective* particularity of the Indian's "soul." Both of these insufficiencies stemmed from the fact that *indigenismo* was, after all, still a literature written by the urban mestizo:

---

5 Following Alain Badiou (2009), I use the term *subject* or *subjectivation* to designate a process whereby individuals become incorporated into historical sequences of radical creation across different domains of thought: the elaboration of new scientific theories, the production of new artistic forms, the emergence of new collective emancipatory political possibilities and new existential-affective rapports. In each case, *subjectivation* appears as an exceptional occurrence to the laws and determinations which structure a given situation, implying a process that is at once negative and affirmative.
6 Mariátegui, José Carlos, *Correspondencia, 1915–1930*, edited by Antonio Melis, Empresa Editora Amauta, 1984, pp. 43.

[I]*ndigenista* literature cannot give us a rigorously truthful version of the Indian. It has to idealize and stylize him. Nor can it give us his own soul. It is still a literature made by mestizos. That is why it is called indigenista and not Indigenous. (Mariátegui 1928)[7]

In short, the transition from *indigenismo* to an Indigenous literature anticipated the passage not only toward a "correct" interpretation of the rural Indian, but a shift in the very *ontological status* of the Indian: from an idealized *object* for the representation of mestizo intellectuals in the urban space, to a historical self-conscious *subject* responsible for its own expression and emancipation.

But rather than a literature deprived of all influence from the urban mestizo or Western world, the overcoming of the idealist impulse entailed, Mariátegui argues, a negotiation with progressive tendencies coming from the global "contemporary scene." Already in an article from 1924 titled "The National and the Exotic" (*Lo nacional y lo exótico*), he denounces the idea that learning from the foreign compromises the authenticity of national expression. Such provincialist allergy to foreign influence, he argues, naïvely imagines that an unmediated or pure "national expression" is possible. Being peripheral but integral to Western culture, to understand the Peruvian context is also then, necessarily, to understand its place in "the reality of the world":

> Contemporary Peru moves in the orbit of Western culture. The mystified national reality is but a segment, a parcel in the vast reality of the world. [...] We have the duty of not ignoring national reality, but we must also not ignore the reality of the world. Peru is a fragment in a world that follows a solidary trajectory. The communities with most aptitude towards progress are always those with the greatest aptitude to accept the consequences of its civilization and its epoch.[8]

This indissociable bind between the local and the global has direct implications for literary practice: it is only insofar as it appropriates the experimentalism of the cosmopolitan period that *indigenismo* emerges, paving the way for an integral consciousness woven from different theoretical registers and modalities of cultural production, both national and foreign. As Mariátegui declares, this

---

7 Ibid.
8 Mariátegui, José Carlos. "Lo Nacional y lo Exótico," in *Mundial*, December 9, 1924. https://www.marxists.org/espanol/mariateg/oc/peruanicemos_al_peru/paginas/nacional.htm

integrative process or synthesis involves a resolution of the perceived opposition between *regionalism* and *centralism*, subtracting the former from *ancestralist nostalgia* and dissociating the latter from *bourgeois occidentalism*:[9] "This regionalism is no mere protest against the centralist regime. It is an expression of the sierra conscience and of the Andean sentiment. The new regionalists are, above all, pro-Indian and they cannot be confused with the old-style anticentralists."[10]

Drawing an analogy with Marx's analysis of the Asian agrarian mode of production in *Pre-Capitalist Economic Formations* (1857–58), Mariátegui classifies all ancestralist views fetishizing a return to the pre-Columbian past as extensions of such a "fictitious, bourgeois fate," which produces a sterile fetishism and brings about no genuine novelty:[11] "What person who follows the development of modern thought with critical lucidity can fail to note that the return to spiritualist ideas, the retreat to Asian paradises, has clearly decadent causes and origins?" (Mariátegui 2011: 224). In contrast, the creative and integrative impetus behind Mariátegui's conception of socialism as an active philosophy is palpable in his assessment of the geopolitical and global cultural context within which Peruvian reality must be inscribed. In the essays comprising *The Contemporary Scene* (*La escena contemporánea*), written between 1923 and 1925, Mariátegui had undertaken a critical assessment of emerging international intellectual and political currents, serving as a platform to think the requirements for a Peruvian socialism by placing Latin American reality in a global context.

Attesting to the inextricability of the local and the global for a socialist interpretation of Peruvian social reality, throughout the *Seven Essays* Mariátegui negotiates with the liberal progressive political and artistic orientations of urban intellectuals during the cosmopolitan phase and their appropriation of such international influences and formal experimentalism. As we noted in our introduction, Mariátegui recognizes above all the progressive spirit of Manuel González Prada: the "least Peruvian of our writers," but

---

9 Mariátegui's own literary, critical and philosophical production was itself always marked by an incessant curiosity and dialogue with emerging global trends as much as local movements. His translations of foreign lyricists—Hugo, Goethe, Heine, among others—and own proto-modernista experiments (including his late collections *Minúsculas and exóticas*, and his unpublished *Orometría*) constitute groundbreaking attempts in literary experimentation against the hegemony of modernismo and other traditional forms in Peruvian literature.

10 Mariátegui 1928, https://www.marxists.org/archive/mariateg/works/7-interpretive-essays/essay07.htm

11 Marx, Karl. *Pre-Capitalist Economic Formations*, translated by Cohen, International Publishers, 1964. https://www.marxists.org/archive/marx/works/1857/precapitalist/index.htm

also the paradigm of an emerging "Peruvian literature" that interrupted the "living anachronism" of the colonial spirit. Igniting a process of aesthetic experimentation and urban modernization, González Prada unabashedly endorsed an *ethical* horizon for destabilizing the lingering feudal heritage in Peruvian social reality. His own artistic and political work creatively draws, Mariátegui argues, from that "passionate and revolutionary" spirit of eighteenth-century Enlightenment philosophy which postulated Reason as a rigorous self-correcting and collective enterprise, in contrast to the "degenerate bourgeois positivism" that devolved from nineteenth-century Romanticism. The latter's elitist inflections and economic conservatism, Mariátegui tells us, implied a regression in relation to the progressivism of Enlightenment rationalism, giving rise to a "domesticated rationalism" that was stagnant and reactive.[12] With this in mind, Mariátegui seconds González Prada's verdict that modernity must constitute a *constructive* response to the medieval, colonial legacy lingering in Peruvian society, even if he resists the ethical-moralist emphasis of the liberal imaginary, insofar as it occludes the primacy of economic determination:

> Spain brought us the Middle Ages: the Inquisition, feudalism, et cetera. Later it brought us the Counter Reformation: a reactionary spirit, a Jesuit method, a scholastic casuistry. We have painfully rid ourselves of most of these afflictions by assimilating Western culture, sometimes obtained through Spain itself. But we are still burdened with their economic foundations embedded in the interests of a class whose hegemony was not destroyed by the War of Independence. The roots of feudalism are intact and they are responsible for the lag in our capitalist development.

This polemic would extend to the understanding of the nature and ultimate aims of emancipatory politics: Mariátegui affirms González Prada's late political writings (after 1886), which were informed by the anarchist ideas of Proudhon and Bakunin. These writings harbored for Mariátegui a "timeless and eternal spirit" that stood against the sociological positivism of the "futurist" generation (Riva Aguero, Prado, García Calderon, Galvez, etc.) and the conservatism of the "*civilistas*," who remained submitted to Hippolyte Taine's thought.[13] In these texts, González Prada castigated the toothless nostalgia

---

12 Ibid.
13 Hippolyte Taine's thought was also characterized in fact by an insistence in the absolute right to property, and accordingly held a reactionary attitude against revolutionary politics in general, and to the Jacobins in particular, rejecting the 1793 French

of *"pasadista"* writers and the vulgarity of a reactionary *"perricholismo"* that perpetuated the colonial heritage and traditional values to justify existing class hierarchies. ("They were characterized, spiritually and ideologically, by a positivist conservatism, an opportunistic traditionalism."[14])

Perhaps more importantly, Mariátegui argues, González Prada rejected the mechanistic positivism of nineteenth-century historical materialism, which tended to deform the creative spirit of socialism into a rigid determinism. Particularly, "in his later years, he realized that idealistic and reformist politics must be solidly grounded in reality and history."[15] This late realization formed a clear precedent to Mariátegui's alternative modernity and his socialist project in the *Seven Essays*, which begins precisely by "taking the least romantic option possible." Thus, while he failed to bring the problem of the Indian into proper focus as a result of adopting a perspective grounded on ethical considerations, González Prada's work was credited for underscoring the nefarious effects that the feudal residues of colonialism had for Peruvian rural populations. The retrograde, ignorant "barbarism" of the mestizo landlord oligarchy, he observed, thwarted the inherent potentials in new generations of mestizos:

> The children of some *hacendados* travel to Europe when they are young. They become educated in France or in England and they return to Peru with all the experiences of civilized people. But as soon as they return to the haciendas, they lose the European polish and proceed with even more inhumanity and violence than their parents.[16]

The limitations that Mariátegui sees in González Prada's conception of modernization were accordingly also those he sees more generally in the liberal and anarchist imaginaries he draws upon: the commitment to urbanization

---

Constitution. According to the sociological positivist outlook, he proposed a scientific understanding of literature as determined through three central concepts: race, milieu and moment (*"race, milieu, et moment"*). See Khan, Sholom J. *Science and Aesthetic Judgment: A Study in Taine's Critical Method*. New York: Columbia University Press, 1953; Katscher, Leopold. "Taine – A Literary Portrait," in *The Nineteenth Century*, Vol. XX, 1886, pp. 51–73.

14 Ibid.
15 Ibid.
16 González Prada, Manuel, "Nuestros Indios," in *Horas de lucha*, translated by Harold Eugene Davis, in "Our Indians," Latin American Social Thought, The University Press of Washington, 1961, pp. 339–340.

offered no solution for the problem of the Indian other than their acculturation in the city under education and professionalization, and their miscegenation with mestizos. Indeed, González Prada unambiguously endorsed the abolition of the *latifundio* and turning the rural Indian into small-property owners of redistributed land, thereby incorporating them to the emerging capitalist economy. After the 1890s—disillusioned with the resilient divide between the rural Indian and the mestizo and the survival of the *latifundio* after the collapse of the Aristocratic Republic—González Prada could conceive of no solution other than the anarchist insurrectional destiny for the Indians to rise violently against the oligarchs.[17] In contrast, for Mariátegui, neither making of the rural Indian "small-property owners," nor educating them in the ways of the city, nor enjoining a headless confrontation with only destruction as its horizon, could be sufficient to conceive of a future economic model for Peru in general, or an emancipatory destiny for the rural Indian in particular.

Other trends in the national cosmopolitan scene introduced dissonant elements into Peruvian literary production, paving the way for the social realist aesthetics of *indigenismo*. The work of Valdelomar, Mariátegui highlights, overtly endorsed an avant-garde practice through the publication of the journal *Colónida* (1916). Above all, Mariátegui recognizes the influence of French symbolism and British aestheticism for *Colónida* writers, and in particular the work of Gabrielle D'Annunzio, thematizing rural poverty and economic struggle with vigorous precision, while diagnosing the decay of Roman art. In his 1900 novel *Il Fuoco*, and under the sway of Nietzsche's vitalism, D'Annunzio had sought to give literary expression to Nietzsche's "overman" in a so-called *superomismo* (literally, self-overcoming), as his characters struggled heroically against the dominant forces of their day in the name of a creative will and subjectivity unbound from reactionary forces. This creative, positive dimension, inherent to the *Colónida* experiment, would be radicalized in Mariátegui's conception of the revolutionary subject as a creative agency that positions itself against the nihilistic tendencies of anarchism as much as the liberal complicity with capitalist urban modernization.[18] For Mariátegui,

---

17 At the same time, González Prada remained firmly liberal in economic matters: however hindered by the social disjunctions affecting its population, the rejection of colonialist protectionism was to be met with a liberal opening of the Peruvian economy to the global market, a trope which would be appropriated and referenced ideologically as overtly Pradista decades later in Leguía's dictatorship after 1919, to justify the submission of Peru to international capital.
18 In this regard, Valdelomar's 1916 *Los hijos del sol* was a paradigmatic exemplar of unctuous ancestralist nostalgia for the pre-Hispanic past.

experimental, creative unruliness thus remained *Colónida*'s lasting value, even if their ideological bent ultimately expressed a flaccid individualism, iconoclasm, corporatism and reformism in political matters aligned with González Prada's Parnassian tendencies when it suited their interests. Still, they took part in what many writers referred to as "a revision of our literary values,"[19] a "belligerent force" that was a necessary though insufficient condition for a new social realist and revolutionary consciousness to emerge. These limitations would naturally extend to the literary representations of the rural setting, which remained still subject to idealist distortions:

> *Colonida* was a negative, disintegrative, belligerent force, expressing the opposition of those writers who objected to the domination of national reputation by an antiquated, official, and pretentious art. [...] Valdelomar does not herald a new era in our literature because too many decadent influences acted on him. Together with Faith, the Sea, and Death, he places Twilight among the "ineffable and infinite" elements that entered into the development of his Inca legends. (Mariátegui 1928)[20]

For Mariátegui, the decadent tendency of Colónida writers to fall back on ancestralist idealizations reflected a tendency toward a depoliticized aestheticism that both failed to address the demands of their concrete social reality and to develop a truly modern aesthetic style. For example, the "pure" poetics exemplified by José María Eguren's symbolism is criticized by Mariátegui for its insensitivity to the history of the Indian, while also lacking a genuine knowledge of Western modernity, making it finally an "echo of the medieval West"; Alberto Hidalgo's naïve avowal of a "pure revolutionary" spirit yields a pure lyricism, whose political inertia or even indifference reflected the limits of the Colonida imaginary. The critique of lyricist abstraction leads Mariátegui to reject the idea of a "pure revolution," distinguishing between liberal and socialist conceptions of revolutionary practice in both politics and poetics:

> Pure revolution, revolution as such, my dear Hidalgo, does not exist in history and neither does it exist in poetry. Pure revolution is an abstraction. There are many revolutions, among them the liberal and the socialist. There is no pure revolution, either as a historical event or as a poetic theme. (Mariátegui 1928)

---

19 Mariátegui 1928, https://www.marxists.org/archive/mariateg/works/7-interpretive-essays/essay07.htm
20 Ibid.

The autonomy of the aesthetic from the political attests to the nefarious legacy of Romanticism, its subjectivism, individualism and idealism, which he ironically designates as the "bourgeois revolution," and which stands in tension with both the liberal revolution inspired by eighteenth-century rationalism, as much as the socialist revolution inspired by historical materialism:

> Romanticism, understood as a literary and artistic movement linked to the bourgeois revolution, becomes individualism in concept and sentiment. Symbolism and decadence have been only romantic stages, and this is also true of modernism in artists who cannot help being extremely subjective. There is a symptom inherent in individualist art that indicates, better than any other, a process of dissolution: the determination with which every art and even every artistic element asserts its autonomy. (Mariátegui 1928)[21]

Taken as a whole, Mariátegui's dual affirmation and criticism of the cosmopolitan stage of Peruvian history is clear: the urban capital, the "daughter of conquest," had become the cradle for a new mestizo intelligentsia that broke from the colonial aesthetics, appropriating emerging trends in the global scene. At the same time, however, these efforts remained incapable of representing their social realities to conceive of a collective, national future adequate to this social world. Thus, achieving independence from the colonial shadow would require not only relinquishing medieval remnants in urban cultural production, but, more radically, a new social realist aesthetics and revolutionary practice that took the emancipation of the rural Indian as its historical foundation, beyond the contours of the urban capital:

> Lima has no roots in an autochthonous past. Lima is daughter of the conquest. But from the moment that it intellectually and spiritually becomes less Spanish in order to become a little cosmopolitan, from the moment it shows concern for contemporary ideas and issues, Lima no longer appears exclusively as the home of colonialism and Hispanism. The new Peruvianness will be created, using the Indian as its historic cement. Its axis will probably rest on Andean stone rather than on the clay of the coast. But Lima, restless and reformist, wants to participate in this creative work. (Mariátegui 1928)[22]

---

21 Ibid.
22 Ibid.

In this regard, the rise of *indigenismo* during the Peruvian cosmopolitan phase is understood as "a precursor of the new spirit, the new conscience."[23] It preserved the experimental impetus of progressive mestizo intellectuals, while defying the individualistic tendencies that divorced aesthetic formal experimentation from social ends. In this context, the "problem of the Indian" slowly becomes crystallized as the unifying thread weaving together intellectual labor in the sciences and arts, and the strategic aims of emancipatory politics, jointly comprising what Mariátegui names the "totality of life":

> If the Indigenous problem is part of politics, economics, and sociology, it cannot be absent from literature and art. One would be mistaken to think of it as an artificial issue simply because many of those who advance it are novices or opportunists. [...] Mere literary erudition does not suffice for a profound interpretation of the spirit of literature. Political acumen and historical perspective are more important. The professional critic considers literature by itself without relating it to politics, economics, the totality of life. Therefore, his investigation does not reach the essence of literary events by exploring their beginnings and subconscious. (Mariátegui 1928)[24]

In his November 1926 article *Arte, revolución, decadencia*, published in the third volume of *Amauta*, Mariátegui endorses Vallejo's verdict in the article *Poesía nueva*, according to which modern art, both in Latin America and Europe, had become a vehicle for technical experiments without social purpose:

> We cannot accept as new any art that merely brings us a new technique. This would mean amusing ourselves with one of the most fallacious modern illusions. No aesthetic can reduce artistic work to a question of technique. New technique should also correspond to a new spirit. If not, the only things that change are the parameters, the decorations. And an artistic revolution does not content itself with formal conquests. (Mariátegui 1926: 3–4)[25]

From this perspective, we might consider an epistemological problem within Mariátegui's dialectical narrative: how could *indigenismo* as a literature be inherently "idealizing" while also constituting a more "authentic" expression

---

23 Ibid.
24 Ibid.
25 Mariátegui, José Carlos. "Arte, revolución y decadencia," in *Amauta*: no. 3, pp. 3–4.

of the Indian spirit? For if being written by mestizos suffices to render literary representations of the Indian inauthentic and idealizing, it would follow that *indigenismo* could be no better off when providing an "accurate" version of the Indian than any other colonial or cosmopolitan form. And yet, while Mariátegui accepts that the representations of the mestizo can never capture the reality or spirit of the Indian and be free from idealization, he rejects an *epistemic antirealism* that would present all such representations as equally idealizing or inauthentic. For just as it is possible to gain proper traction on "the problem of the Indian" by placing it in its proper economic context, so it is possible for a mestizo poet to express the grief of the rural world without relapsing into sentimentalist idealization.

Assessing Vallejo's poetry, which he takes to be paradigmatic of the nascent *indigenista* aesthetic, Mariátegui recognizes its authenticity insofar as it escapes the "ancestralist" nostalgias promoted by *pasadista* writers, capturing the alienation and strife of the rural setting:

> His nostalgia, conceived in lyric purity, should not be confused with the literary nostalgia of the *pasadistas*. Vallejo's nostalgia is not merely retrospective. He does not yearn for the Inca empire in the way that *"pasadismo" perricholesco* yearns for the viceroyalty. His nostalgia is a sentimental or a metaphysical protest; a nostalgia of exile, of absence. (Mariátegui 1928)[26]

Rather presenting an ideal depiction of past traditions, for Vallejo, the poetic act carries a subversive sign of "metaphysical protest" on behalf not only of the rural Indian but of humanity as a whole, traversing the division between the individual and the collective, the regional and global, the particular and the universal (cf. Chapter II).

For Mariátegui, the overcoming of all ancestralist nostalgias through an authentic poetic voice capturing the alienation of the Indian is continuous with *a politics of vindication*: "The authentic *indigenistas*—who must not be confused with those who exploit Indigenous themes for sheer exoticism, collaborate, consciously or not, in a political and economic politics of vindication, not of restoration or resurrection."[27] Above all, Mariátegui highlights the import

---

26 Mariátegui 1928, https://www.marxists.org/archive/mariateg/works/7-interpretive-essays/essay07.htm
27 Ibid.

of symbolism in Vallejo's poetry, as an expressive form "better suited than any other to interpret the Indigenous spirit," while also including "elements of expressionism, Dadaism, and surrealism."[28] Binding a certain melancholy before the rural setting to a universal address, Vallejo confronts human finitude while avoiding Western skepticism and nihilism:

> There is no relationship or affinity between him and the nihilism or intellectual skepticism of the West. The pessimism of Vallejo, like the pessimism of the Indian, is not a belief or a feeling. It is tinged with an oriental fatalism that makes it closer to the Christian and mystic pessimism of the Slavs. (Mariátegui 1928)[29]

Throughout Vallejo's *Los heraldos negros* and *Trilce*, existential solitude and familial abandon within the Andean world thereby coincide with a cosmic empathy and generic address for mankind writ large, so that the "poet of a race" becomes at once the "poet of his era":

> This pessimism is full of tenderness and compassion, because it is not engendered by egocentricity and narcissism, disenchanted and exacerbated, as is the case almost throughout the romantic school. Vallejo feels all human suffering. His grief is not personal. His soul is "sad unto death" with the sorrow of all men, and with the sorrow of God, because for the poet it is not only men who are sad. [...] Vallejo, from this point of view, belongs not only to his race but also to his century, to his era.[30] (Ibid.)

That the "poet of a race" could emerge within the cosmopolitan context meant that, for Mariátegui, mediation with foreign forms was not incompatible with the emergence of a national literature or with the realism required for such a literature to emerge. Rather, it is by linking its local economic and social context to a transnational horizon and address that the *indigenista* current expresses as its most distinctive trait:[31]

---

28 Ibid.
29 Ibid.
30 Ibid.
31 Doubtlessly, for Mariátegui, the fatalism that characterizes Vallejo's early work would also signal, however, its status as a transitory phase in the process of the Indigenous self-awakening: expressing the animus of Indigenous suffering, but falling short of expressing the possibility for any kind of emancipatory gesture or process of radical transformation. One can only surmise that, had Mariátegui been exposed to Vallejo's

The development of the *indigenista* current does not threaten or paralyze other vital elements of our literature. *Indigenismo* does not aspire to preempt the literary scene by excluding or blocking other impulses and manifestations. It represents the trend and tone of an era because of its sympathy and close association with the spiritual orientation of new generations who, in turn, are sensitive to the imperative needs of our economic and social development.[32]

This integral practice is what Mariátegui conceives under the title of an "active philosophy," of which socialism was the concrete historical expression. The following diagram captures the dialectical periodization proposed by Mariátegui:

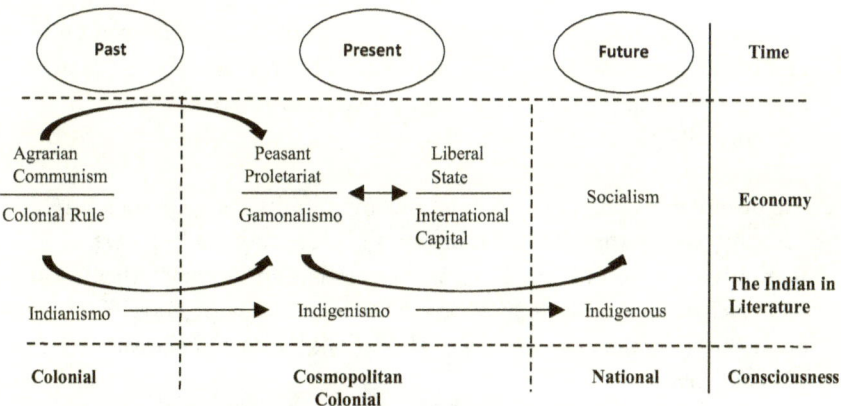

Diagram 1.1 Mariátegui's Dialectics of Peruvian History.

An active philosophy: Creative antagonism, myth and faith

At the surface, it might seem as if Mariátegui's realism or materialism is classically Marxist or "orthodox," insofar as it endorses a kind of "economicist" historical determinism, from which he seeks to draw political and aesthetic imperatives. After all, prioritizing class determination, he argues, was the same as taking "the least romantic and literary position possible,"[33] in what

---

later work, in which cosmic melancholy gives way to a universal humanist jubilation, his avowal of the poet would have been even greater.
32 Ibid.
33 Ibid.

concerns the interpretation of Peruvian history. And as we have seen, the *Seven Essays* diagnose a central contradiction separating the rural and urban worlds, leading to the imperative to abolish the rule of the *gamonales* in their complicity with state power, while affirming the Indian's "right to the land."

> As long as the vindication of the Indian is kept on a philosophical and cultural plane, it lacks a concrete historical base. To acquire such a base—that is, to acquire physical reality—it must be converted into an economic and political vindication. Socialism has taught us how to present the problem of the Indian in new terms. We have ceased to consider it abstractly as an ethnic or moral problem and we now recognize it concretely as a social, economic, and political problem. And, for the first time, we have felt it to be clearly defined. [...] By identifying it as primarily a socio-economic problem, we are taking the least romantic and literary position possible. We are not satisfied to assert the Indian's right to education, culture, progress, love, and heaven. We begin by categorically asserting his right to land.[34]

These pronouncements imply a strict incompatibility between socialism and philosophy, where the latter is understood as an "ethical" or abstract discourse only capable of trafficking in "romantic and literary" idealizations. Yet the disavowal of philosophy in this sense contrasts with Mariátegui's declaration of the identity of his "political passions" with a *philosophical* or even *religious* endeavor:

> I declare without hesitation that I bring to literary exegesis all my political passions and ideas, although in view of the way this word has been misused, I should add that my politics are philosophy and religion.[35]

What is at stake in this apparent contradiction is the rejection of a particular vision of philosophy as an abstract discipline, rooted in a toothless prioritization of ethical or moral considerations, and an affirmation on the contrary of what Mariátegui names an "active philosophy," which binds scientific, political and artistic activity in generating new models of collective social organization and expression. In what will become a recurrent trope throughout *indigenista* literature, Mariátegui systematically adapts theological concepts to a secularized context, in order to think of a new kind of revolutionary

---

34 Ibid.
35 Ibid.

subjectivity and practice. In a 1930 article titled *Is There an Uneasiness Proper to Our Epoch?* (*Existe una inquietud propia, de nuestra época?*), published in the periodical *Mundial*, Mariátegui contrasts the revolutionary conviction of socialist thinkers to the reactionary spirit of that "fictitious faith, intellectual and pragmatic, of those who find equilibrium in dogmas and in the old order," and defends the heroism of a militant, revolutionary subject who "dangerously struggles for the victory of a new order."[36] The irony is that the "authentic faith" proper to socialism takes the rejection of dogmatism as its central principle.

Inspired by the so-called romantic Marxists, and in particular Georges rekindling of the category of *myth* within political discourse, Mariátegui conceives of artistic and intellectual creation as part of an integral "revolutionary mission." In the words of David Sobrevilla (2012), we can say that myth for Mariátegui was part of a "construction of images," capable of guiding revolutionaries in their emancipatory mission.[37] Particularly, in a 1925 text titled *Myth and Man*, Mariátegui correlates the revolutionary spirit and the subjective "force of myth", castigating the conservatism of the bourgeois-liberal imaginary for its lack of an "authentic myth." Indeed, though disruptive of the colonial aesthetic mode, liberalism promoted an exhausted, "fictitious faith" that devolved in a covert nihilism that could not rise to "the creative power of the proletariat": (Mariátegui 2011: 387)

> The bourgeoisie no longer has any myths. It has become incredulous, skeptical, nihilistic. The reborn liberal myth has aged too much. The proletariat has a myth: the social revolution. It moves toward that myth with a passionate and active faith. The bourgeoisie denies; the proletariat affirms. The bourgeois intellectuals entertain themselves with a rationalist critique of the method, theory, revolutionary technique. What a misunderstanding! The strength of revolutionaries is not in their science; it is in their faith, in their passion, in their will. It is a religious, mystical, spiritual force. It is the force of myth. (Ibid.)

---

36 Mariátegui, José Carlos. "Existe una Inquietud Propia, En Nuestra Época," in *Mundial*, March 29, 1930, available at https://www.marxists.org/espanol/mariateg/oc/el_artista_y_la_epoca/paginas/existe%20una%20inquietud%20propia.htm#1a

37 Sobrevilla, David, "La visión del mito en José Carlos Mariátegui, Mariano Ibérico y Luis Alberto Sánchez," in *Escritos Mariáteguianos*, Universidad Inca Garcilaso de la Vega, 2012.

The "priests of the revolution," Mariátegui tells us, are guided by an authentic faith insofar as they also form part of the creation of an unprecedented myth, capable of bringing about a collective historical transformation.

In his text "The Science of Revolution" (which form part of his collection *In Defense of Marxism*, and is titled after Max Eastman's book relating psychoanalysis and Marxism), Mariátegui describes Marxism as enacting not a transition from a "utopian" conception of socialism to a "scientific" one; rather, the transition is from a utopian socialism to a *socialist religion*:

> Marx examines the material world the same way a priest examines the ideal world, with the hope of finding his own creative aspirations in it, and in the contrary case, to see how to transplant them in it. In his intellectual system, Marxism does not represent the passage of utopian socialism to scientific socialism; it does not represent the substitution of a non-practical evangelization for a better world by a practical plan, helped by a study of actual society, and indicating the means of replacing it with a better society. Marxism constitutes the passage of utopian socialism to socialist religion, a scheme destined to convince the believer that the universe itself automatically engenders a better society and that he, the believer, does not have to do anything more than follow that universe. (Mariátegui 2011: 233)

These passages clarify the precise sense in which *indigenismo* approximated the realist and revolutionary disposition required for a socialist future. Mariátegui explicitly references Sorel's secularized concept of myth and religious practice in his appraisal of Valcárcel's *Tempest in the Andes* (*Tempestad en los Andes*), which, "lacking doctrinarian *a priorisms*," displays "something of a gospel, and even something of an apocalypse. It is the work of a believer."[38] At the same time, Mariátegui repeatedly insists that socialist philosophy must itself be transformed by attending to changing historical circumstances, reflected in a concrete socioeconomic reality. Faith in socialism thus becomes, in a kind of dialectical inversion, a call for fidelity to *constructive heresy*, where practical subversion becomes indissociable from theoretical revision.

---

38 Mariátegui, José Carlos. "Prologo" in *Tempestad en Los Andes*, edited by Luis. E Valcarcel, 1927. My translation. Available at: https://www.marxists.org/espanol/mariateg/1927/oct/10.htm).

In *Modern Philosophy and Marxism*, Mariátegui thus defines the singular "law" that socialist religious practice follows: that of a dynamic, self-revising practice of theory and theory of practice, examining the historical structures under which individuals and collectives are submitted. This law, he claims, expresses the core of Marxism as "the gospel and method of a mass movement":

> Marxist criticism studies capitalist society concretely. As long as capitalism has been transformed definitively, Marx's canon remains valid. Socialism or, rather, the struggle to transform the social order from capitalist to collectivist, keeps this critique alive, continues it, confirms it, corrects it. Any attempt to categorize it as a simple scientific theory is in vain since it works in history as the gospel and method of a mass movement.[39] (My translation)

Heavily influenced by the Parisian *Clarté* group (directed by Henri Barbusse) and Italian syndicalism (Croce, Papini), Mariátegui seeks to adapt the tenets of Marxist philosophy to Peruvian social reality by weaving together different theoretical registers and disciplines, always attentive to progressive and revolutionary tendencies in science, the arts and politics.[40]

In *The Contemporary Scene*, and commenting on Barbusse's work, revolution was inherently linked to a creative disposition. But rather than contrasting the myth-creating disposition of socialist religion to the "utopian socialism" that preceded the advent of Marxism, here the "revolutionary duty" is understood as the intrication of a "utopian" and "active" rather than passive "Intelligence":

---

39 Mariátegui, José Carlos. "La filosofía moderna y el Marxismo," in *Defensa del Marxismo*, 1974, https://www.marxists.org/espanol/mariateg/oc/defensa_del_marxismo/paginas/iv.htm. "La crítica marxista estudia concretamente la sociedad capitalista. Mientras el capitalismo no haya trasmontado definitivamente, el canon de Marx sigue siendo válido. El socialismo, o sea la lucha por transformar el orden social de capitalista en colectivista mantiene viva esa crítica, la continúa, la confirma, la corrige. Vana es toda tentativa de catalogarla como una simple teoría científica, mientras obre en la historia como evangelio y método de un movimiento de masas."

40 See in particular the chapter titled *La Revolución y la Inteligencia* (*The Revolution and the Intelligentsia*), from *La Escena Contemporanea*. Barbusse's influence can be seen already in Mariátegui's involvement and direction of *Claridad*, succeeding Haya de la Torre, before his definitive break with the APRA in 1928. It is also worthy of note that in 1927 Vallejo sent Mariátegui a copy of Barbusse's *Fait Divers*.

> Barbusse reminds intellectuals of the revolutionary duty of Intelligence. The function of Intelligence is creative. [...] The innumerable army of the humble, of the poor, of the miserable, has been placed resolutely in the march towards Utopia that Intelligence, in its generous, fecund and visionary hours, has conceived. (Mariátegui 1925)[41]

Focusing on Barbusse's "reinvention of the epic" in *Les Enchainements*, Mariátegui notes that the work's formal ambiguity, straddling the line between poetry and the novel, awakens "the epic, larval and amorphous still of a proletariat civilization," a collectivist clamor or "multitudinous sentiment"[42] (Mariátegui 1925). It is not the epic of the heroic individual that is at stake here, but rather a new generic and universal humanity that Mariátegui calls simply "the multitude."[43]

In continuity with this universalist conception of a collective and genetic subjectivity, and inspired by Barbusse's reinvention of the epic, in the article *Modern Philosophy and Marxism* Mariátegui mentions several philosophical orientations that amplify the synthetic horizon and integrative scope of socialism:

> Vitalism, activism, pragmatism, relativism: none of these philosophical currents, insofar as what they bring to the revolution, have remained marginal to the Marxist intellectual movement. (Mariátegui 2011: 196)

And in two texts titled *Marxist Determinism (El determinismo Marxista)* and *Freudianism and Marxism (Freudismo y Marxismo)*—compiled in his *In Defense of Marxism (Defensa del Marxismo)*—Mariátegui again rejects a determinist conception of socialism, asserting the self-revising nature of Marxist theory and practice. In the course of a commentary on the work of Max Eastman, he draws an analogy between the critique of ideology elaborated by Marx and the analysis of the unconscious drives that animate the psychoanalytic study of libidinal forces by Freud. Against crass interpretations that find in Marxism a form of historical determinism, he underlines how the economic and social history of different modes of production led Marx to reject a narrow economism, turning ideological critique against dogmatism and determinism. He

---

41 Mariátegui 1925, my translation. https://www.marxists.org/espanol/mariateg/oc/la_escena_contemporanea/paginas/les%20enchainements.htm#1a
42 Ibid.
43 Barbusse, Henri. "El presente y el porvenir," in *Amauta*: no. 8, pp. 9–11.

argues that "the dialectical principle on which all of the Marxist conception is based excludes the reduction of the historical process to a purely mechanical economics" (Mariátegui 2011: 221). Following Jacoby, Mariátegui thus calls for a "dialectical loyalty" to the voluntarist spirit of Marxism, which emphasizes the *active* role of the revolutionary subject against a "passive" historicism that reduces historical dynamism to mechanistic law:

> The voluntarist character of socialism is not, in truth, less evident, although it is less understood by critics, than its determinist background. [...] [E]very word, every act of Marxism harbors an accent of faith, of will, of heroic and creative conviction, whose impulse it would be absurd to search for in a mediocre and passive determinism.[44]

Mariátegui's analogy with the psychoanalytic cure is related to this voluntarist conception of revolutionary agency, inspired by Sorel's syndicalism: he argues that denunciations of Marx's supposed "pan-economism" (resting on a simplification of his understanding of the economy) mirror denunciations of Freud's alleged "pan-sexualism."

Mariátegui draws a further analogy between the psychoanalytic repression of trauma in the unconscious and the false consciousness promoted by ideological dogmatism in all its forms, including that characteristic of an ossified, "dogmatic" pseudo-Marxism. For just as the internalization of trauma in the unconscious designates the process whereby the normative order of law and repression begins to function autonomously in the body, the concept of "ideology" represents "the deformations of social and political thought produced by repressed motives" (Mariátegui 2011: 220). This leads Mariátegui to declare that socialism is but an extension of psychoanalysis, taking the latter beyond the individual to the collective domain, such that "the economic interpretation of history is not anything more than a generalized psychoanalysis of the social and political spirit."[45] The psychoanalytic therapeutic procedure through which the traumatic effects of the unconscious become displaced in the psychic economy thus mirrors the critical process of subversion at the political level, which displaces the economic organization of society: socialism as an active philosophy unearths the repressive mechanisms required for collective emancipation, just as psychoanalysis unearths and

---

44 Mariátegui, José Carlos. *Marxist determinism*, translated by Celina María Bragagnolo, 1928, https://www.marxists.org/archive/mariateg/works/1928/marxist-determinism.htm

45 Ibid.

displaces libidinal torsions of the individual psyche. As Alain Badiou writes in his 1975 work *Theory of the Subject*, deepening the analogy proposed originally by Mariátegui, identifying the continuity between psychoanalysis and Marxist practice amounts to identifying a common *epistemological role* in the categories of the *hysteric* and the *proletariat*, as central figures of the *subject*: both carry within themselves a fracture with the stable ideological notions that identify individuals and collectives within a given cultural and socioeconomic order: "It is beyond doubt that Freud's unconscious and Marx's proletariat have the same epistemological status with regard to the break they introduce in the dominant conception of the subject"[46] (Badiou 2009: 115).

This process of individual and collective subjective liberation, Mariátegui argues, becomes intrinsic to the literary creative process. In a text titled *"Freudianism" in Contemporary Literature*, he claims that modernist literature harbors a subversive spirit that sides with the pursuit of unqualified human freedom, citing the works of Pirandello and Proust, which reflect simultaneously a process of psychic liberation and social critique.[47] In sum, a revisionary, multidisciplinary and antidogmatic pathos was central to Mariátegui's understanding of socialism as an "active philosophy," concentrating the voluntarist and affirmative creative spirit that Flores Galindo summarizes as "that hope in the future which does not repose in the laws of the dialectic, not in the conditioning of the economy, but rather on collective wills" (Flores Galindo 1980: 14).[48] The identification of philosophy and religion with socialist practice should therefore not indicate what was often imputed against Mariátegui: an "intellectualist" reification of theoretical principles that operated in comfortable distance from the Andean world that he claimed to speak for.[48] Flores Galindo argues that this aspect of Mariátegui shows, beyond any

---

46 Badiou, Alain. *Theory of the Subject*, translated by Bruno Bosteels, Continuum, 2011.
47 Mariátegui, José Carlos, El "Freudismo" en la literatura contemporánea, published in *Variedades*, August 14, 1926, https://www.marxists.org/espanol/mariateg/oc/el_artista_y_la_epoca/paginas/el%20freudismo.htm
48 This line of criticism, one would do well to remember, was not only that proposed by political rivals or posterior critics, but often sprung from fellow sympathizers of Marxism and even from Mariátegui's own collaborators. Perhaps the clearest case is that of Martinez de la Torre, who in his correspondence with the exiled Mario Nerval, targeting Mariátegui's incipient efforts through the publication of *Amauta*, proposes a vigorous 'attack against intellectuals and petit bourgeoisie professionals who pretend to lend their "intelligence" to the movement, being their labor, within it, precisely negative. To the inert intelligence we ought to oppose the "active intelligence."' See Martínez de la Torre, Ricardo, *"Apuntes para una interpretación marxista de la historia social del Perú,"* Volume III, Empresa Editorial Peruana, 1947."

doctrinal affiliation with Marxist theory or any specific analytic categories for approximating social reality, that for Mariátegui what remained central was the power of the revolutionary subject to affirm its will against all closed systems, against dogmatism and determinism:

> Facing the necessity to summarize what's essential in Marx, [Mariátegui] did not think in any analytic category (merchandise, for instance), or discipline (historical materialism), nor even in a method (the dialectic), but strictly its "exceptional merit" was to have discovered the proletariat; that is, the revolutionary subject. (Flores Galindo 1980: 54, my translation)[49]

In the editorial opening to the 17th volume of *Amauta*, Mariátegui reiterates that the collective labor of the journal was to serve both a site for intellectual explorations, but also for new social movements, alluding to the generic "multitude" of the revolutionary, collective subject to come: "*Amauta* is not a diversion nor a game between intellectuals: it professes a historical idea, it confesses and active and multitudinous faith, it obeys a contemporary social movement"[50] (Mariátegui 1928). The coming revolution had to be, he argues, a movement toward integration, resisting the fragmentation of the working class which sent European socialism into a crisis.[51]

These considerations lead us to reconsider the sense in which Mariátegui's socialism remains subordinated to a "nationalist" project. For when defining the construct of a "national consciousness," coeval with the emergence of an Indigenous literature beyond *indigenismo*, Mariátegui was careful to reject the essentialist concept of the "nation." The search for a "national identity" was to be conceived as a *task* to be realized, rather than as an essence from which to draw an imaginary unity. Referencing De Sanctis, he claims that "the idea

---

49 "En su Defensa del marxismo, puesto frente a la necesidad de resumir lo esencial del pensamiento de Marx, no pensó en ninguna categoría de análisis (mercancía por ejemplo), en ninguna disciplina (la economía política), tampoco en algún nuevo continente científico (el materialismo histórico), ni siquiera en un método (la dialéctica), pensó estrictamente en que su 'mérito excepcional' consistía en haber descubierto al proletariado, es decir al sujeto de la Revolución."
50 Mariátegui, José Carlos. "Aniversario y Balance," in *Amauta*, vol. 17, 1928. https://www.marxists.org/espanol/mariateg/1928/sep/aniv.htm
51 Mariátegui, José Carlos, "La Crisis doctrinal del socialismo," in *La Escena Contemporánea*, 1925, my translation. https://www.marxists.org/espanol/mariateg/oc/figuras_y_aspectos_de_la_vida_iii/paginas/la%20crisis%20doctrinal.htm

of a national literature is an illusion. Its people would have to be as isolated as the Chinese are supposed to be. [...] Greek poetry has Asiatic elements, Latin poetry has Greek, and Italian poetry has both Greek and Latin."[52] Mariátegui's opening statement in *Amauta*, in 1926, declares the overt mission of the journal as that of coordinating the efforts of progressive Peruvian intellectuals, activists and writers with the ideas and works of foreign thinkers, ideological currents and artistic experiments, implicitly referencing Barbusse's avowal of a new form of "Intelligence" continuous with interdisciplinarity:

> Beyond differences, all these spirits lay forth what binds and groups them: the will to create a new Peru within a new world. Intelligence, the coordination of the most volitional of these elements, progress gradually. The movement—intellectual and spiritual—acquires organic integrity little by little. With the apparition of *Amauta*, it enters into a definitional phase. [...] But we always consider Peru within the panorama of the world. We shall study all the great movements of renovation: political, philosophical, artistic, literary, and scientific. All that is human is ours. This magazine will bind all the new men from Peru, first with other peoples of the Americas, and then with the peoples from the world as a whole.[53] (Mariátegui 1926)

Further developing this point, in a 1929 article titled *The Mission of Israel* (*La misión de Israel*), published in *Mundial*, Mariátegui speaks of "dialectical negation" or purely exclusionary relationship between "internationalism" and "nationalism." Conceiving of the necessity to forge a national consciousness that would restore the social divisions lingering in the Andean nations, such a dialectical negation implies that the internationalist stance proper to socialism nevertheless is capable of recognizing nationalism as what he names "an epoch's historical necessity."

> Internationalism is the same as supranationalism. Internationalism is not, as is imagined by many obtuse leftist and rightists, the negation of nationalism, but its overcoming. It is a dialectical negation, in the sense in that it contradicts nationalism; but not in the sense

---

52 Ibid.
53 Mariátegui, José Carlos. "Presentación de *Amauta*," in *Amauta*, year 1, no. 1, 1926, my translation. https://www.marxists.org/espanol/mariateg/1926/sep/amauta.htm

that it condemns or disqualifies it as an epoch's historical necessity.[54] (Mariátegui 1929)

Such an account of "dialectical negation" concentrates the relation between the local and the global that Flores Galindo has identified as the fundamental axis around which Mariátegui's entire thinking finally revolves: that of the encounter between "Marxism and nation." It is in the articulation of these two polarities that Flores Galindo finds a universal dimension in Mariátegui's thought, which binds the construction of the nation to the global horizon of revolutionary thought:

> As it so happens, precisely coming from his peculiar articulation between Marxism and Nation, Mariátegui ended up elaborating a specific way—Peruvian, Indoamerican, Indigenous—to think Marx and, as always, precisely by virtue of being all the more Peruvian became universal; such that he was able to propose a Marxism as different as that of Gramsci and Lukacs, and as valuable as either, thanks to which Peru began to appear in the geography of socialism. (Flores Galindo 1980: 12)[55]

The development of a national consciousness required, however, that workers themselves awaken a sense of class consciousness. In his 1927 *Message to the Worker's Congress*, Mariátegui speaks of the theoretical tasks of Marxism (to describe the economic-social contradictions which divided the nation through the internationalist lens of socialism) as a practical one in the local sphere (to enable the organization of urban and rural workers, and intellectuals and activists):

> It is necessary to create a class consciousness. The organizers know well that most workers have a spirit of cooperation and mutualism. This spirit should be developed and educated until it is converted into a class spirit. The first thing that must be overcome and defeated is the anarchoid, individualistic, egoistic spirit, which besides being profoundly

---

54 Mariátegui, José Carlos. "La misión de Israel," in *Mundial*, May 3, 1929, my translation. Available at: https://www.marxists.org/espanol/mariateg/oc/figuras_y_aspectos_de_la_vida_iii/paginas/la%20mision.htm#*a

55 "Pero ocurre que, precisamente a partir de su peculiar articulación entre marxismo y nación, Mariátegui acabó elaborando una manera específica -peruana, indoamericana, andina- de pensar a Marx y, como siempre, precisamente por ser más peruano se convirtió en universal; de manera que consiguió proponer un marxismo tan diferente como el de Gramsci y el de Lukács, y tan valioso como ambos, gracias a lo cual el Perú recién comenzó a figurar en la geografía del socialismo."

antisocial, does not constitute anything but the exacerbation and degeneration of the old bourgeois liberalism; the second thing that must be overcome is the spirit of corporatism, of a trade, of job category. (Mariátegui 2011)[56]

Within this general program, as Galindo (1980) argues, a Peruvian "national socialism" rejects the hope of prolonging an agonizing Andean tradition, seeking instead to reconstitute the social bond of Peruvian society outside the prescribed liberal fate of capitalist modernity.

Such a reconstitution would not produce an *abstract* or *absolute negation*, but rather a qualified, *concrete negation* of the arc of Western history, reconciling the "open spirit of modern culture" with the pursuit of a national destiny.

> The critique of the West will not derive in an absolute negation, just because Mariátegui distinguished western culture and capitalism. The decadence, the dusk and finality responded to an economic system and not to a culture's cultural conquests. The West did not have to follow the paths of capitalism. [...] The problem was to harmonize this open spirit to modern culture, with the independence and defense of national elements. (Flores Galindo 1980, 43)[57]

But while Mariátegui rejects ancestralist nostalgia and provincialism in all of their forms, as much as occidentalist decadence, he argues that it is only by forging the conditions for a constructive mediation between the Western and pre-Hispanic worlds that Peru enters a "universal path," through which it simultaneously approximates the construction of a national identity for itself.

> From abroad we simultaneously receive various international influences. Our literature has entered a period of cosmopolitanism. In Lima, this cosmopolitanism is reflected in the imitation of corrosive Western decadence and in the adoption of anarchical *fin-de-siècle* styles. But under this swirling current, a new feeling and revelation are perceived. The universal, ecumenical paths we have chosen to travel, and for which we are reproached, take us ever closer to ourselves. (Mariátegui 1928)[58]

---

56 Mariátegui, José Carlos. *José Carlos Mariátegui: An Anthology*, edited and translated by Harry E. Vanden and Marc Becker, NYU Press, 2011, p. 184.
57 Ibid., p. 232.
58 Ibid.

Giving a central role to aesthetic creation in this process, in a correspondence from Vallejo to Mariátegui, dated 10 December 1926, the *indigenista* literary production becomes identified as part of a common aspiration to "densify more and more the healthy Peruvian inspiration of our action before the continent and the world."[59] In the next section, I examine how this programmatic imperative leads Mariátegui to revise the Marxist conception of the proletarian subject and of the emancipatory process to come, generating new political and intellectual modes of collective action to facilitate the integration of the working class with intellectuals and activists.

Toward a Peruvian Socialism: The Indian Proletariat Subject and the Coming Nation

Mariátegui's own statements notwithstanding, and being mindful of his failure in predicting the future of Peruvian society, it seems plausible to suggest that the dialectical narrative forecasting a socialist, national phase at the end of history was but another idealization issued by mestizo intellectuals from the urban setting. The socialist imaginary would have reiterated a structural invariance common to socialism and liberals alike: to conceive of "realism" in the model of a specific theoretical and political orientation, which furthermore serves to prescribe the future for a given society. This is what we might call *the myth of authentic representation*, according to which the very attempt to escape idealization as a whole in the name of a "realism" or "authentic" account of a social-historical world through a privileged theoretical and political framework cannot but generate another form of idealization. It would follow that Mariátegui's dialectical narrative of Peruvian history, his description of the rural Indian and the anticipation of a modern nation nurtured by Indigenous cooperativism would have been an idealization underwritten by his own Marxist commitments. With this in mind, perhaps a reconsideration of Peruvian literary history enjoins us to separate *indigenismo* from the place assigned to it by socialist imaginary, situating it instead within a wider theoretical and historical frame.[60]

---

59 Vallejo, César. *Letter to José Carlos Mariátegui*, December 10, 1926, my translation. https://www.marxists.org/espanol/vallejo/cartamar.htm

60 Departing from Mariátegui's terminological frame and dialectical methodology, Ismael Marquez, for instance, situates *indigenismo* within a common alternative, four-stage periodization, which aims to place it in a more ideologically neutral context of cultural production. The first category, that of *Indianismo*, corresponds to the nineteenth-century "Romantic" colonial literary production about the Indian, surrendered to nostalgic representations, with no discernible political agenda oriented

As many commentators have noted, such a gesture would also have the advantage of interpreting Mariátegui's thought within a wider historical spectrum that thinks of political and sociocultural frictions in Latin America, once two of his fundamental assumptions are questioned: (1) that there is an essential, integral "reality" which only the Indians themselves can express or communicate, and (2) that the specific revolutionary fate anticipated and imagined by socialism for the rural Indian is but the inevitable result of them achieving a kind of "historical self-consciousness" conforming to the socialist political imaginary and its prescriptive tenets. If these assumptions are suspended, then it would appear that *indigenismo* could only constitute a "more authentic" representation of the rural Indian than those "idealized" ancestralisms it claimed to supersede insofar as the future of the rural Indian, in particular, and the nation in general, coincided with the collectivist tenets of socialism, never mind its "adaptation" to the Peruvian context.

This suggestion, however, operates under the assumption that representation comprises a monolithic gaze, camouflaging its own idealization as authentic representation. Nothing seems to support this thesis but the assumption that every attempt at representation results in an epistemological and pragmatic impossibility, as a result of theoretical mediation. With this in mind, we claim that although one must be wary of what Efraín Kristal (1987) names, following Bourdieu, the "effect of realism" that plagues *indigenista* authors when construing an image of the rural Indian and its future on the basis of given ideological biases, one must be equally wary of an "effect of antirealism" that reifies the rural Indian as an ineffable Otherness, rendering every discourse or theory as equally idealizing or epistemically impotent when attempting an approximation. Indeed, it is trivially true that in its descriptive and projective dimensions, Mariátegui's narrative follows those specific theoretical ideals that determine his understanding of national and global history.

---

toward the restitution of Indigenous values and lacking any effort to confront the socioeconomic hegemony of the urban elites. It is only with the second category, *indigenismo*, that the political goal of vindicating the oppressed Indian becomes defined and an overt aim. Third, in Marquez's periodization we find the "Indigenous literature" to be written by the self-representing Indian writers to come, but which historically never arrived; indeed, this stage becomes not so much a step beyond *indigenismo*, as Mariátegui conceived, but an integral part of the imagination of *indigenista* urban writers, in the broader sense defined above. A fourth category, that of neoindigenismo, designates representations of the Indian produced after the 1950s, roughly after the publication of Arguedas's *The Deep Rivers* (1958). This last phase assimilates elements of magical realism and modernist literature to depict "mythological" facets of Indigenous culture and construe its imagined vindication with an exacerbated sense of lyricism and a disposition toward formal experimentation.

But it doesn't follow that because every representation must be conditioned by given theoretical principles and political imperatives, every such representation must be equally distorting or idealizing. Even so, it must be said that Mariátegui's assumption that only the Indians are able to represent themselves supposes that a social or ethnic group has a kind of privileged access to their own psychic or social reality, which cannot be adequately captured by those who do not inhabit it. Yet it is unclear why self-representation would be somehow immunized from distortion or idealizations; is not the central lesson we have learned from both Marx and Freud, as Mariátegui recognizes, that our collective and individual self-understanding remains shrouded by impersonal-structural conditions and causal factors to which we do not have direct access, but require precise theoretical-analytic intervention?

In any case, since every external representation and projection appears conditioned by background assumptions and imperatives, at the outset of the *Seven Essays*, Mariátegui not only accepts that he is guided by specific political and philosophical convictions, but affirms that the presumption of neutrality is part of a hermeneutic illusion that denies its inherent biases: "My criticism renounces any pretense of impartiality, agnosticism—if indeed any criticism can be so—which I absolutely do not believe. All criticism is informed by philosophical, political, and moral concerns" (Mariátegui 2011: 407). Above all, however, the antirealist position not only assumes that knowledge of a different cultural–social–economic context is a misnomer, but misses how interpretation can be construed not only in *representational* terms—as the *correct* depiction of a particular reality by a descriptive framework—but in terms of the *constructive* task of imagining and forging new possibilities for theoretical and practical agency. Surely, to imagine a future is to project an ideal horizon concerning a possible world on the basis of implicit assumptions or explicit theoretical principles. But again, from this point nothing follows about the plausibility or desirability of specific visions of literary creation or philosophical analysis in its relation to political projects.

This point is of considerable importance, since Mariátegui repeatedly suggests that the transition from *indigenismo* to an Indigenous literature would not merely constitute the transition from an *incorrect representation* of the Indian to a more correct one. Rather, he conceives the emancipation of the Indian as premised on the rural Indian achieving independence from the representations of mestizo writers. The reduction of *indigenismo* to idealization thus underestimates how the dialectical method, as Alain Badiou argues, affirms the task of creative *ideation* against representational *idealization*, such that "a dialectical mode of thinking will be recognized by its conflict with representation."[61] And although grounded in the empirical methods of the social sciences, as we have seen, Marxist practice requires also the revision of theory in light of changing historical circumstances. As Mariátegui writes in *The Liberal Economy and the Socialist Economy*:[62]

> And it cannot be said, on the other hand, that Marxism as a *praxis* currently relies on the data and premises of Marx's economy studies, because the theses and debates of all its congresses are not anything other than a continual reintroduction of the economic and political problems, according to the new aspects of reality.[63]

Above all, Mariátegui systematically avoids the temptation of framing a general solution for a Peruvian socialism, rejecting the "linear conception of history that all countries must necessarily pass through the same process of political and economic development in the formation of a civil society sufficiently strong to support the apparatuses of the state" (Bosteels 2012: 7). In the Preface to *The Contemporary Scene*, Mariátegui had already unambiguously declared:

> I do not think it is possible to imagine the entire panorama of the contemporary world in one theory. [...] We have to explore it and know it, episode by episode, facet by facet. Our view and our imagination will always be delayed in respect to the entirety of the phenomenon. Therefore, the best way to explain and communicate our time is one that is perhaps a little bit journalistic and a bit cinematographic. (Mariátegui 2011: 30)[64]

---

61 Badiou, Alain. *Peut-on penser la politique?*, Le Seuil, 2008, p. 86. Translated by Bruno Bosteels (Bosteels 2012: 70).

62 Mariátegui, José Carlos. "La economía liberal y la economía socialista," in *Defensa del Marxismo*, my translation. https://www.marxists.org/espanol/mariateg/oc/defensa_del_marxismo/paginas/ix.htm

> "Y no se diga, de otro lado, que el marxismo como praxis se atiene actualmente a los datos y premisas de la economía estudiada y definida por Marx, porque las tesis y debates de todos sus congresos no son otra cosa que un continuo replanteamiento de los problemas económicos y políticos, conforme a los nuevos aspectos de la realidad."

63 Ibid.

64 In several texts from *Mundial* and *Variedades* from the same year, Mariátegui repeatedly referenced cinematic production (particularly, the work of Chaplin) as an example of a contemporary artistic form in which national concerns could be integrated

With this broadly "historicist" and antiessentialist conception of socialist practice in mind, there could be no preexisting essential unity attributed to the Indigenous populations that could be assumed in advance of the labor of creative antagonism, just as there could be no pure "essence" incarnating the Peruvian national consciousness to come, prior to its construction. Against such essentialist idealizations, the disaggregation of Indigenous workers and intellectuals, both urban and rural, must be taken as the factual basis that explains why the Peruvian proletariat has not yet become capable of a national organization or of overcoming its social contradictions:

> The Indigenous congresses, misled in recent years by bureaucratic tendencies, have not yet formed a program, but their first meetings indicated a route for Indians of different regions. The Indians lack a national organization. Their protests have always been regional. This has contributed in large part to their defeat. Four million people, conscious of their numbers, do not despair in the future. These same four million people, though they are nothing more than an inorganic mass, a dispersed crowd, are unable to decide its historical course. (Mariátegui 2011: 152)

To find the means to carry forth this organizational mission required an act of "heroic creation"—in the impersonal sense in which Barbusse redefines the subject of the epic narrative—and through which socialism becomes not merely transposed to the Andean world, but singularly adapted to it. As Mariátegui writes in the introduction to the third-anniversary volume of *Amauta* in 1928: "We don't want, certainly, that socialism will be in America, mere doubling and copying. It must be heroic creation. We must give our lives with our own reality, in our own language, the Indoamerican socialism. Herein lies a mission worthy of a new generation."[65]

The integration of the "inorganic mass" which composes the Indigenous populations required forging new institutions through which intellectuals and

---

and seen within a wider international context, an example which he extends to the "journalistic" task of activists and thinkers to interpret their local realities.

65 Mariátegui, José Carlos, "*Aniversario y balance*," in *Amauta*, Year III, no. 17, 1928, my translation. https://www.marxists.org/espanol/mariateg/1928/sep/aniv.htm

"No queremos, ciertamente, que el socialismo sea en América calco y copia. Debe ser creación heróica. Tenemos que dar vida, con nuestra propia realidad, en nuestro propio lenguaje, al socialismo indoamericano. He aquí una misión digna de una generación nueva."

workers could cooperate toward common goals.[66] To achieve this, the political intelligentsia of the urban centers would have to play a different pedagogical role than that imagined by liberal progressives: to facilitate the organization of the disarticulated peasantry, not only through the agency of the *party*, but of a new *syndical* organization which would awaken "class consciousness" for urban and rural workers:

> But the great masses of peasants are disorganized; they have multiple problems to resolve. [...] In order to focus and resolve these problems, it is necessary to organize and educate the masses as to their class role, and to gather them in peasant leagues and peasant communities that lead to the creation of the *National Federation of Peasant Leagues* [...] the Indian will be a militant in the union movement, that is, a soldier who fights for the social liberation of his class. The objective of communities will then be able to realize the full potential of their capabilities, and to bring the federation of all the communities into a single common defense front. (Mariátegui 2011: 347–49)

At the conceptual level, this involves reconceiving the scope and place of the category of the working class within Peruvian society, in light of the development of its economy and society since colonial times. In particular, Mariátegui complicates the division of the social terrain in terms of the binary contradiction between an *industrial proletariat* and the *capitalist bourgeoisie*. This classical conception, Mariátegui argues, betrays a fivefold socioeconomic structure, derived from the thwarted colonial heritage and pre-Hispanic world: (1) a subordinate and exploited multiplicity of Indigenous communities, with their persisting cooperativist labor practices and collective property modalities, dating back to the "agrarian communism" of the *ayllu*; (2) the semifeudal control of landowning *gamonales*, with their "medieval" and semifeudal institution of serfdom, in complicity with the state, derived from colonial times; (3) the indifference and complicity of the republican state and the new creole and mestizo bourgeoisie, whose power stems from the urban centers, ultimately

---

66 Bruno Bosteels (2012) has suggested that, had he been aware of the emergence of Indigenous revolts across the continent, Marx himself could have amended his colossal dismissal of Latin America, recognizing the inherent potential in pre-Hispanic communitarian forms of property and labor. After all, it was an appreciation of the emerging rural peasant uprisings in countries with such a colonial heritage that led Marx—after 1870, in his studies on Ireland, China, Russia and others—to revise the thesis according to which the socialist revolution was first to emerge from the most industrially developed countries with a consolidated industrial proletariat class.

subordinated to the interests of international market capitalism; (4) the urban working classes, including both the nascent industrial proletariat class and those subjugated by colonially derived forms of coastal oligarchic rule; (5) the intellectual mestizo class, centered again in the cities, who were charged with the mission to allow urban and rural workers to coalesce, and to generate the conditions for a new cultural production to emerge outside the urban mestizo centers.

Attending to this internal structure complicates the Marxian picture in an essential way: the persistence of a semifeudal system attested to the lingering colonial vestiges of premodern social forms and values, and their hegemonic power over pre-Hispanic collectivist productive modalities in the rural economy. But while the former designated a precapitalist residue composing the coastal and rural oligarchies, for Mariátegui the latter indicated the potentials in Indigenous traditions to lay the foundations for a *post-liberal economy*, rooted in "habits of cooperation and solidarity that are the empirical expression of a communist spirit" (Mariátegui 2011: 98). Such traditions comprise, above all, "a formidable productive machinery," measurably superior to the aberrant marriage of capitalism and *gamonalismo* which fractured the nation (Ibid.).

This position marked a clear divergence and friction with the more orthodox, Marxist–Leninist line pursued by the Latin American *Komminterm*, proposing not only to widen the base of the organization of the party through the inclusion of other sectors of society, such as the rural peasantry, but peddling a reformulation of the shape of the revolutionary politics to come. It gave way to a more capacious concept of the proletariat class and of the dynamics of class struggle than that specific to the strife of industrial wage laborers in an urban context. As Flores Galindo writes:

> This communal collectivism could serve as the base for the development of socialism in Peru. This was a fundamental thesis, since from it followed a very peculiar image of Peruvian society. While for the International it could be simply defined as "semi-colonial and feudal," for the Peruvian socialists it pertained to a world in which a nascent capitalism coexisted with the feudalism inherited from the colony and the agrarian communism that gave life to the great peasant masses. The collectivist traits allowed the rural populations to listen and partake in the socialist thought; it is for this reason that the term "proletariat" acquired a more generic meaning—as has been remarked by Robert Paris—for Peruvian socialists, including in its interior both workers as well as farmers. (Flores Galindo 1980: 31)

By amplifying the concept of the working class, the rural Indian would pass from being a blind spot, lacking even the status of wage laborers, to an identifiable agency in the political process, mediated by the organization of the party and syndicate. The association of workers thus constituted the political obverse of the multidisciplinary intellectual integration envisaged through the serial publication of *Amauta* and *Labor*, which had an important precedent: in 1918—before his involvement with French and Italian syndicalism—Mariátegui had cofounded the partisan newspaper *La Razón*, which supported worker and student strikes. Following the May 1919 worker's strike in protest against rising food costs, Mariátegui led the formation of the *Peruvian Regional Labor Federation* in 8 July, leading to a mass demonstration congregating in his honor.[67] The periodical was short lived, but it prefigured how Mariátegui would seek to coordinate the labor of intellectuals with the collectivization of rural and urban workers. This ideal would become an overt strategic objective for the journal *Amauta*, leading to a specification of the role of the Indigenous proletariat class.

In this regard, Mariátegui noted that the urban working class had already begun to cooperate with the syndical movement, which in turn potentiated latent "militant aspects" in the rural Indian peasantry:

> The working class avant-garde makes use of those militant aspects of the Indigenous race, which in the mines or urban centers, and particularly in the latter, come into contact with the syndical and political movement. They become assimilated to its principles and are capacitated to play a role in the emancipation of races.[68]

In an essay titled *The Proletariat of Spirit* (*El proletariado del espiritu*), published in the 15th volume of *Amauta*, Luis Aragón argued that, beyond a coalition

---

67 With regard to the May 1919 general strike, Mariátegui deemed this to be a historic event "whose experience led the proletariat to its first attempt at a national syndical organization, under the principle of class struggle."

   Mariátegui, José Carlos. "Presentación a *El Movimiento Obrero* in 1919," published in *Amauta*, 1928.

   "El proceso del 'paro de las subsistencias,' cuya experiencia condujo al proletariado a su primera tentativa de organización sindical nacional, bajo el principio de la lucha de clases, está aquí explicado en sus principales factores y aspectos."

68 Mariátegui, José Carlos. "El problema de las razas en America Latina," in *Tesis Ideológicas*, my translation. https://www.marxists.org/espanol/mariateg/oc/ideologia_y_politica/paginas/tesis%20ideologicas.htm

between intellectuals and workers, ultimately socialism enjoined their *identity* under the name of a "global proletariat."[69] And although Indigenous communities were still in the course of being organized into a united front, the cooperativist productive modalities that persisted across disparate Indigenous populations under the *latifundio* could be potentiated through the labor of syndical organization[70] and the progressive consolidation of the socialist party. With regard to the latter, *The Programmatic Principles of the Socialist Party* (1928) outlined a "doctrinal declaration" that at once placed the problematic of the Peruvian working class in the context of international proletariat struggle, at the same time indicating the singular character of the Peruvian situation. It thus reiterated the need to reconcile Indigenous cooperativism with the productive demands of modern civilization against restorative projects:

> [L]ike the stimulation that freely provides for the resurgence of Indigenous peoples, the creative manifestation of its forces and native spirit, does not mean at all a romantic and anti-historical trend of reconstructing or resurrecting Inca socialism, which corresponded to historical conditions completely bypassed, and which remains only as a favorable factor in a perfectly scientific production technique, that

---

69 Aragón, Luis. *El proletariado del espíritu*, in *Amauta*: no. 15, 1928, pp. 3–5.
70 Mariátegui, José Carlos, *Estatutos de la Confederación General de Trabajadores del Perú*, 1929, https://www.marxists.org/espanol/mariateg/oc/ideologia_y_politica/paginas/estatutos.htm

> With regard to the syndical organization of the working class, Mariátegui defended a unionist and federalist separatism in Peru. Throughout the different issues of *Labor*, two essential articles from 1929 begin to frame the problem of a syndical coalition, in critical relation to the European experience: *Origen y desarrollo de los sindicatos de oficio* and *Sobre los comites de fábrica y sindicatos de industria*. Placing the problematic of the coordination between industrial workers and the peasantry at its center, these provisory meditations would result in the 17 May 1929 *Estatuto and Programa de Lucha*, laying out the foundation of the *Confederación General de Trabajadores del Perú* (CGTP). The syndical movement would thus complement the labor of the party, tilting the political process through legal reform, while keeping the socialist horizon in place.

> The creation of the CGTP concretized a long sequence in which attempts at unification for Peruvian workers finally take place, a process dating back to the 1913 *Maritime and Terrestrial Federation* in Callao, passing through the *First Workers' Congress* in Lima in 1922 and the formulation of the *Local Labor Federation* during the same year, finally leading to the anarcho-syndicalist inflections of the 1923 *Regional Indigenous Workers Federation* and of the 1926 *Local Labor Congress*. The CGTP's efforts were both pedagogical and tactical: collective action toward local reform was to be put to the service of the development of a general "class consciousness," through which urban and rural workers would integrate themselves also to the international proletariat revolution.

is, the habits of cooperation and socialism of Indigenous peasants. Socialism presupposes the technique, the science, the capitalist stage. It cannot permit any setbacks in the realization of the achievements of modern civilization but, on the contrary, must methodically accelerate the incorporation of these achievements into national life. (Mariátegui 2011: 239)

As noted by César Ugarte, Mariátegui would then identify the following essential traits associated with the communitarian practices in rural Indigenous communities to be appropriated and potentiated within a socialist, modern national project:

Collective property of the land labored by the "*Ayllu*" or group of families, though still divided in non-transferable lots; collective property of water, arable lands and forests by the tribe, that is, the federation of established *ayllus* surrounding a single village, common cooperation in work, individual appropriation of crops and yield. (Mariátegui 1928)[71]

The organization of the *ayllu* as a collective labor unit would thus support a different productive model than the liberal proposal to make of the rural Indian small-property owners, for the latter ultimately liquidated their native traditions and the potentials inherent in their productive modalities. Moreover, Mariátegui contrasts the cooperativist ideal with those "spiritualist ecstasies" that distort the problem of the Indian by occluding the question of property rights and labor:

In Peru, communal property does not represent a primitive economy that has been gradually replaced by a progressive economy founded on individual property. No, the communities have been stripped of their land for the benefit of the feudal or semifeudal large landholdings that are constitutionally incapable of technical progress. [...] The community, however, on the one hand leads to an effective capacity for development and transformation, and on the other hand is presented as a system of production that keeps alive in the Indians the moral stimuli needed for their maximum performance as workers. (Mariátegui 2011: 99)

---

71 Mariátegui 1928, https://www.marxists.org/archive/mariateg/works/7-interpretive-essays/essay03.htm

These "practical reasons," however factually controversial in the last instance, led Mariátegui to postulate the relative advantage of the Indian's cooperativist productive model in comparing coastal and rural agricultural yield, attending in particular to the produce of cotton and sugar plantations in the Peruvian south. The latter's "measurable superiority" provided economic evidence, he argued, against the liberal prospects of fragmentation of the land into parcels for small-property ownership:

> The sugar and cotton *latifundios* cannot be divided into parcels to make way for small properties—a liberal and capitalist solution of the agrarian problem—without negatively impacting yield and its profitable functioning based on the industrialization of agriculture. The collective state management of these enterprises is, however, perfectly possible. (Mariátegui 2011: 250)

It is in continuity with this appropriative principle and productivist appraisal that the 1928 *Program of the Socialist Party* conceived of the integration of a modern national project with the labor practices and structures that organized the labor of peasant populations, fixing a horizon beyond the disjunction between capitalist modernity and the ancestralist restoration of "agrarian communism":

> Socialism finds the same in the subsistence of the community in the great agrarian enterprises, in the elements of a socialist solution to the agrarian question, a solution that would have tolerated in part the exploitation of the land by small peasants, there where *yanaconazgo* or small property ownership recommend discarding individual management, to the extent that a collective management is advanced, in those areas where that kind of exploitation prevails. But this, the same as the stimulation that lends itself to the free resurgence of Indigenous thought, to the creative manifestation of its forces and native spirit, does not mean at all a romantic and ahistorical tendency of construction or resurrection of Incan socialism, which corresponded to historical conditions that have been completely overcome, and which remains only as an appropriable factor within a perfectly scientific technics of production.[72]

---

72 Mariátegui, José Carlos. "Programa del Partido Socialista Peruano," in *La organización del proletariado*, Comisión Política del Comité Central del Partido Comunista Peruano, 1967, my translation. https://www.marxists.org/espanol/mariateg/1928/oct/07a.htm

In its broadest philosophical implications, the rural Indigenous populations become in this framework recognizable as part of a more broadly defined proletariat class, once one revises the dialectical materialist *theory of contradiction* to account for how gamonalismo and Indigenous cooperativism coexisted within a "capitalist" state in the Peruvian nation.

To understand this operation, and following Alain Badiou (2011), we note that the Marxist inscription of contradiction in a *materialist* register was given two distinct formulations, continuous with the critique of capitalist economies: (1) *the fundamental contradiction*—expressing the structural relation between the forces of production, as well as the objective dynamics of private accumulation/control over the means and ends of production under capitalism; (2) *the principal contradiction*—expressing the historical relation between the proletariat and bourgeoisie, as the subjective dynamics of class struggle:

> The specification of the fundamental contradiction gives us a definitional construction in the following manner: capitalist is any social formation in which the private appropriation of the means of production tends to constitute a barrier to the necessary and growing socialization of the productive forces. Under capitalism, the competitive dispersion of property (the multiplicity of subject-profits) enters into a restrictive collision with the process of the organic concentration of the means of production. There you have, the classics say in one voice, what constitutes the base of the social history of humanity. All the rest is superstructure.
>
> The specification of the principal contradiction provides us with an entirely different definition of capitalism. Capitalist is any society in which

---

"El socialismo encuentra, lo mismo en la, subsistencia de las comunidades que en las grandes empresas agrícolas, los elementos de una solución socialista de la cuestión agraria, solución que tolerará en parte la explotación de la tierra por los pequeños agricultores, ahí donde el yanaconazgo o la pequeña propiedad recomienden dejar a la gestión individual, en tanto que se avanza en la gestión colectiva de la agricultura, las zonas donde ese género de explotación prevalece. Pero esto, lo mismo que el estímulo que se presta al libre resurgimiento del pueblo indígena, a la manifestación creadora de sus fuerzas y espíritu nativo, no significa en lo absoluto una romántica y antihistórica tendencia de construcción o resurrección del socialismo incaico, que corresppndió a condiciones históricas completamente superadas y del cual sólo quedan como factor aprovechable dentro de una técnica de producción perfectamente científica, los hábitos de cooperación y socialismo de los campesinos indígenas. El socialismo presupone la técnica, la ciencia, la etapa capitalista, y no puede importar el menor retroceso en la adquisición de las conquistas de la civilización moderna, sino, por el contrario, la máxima y metódica aceleración de la incorporación de estas conquistas en la vida nacional."

the central class conflict, the one that organizes political life, opposes the bourgeoisie and the proletariat. Such is, the classics state unanimously, the motor of the social history of humanity. The rest is ideology.

Base and motor. Two contradictions, two definitions, a single object—capitalism—and a single doctrine, Marxism. (Badiou 2011: 26)

Badiou notes that the category of the "proletariat" plays a definitional role in both formulations: first as the "objective" base of the productive force against *capitalist* control, and second as the opposing "subjective" polarity in the proletariat's class struggle against *bourgeois* hegemony. In its structural-objective and historical-subjective sides, the working class thus refers, respectively, to (1) an "arrangement of places, quantities, invariants" (base), and (2) a militant, revolutionary agency (the "motor" of change) that introduces a "coefficient of torsion," that is, a strong "qualitative shift" in the organization of places that determine the fundamental contradiction. The proletariat therefore not only opposes the bourgeoisie negatively, in their *structural* objective placement, but becomes an active subjective *force*: "Strong difference (the subjective project of the proletariat, that is, communism, cannot be represented by the bourgeoisie)/Class struggle, and not a simple binary distinction of the social./ Reversible asymmetry, within the problematic of the revolution."(Ibid: 27) This subjective force cannot be reduced to an anarchic fulguration that emerges *ex nihilo*; rather, it is conditioned by the structural dynamics specified by the fundamental contradiction. In this sense, the two contradictions are not intelligible apart from each other: the fundamental contradiction without the principal contradiction only describes a synchronic objective order of established positions; the principal contradiction without the fundamental is in turn a volitional coefficient stripped from all contextual, strategic and programmatic specificity. In short, taken together, "the definition of capitalism ultimately leads to the divided definition of the working class."[73]

Following these indications, we can better understand how Mariátegui's heterodox socialist practice adapts the terms of both the fundamental and principal contradictions to the Peruvian context to understand both its structural basis (the socioeconomic analysis and grounding) and its subjective agency (the rural and urban proletariat). The Indigenous populations working under the latifundio constitute the principal "motor" of class struggle, which leads to "strong qualitative difference" in the structuration of Peruvian society—not

---

[73] Badiou, Alain, *Theory of the Subject*, translated by Bruno Bosteels, Continuum, 2012, pp. 27.

only a *negation* of the existing socioeconomic order, but a *positive* and *affirmative* act, again reiterating this as an act of "faith":

> All great human ideals have started with a denial, but they also have been an affirmation. [...] It is with pessimistic and negative spirits of this nature that our optimism of the ideal refuses to let us be confused. Negative attitudes are absolutely sterile. Action is made of negations and affirmations. The new generation in our America and around the world is, above all, a generation that shouts its faith, sings its hope. (Mariátegui 2011: 231)

The inextricability of negation and affirmation places Mariátegui's "active philosophy" and secularized conception of myth and faith in the company of contemporary attempts to reconstitute a creative conception of materialist dialectics, refusing the isolation of the insurrectionary dynamics of class struggle from the constructive labor of thought. As Badiou (2007) argues, the materialist dialectic must account for the role played by the subject in the political process, which is at once antagonistic and creative: *concrete negation* includes not only the *destruction* of the old world, but a movement of *subtraction*, through which new structures are materialized as part of creative novelty:

> All creations, all novelties, are in some sense the affirmative part of a negation. "Negation," because if something happens as new, it cannot be reduced to the objectivity of the situation where it happens. So, it is certainly like a negative exception to the regular laws of this objectivity. But "affirmation," affirmative part of the negation, because if a creation is reducible to a negation of the common laws of objectivity, it completely depends on them concerning its identity. [...]
>
> I name subtraction the affirmative part of negation. [...] Clearly, this subtraction is in the horizon of negation; but it exists apart from the purely negative part of negation. It exists apart from destruction. In any case we name subtraction this part of negation which is oriented by the possibility of something which exists absolutely apart from what exists under the laws of what negation negates.
>
> So, negation is always, in its concrete action—political or artistic—suspended between destruction and subtraction. That the very essence of negation is destruction has been the fundamental idea of the last century. The fundamental idea of the beginning century must be that the very essence of negation is subtraction.[74] (Badiou 2007)

---

74 Badiou, Alain. *Subtraction, Destruction, Negation*, presented at UCLA, 2007. Available at: http://www.lacan.com/badpas.htm

The semantic resonance should appear more than superficially obvious: Badiou's emphasis on "affirmation," "subjective creation" and "fidelity" to a creative act is continuous Mariátegui's affirmative conception of "creative antagonism," his account of revolutionary "faith" and the ideation of a new "living myth."

What underlies this shared rhetoric, beyond terminological and affective affinity, is the vocation to define a new conception, the subject, where theological and voluntarist vocabularies are repurposed to a secular, universalist register that evades exhausted essentialisms or dogmatisms. In his 1975–76 book *Theory of the Subject*, Badiou diagnoses two possible and corresponding deviations from the materialist dialectic in relation to the fundamental and principal contradictions. An "active materialism," he argues, cannot remain content with the reflective operation given by the metaphor of thought as a "mirror," according to which the subject merely *represents* the world in its structural composition. But neither can it fetishize the complementary image of the "asymptote," as an indomable excess to all representation. Materialism, that is, can be neither *structuralist-dogmatist* nor *dynamicist-anarchist*: it must produce a concept of practice in which revolutionary agency is irreducible to the structural logic of places that represents an existing situation, while nevertheless remaining grounded in the latter. Resisting the logic of representation, the dialectic must nevertheless retain from the representational image of "the mirror" the possibility of an address to the Real in its structural basis.

This is the key to salvaging realism from the skeptical relativization that renders different cultural, socioeconomic worlds incommensurable with regard to each other: it is always possible to *positivize* into the order of knowledge that which, within the hegemonic structure, appears as its remainder, within a new structural distribution:

> [W]hat we did not know before was determined as a remainder of what has come to be known, at the crossover between the nameless movement through which the real appears as a problem and the retroaction, named knowledge, which provides the solution [...] there is no unknowable, even though all knowledge demands its position. (Badiou 2011: 201)

As Badiou further elaborates, in the process of subjectivation, thinking appropriates the un-representable point of a situation by "supplementing" it with a new presence:

> The real of knowledge is at all times that which is impossible to know. But that is precisely what asymptotically fixates the future of the reflection. This impossible, therefore, will be known, all the while being

placed in the position of possibility (of reflection) by the new supplement in its field.[75]

And it is the same for Mariátegui's rejection of subjective sublimation as a self-sufficient force, in the name of a synthetic, integrative discipline.[76] For as we saw in the first section, it was precisely the overemphasis on a purely destructive conception that was responsible for anarchic avowals of violence against the mestizo hegemony, as in the late work of González Prada. As Mariátegui writes in his 1928 essay *The Heroic and Creative Sense of Socialism*—prologue to Valcárcel's *Tempest in the Andes*—it is not toward a *destructive* disposition that the proletariat must orient itself, but rather toward building a "superior social and economic order," composing itself in a collective, "human effort":

> A new civilization cannot arise from a sad and humiliated world of miserable helots with no greater merits or faculties than their servility and misery. The proletariat only enters history politically, as a social class, at the moment it discovers its mission to build a superior social order with elements gathered by human effort, whether moral or amoral, just or unjust. And it has not gained this ability miraculously. It has won it by situating itself solidly on the terrain of the economy, of production.[77]

If, for Mariátegui, "the bourgeoisie no longer has any myths," this ultimately means that, as Badiou would write decades later, that "[t]he bourgeoisie has no longer been a subject for quite some time" (Badiou 2011: 200). The "peasant proletariat subject" cannot be thus reduced to an insurrectionary force which negates the *latifundio*: it is its *concrete negation*, leading to the advent of a new national and collective consciousness.

The subject commensurate with the rise of an Indigenous literature would accordingly not merely stand as the polar opposite of the mestizo, but signal a new collective consciousness within which the structural terms of the contradiction are rendered inoperative. In this regard, the function of *indigenismo*

---

75 Ibid.
76 Mariátegui parallels Gramsci's rejection of an economicist determinism, and the latter's appeal to underlying "laws of History" in *The Revolution against Das Kapital*—as well as from Sorel's rejection of the idea that the dialectic unfolds as an organic development in socioeconomic sphere, analogous to the evolutionary process of natural selection.
77 Mariátegui, José Carlos, "The Heroic and Creative Sense of Socialism," translated by Harry E. Vanden and Marc Becker, in *Mariátegui: An Anthology,* Monthly Review Press, 2011, pp. 212-13.

can be seen as anticipating and imagining the figurations of the coming subject as much as the coming nation, just like the labor of the intellectual and political activist mestizo is to help prepare the conditions for the emancipation of the rural Indian. Nevertheless, this figuration cannot be conceived independently of the concrete forms of alienation distinctive of the postcolonial Peruvian situation, requiring a complication of the traditional Marxist structural analysis as much as a reconception of the forms of agency required for political action. The action of the mestizo revolutionary subject is precisely to prepare the conditions for the emergence of the Indian revolutionary proletarian subject, as the emblem of a new "national consciousness."

To sum up, we can see how the re-elaboration of the central Marxist categories—contradiction, negation, subject, antagonism, class struggle—attending to the role of revolutionary mestizo and the rise of a new figure of the Indian proletariat revolutionary subject gave way to a unique conception of dialectical and materialist philosophy, within which *indigenista* literature appears not only "realist" in the narrow, representational sense in which it correctly captures the "Indian spirit." Beyond that restricted notion of realism, it serves the utopian labor of imagining an alternative modernity, within which the historic alienation of the rural Indian, and their division from both urban workers and mestizos, would be definitively overcome, rekindling inherent potentials in their own traditions and productive modalities.

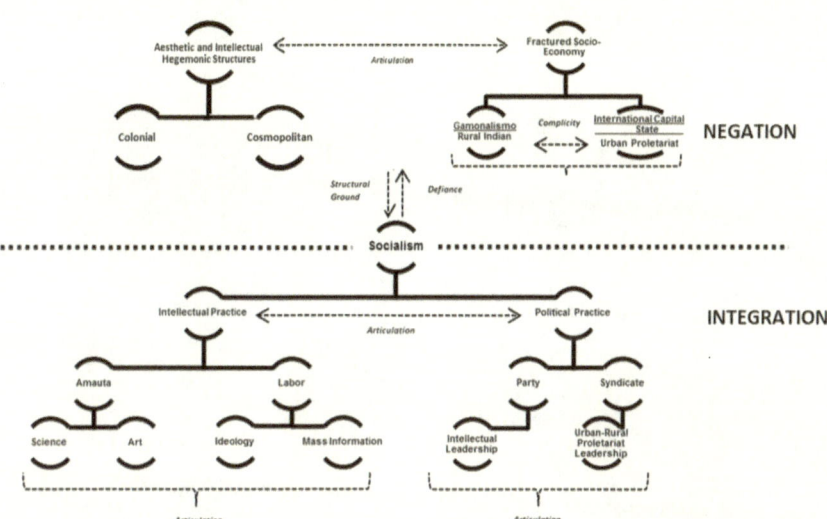

Diagram 1.2 Mariátegui's System.

Diagram 1.2 illustrates how Mariátegui conceives of the relation between intellectual-artistic and political practice as part of the integrative practice of socialism qua active philosophy.

Our elucidation of the peculiarities of Mariátegui's socialist conception as an "active philosophy," and its proximity to contemporary attempts to reconstitute dialectical materialism, however, by no means entails that his vision of revolution could be simply transposed to understand Peruvian reality today. If anything, to subscribe to the dynamic and revisionary conception of philosophy that Mariátegui elaborates entails, above all, that we should treat his work in the same way as he treated Marx: amending its postulates and scope in light of changing historical circumstances, attending to both the peculiarities of one's local context, but also of the global "contemporary scene."

It goes without saying that Peruvian history from the 1930s onward did not follow on the paths that Mariátegui's dialectical narrative anticipated. The negation of the "liberal phase" by a socialist society, nurtured by elements of Indigenous cooperativism, would not come to fruition. And the overcoming of *indigenismo* by an "Indigenous literature" did not take place. By the end of the century, revolutionary politics would become the avatar for humanitarian horror and sectarian fragmentation, rather than a horizon for national integration and a plausible vision for collective life beyond social–economic divisions. Attending to the divergent paths that history has taken ought, then, to be the starting point in attempting a critical reckoning with Mariátegui's work.

Chapter 2

FROM EXISTENTIAL DESPAIR TO COLLECTIVE JUBILATION: CÉSAR VALLEJO'S MATERIALIST POETICS

> Hay un timbre humano, un sabor vital y de subsuelo que contiene a la vez la corteza indígena y el sustrátum común a todos los hombres, al cual propende el artista, a través de no importa que disciplinas, teorías o procesos creadores. [...] A ese rasgo de hombría y de pureza conmino a mi generación.
> —César Vallejo, *Contra el secreto profesional: A propósito de Pablo Abril de Vivero*, 1987.

Introduction: Vallejo's Universalist Poetics and the Question of *Indigenismo*

As we saw in the previous chapter, José Carlos Mariátegui lauds César Vallejo's first two poetic collections for having forged a new lyrical style within an emerging intellectual avant-garde, capturing with unprecedented authenticity the rural Indigenous sentiment and spirit. Such was the nascent role of *indigenismo* during the "cosmopolitan period" of Peruvian history, defined by its experimental tendencies, which broke with the dependency on Spanish and colonial aesthetic forms. Following Antenor Orrego's verdict, Mariátegui affirmed Vallejo's "poetic liberty" and "the triumph of the vernacular in writing" against the ornamental excesses of colonial literature, in which the voice of the rural Indian was first rendered legible.

For Mariátegui, Vallejo's works attest to the emergence of a "genuine Americanism," pointing to the Indigenous literature to come, beyond the representations of the rural Indian provided by the urban mestizo:

> Vallejo is a poet of race. In Vallejo, for the first time in our history, Indigenous sentiment is given pristine expression. [...] But the Indian is the fundamental, characteristic feature of his art. In Vallejo there is a genuine Americanism, not a descriptive or local Americanism. Vallejo does not exploit folklore. Quechua words and popular expressions are

not artificially introduced into his language; they are spontaneous and an integral part of his writing. It might be said that Vallejo does not choose his vocabulary. He is not deliberately autochthonous. He does not delve into tradition and history in order to extract obscure emotions from its dark substratum. His poetry and language emanate from his flesh and spirit; he embodies his message. Indigenous sentiment operates in his art perhaps without his knowledge or desire.[1] (Mariátegui 1928)

Challenging the idea that Vallejo's work is primarily defined by its ethnic, Peruvian or Americanist character, some critics have pointed instead to its universal dimension: the way the poet addresses human reality writ large, and engages in a formal experimental spirit that communicates with literary, philosophical and political experiences from around the world. Rafael Gutiérrez Girardot (2003), for instance, has insisted in that Vallejo's works must be understood alongside aesthetic and intellectual currents transpiring in Western culture at the turn of the century, bearing witness to the "destructiveness of the epoch" that afflicted the human race as a whole:

> Universality is precisely what characterizes César Vallejo's work, which is not to suppress his Peruvian, Indigenous, American, Hispanic identity […] the critical orthodoxy reduced Vallejo to a merely Hispanic-American or Peruvian phenomenon, depriving him thus of that universality which is not the one of a vague and general "humanity," but the concrete one of his contemporaneity and of his participation in the perception and formulation of the destructiveness of the epoch with those few poets from other cultural traditions that suffered it. (Gutiérrez Girardot 2003: 6, my translation)

Although these statements doubtlessly point to a crucial aspect in Vallejo's work, particularly its tragic and "existentialist" quality, they nevertheless fall victim to an equally counterproductive one-sidedness. For what Mariátegui conceives as the emergence a "genuine Americanism" in Vallejo's work in particular, and *indigenismo* more broadly, was precisely the indissociable nature of its universal and its regional scope, carrying the expression of the Indigenous problematic beyond telluric nostalgias. The regionalist expression of literary *indigenismo* and its universal dimension were thus not to be understood as incompatible characterizations between which one must choose; they

---

[1] Mariátegui 1928, https://www.marxists.org/archive/mariateg/works/7-interpretive-essays/essay07.htm

constitute simultaneous aspects of a singular poetic voice, fractured between a general human predicament and the contrivances of the poet's local and regional experience.

Attempting to traverse the disjunction between these dimensions in Vallejo's work, recent commentary has traced deep connections between his early poetry, in which local and regional themes appear more prescient, and the overt universalism of his late political poetry. But to map the connections between the local and the universal merely diachronically, as successive phases in Vallejo's oeuvre, also risks obfuscating how both dimensions are inextricable, as part of a coherent, if also conflicted, development. For just as many of the "Paris poems" continue to evoke a rural Indigenous sentiment and localize the poetic voice in its cultural and bodily matrix, the poems comprising *Los Heraldos Negros* and *Trilce* address themes that extend beyond such concerns to think of the human condition as a whole, also interrogating the possibility of its collective destiny. Which is to say that the preoccupation with the destiny of mankind in general is also articulated in response to the poet's local and personal experience, binding the poet to a history, a time and place.

Following this basic insight, in what follows I propose a more nuanced articulation between Vallejo's response to the Peruvian and rural Indigenous context, his persistent existential "cry of protest" for mankind, his literary avant-gardism and his endorsement of a collective-revolutionary destiny for global humanity. Only in seeing these dimensions as part of a coherent intellectual development can one understand the impetus behind Vallejo's contribution not only to poetry or literature, but to "the problem of the Indian" within the nascent spirit of *indigenismo*, as conceived by Mariátegui. Following Linda Nochlin, Tom Gunning and Michelle Clayton, we argue that if Vallejo defies the central tenets of the Latin American tradition as much as those of "literary modernism," it is insofar as he ultimately seeks to reconcile the two opposing dispositions of the modernist artistic project: a *nostalgia for the past* and a *passion for the future*.[2] Nostalgia and passion: the wound of loss that marks human finitude, and the jubilation of collective being against the destructive force of time and the limits of the body. In its last expression, Vallejo's universalism is not one that merely identifies invariances across human experiences, or which bears witness to the universal spirit of his historical moment, as Gutiérrez Girardot suggests. Rather, it elaborates the

---

2 Clayton, Michelle. *Poetry in Pieces: César Vallejo and Lyric Modernity*, UC Press, 2011, Chapter I.

construction of a new lyric idiom as the aesthetic counterpart of the project to forge a new collective humanity, in Mariátegui's sense, guided by the clamor for liberty and justice, beyond national or ethnic determinations. For Vallejo did not awaken an "authenticity of expression" insofar as he ruminated on the idiosyncrasies of the rural setting, fetishizing its cultural environs, mourning its ancestral greatness or vituperating against the Western hubris of the city. Rather, Mariátegui already tells us, his lyric voice is at once an expression of the Andean world and also a statement on behalf of mankind as a whole, so that "the poet of a race" is *at the same time* "the poet of his era":

> This great poet, lyrical and subjective, acts as an interpreter of the universe, of mankind. There is nothing in his poetry reminiscent of the egoistic, narcissistic lament of romanticism. The romanticism of the nineteenth century was basically individualistic; the romanticism of the 1900s is, on the other hand, spontaneous and logically socialist, unanimist. Vallejo, from this point of view, belongs not only to his race but also to his century, to his era. (Mariátegui 1928)[3]

Although Mariátegui's premature death meant he could never be exposed to Vallejo's later poetry and his continuing engagement with Marxism, already his early works took an essential step toward the overcoming of the "dead myths" of liberal writers, prefiguring that "national consciousness" in which the mimetic colonial impetus would finally be overcome and an original Peruvian literature would come into view.

In the first section, I clarify how Mariátegui's reading of Vallejo's early poetry can be further nuanced by attending to his depiction of a poetic subject affected by alienation and traversed by different possible relations to nostalgia. In the second section, I show how in *Trilce* the first figure of the poetic subject, burdened by loss and finitude, becomes the basis for a poetic language that thinks the "material bases of experience" (Clayton), where the lyric voice and subject unravels, reduced to the arrest of libidinal drives and bodily functions. At the same time, Vallejo prefigures an embryonic process whereby the inconsistency of the incarnate, finite individual becomes incorporated to minoritarian struggle and collective subjectivity. In the third section, I explore the extension of Vallejo's collectivist insights into aesthetic and political theory during his European exile, focusing on several of the essays compiled under *El arte y la revolución*, in which he qualifies his appropriation of socialist philosophy

---

3 Ibid.

toward a universalist vision against partisan dogmatisms. In the fourth and fifth sections, I respectively trace the figure of new militant Indian revolutionary subject in *El Tungsteno*, and of the global proletariat collective subject in *Poemas humanos*, in which nostalgic arrest is progressively supplanted by a subversive furor and affirmative jubilation. Taken together, we can see how the nostalgic address to the local scene and the rural Indian world that appears since his earlier poetry becomes mediated by a constructive vision of revolutionary politics, against the dogmatism of European Bolshevism. In the sixth and final section, I show how the universalist aspirations of Vallejo's "communist poetry," as Alain Badiou calls it, result in the production of a generic human subject across his final poetic collection, *Spain, Take Away from Me This Cup*, written in response to the Spanish Civil War of 1936–39. At its lyrical apex in this collection, Vallejo's poetic voice acquires a cosmic and universal scope, celebrating the integrity of Man against both the lawfulness of nature and culture, traversing all strata that bind individuals and groups to contingent orders of identity, including those of race and nation.

Vallejo's Cry of Protest: Nostalgia, Temporality and the Subject of Loss

The nostalgia of absence

For Mariátegui, the definitive interruption of Romantic literary approximations to the rural Indian demanded a definitive cessation of the *ancestralist nostalgia* characteristic of "*pasadista*" writers and of the liberal victimization of the Indian that made of acculturation and miscegenation their singular destiny. The ancestralist disposition, Mariátegui tells us, merely longed for a return to an idealized past and obviated the broken relation to this past in the present. The liberal disposition, in turn, sought to directly thematize the subjugated present of the rural Indian, but victimized the latter to the point of depriving it of a real future, embracing assimilation under the Westernizing process of capitalist modernization. In contrast to the idealization inherent to both liberal and ancestralist approaches, Mariátegui argues, Vallejo's poetic voice expresses a unique *nostalgia of absence*, through which alienation becomes not only a passive mourning, but an act of "metaphysical protest":

> Very well, Vallejo is supremely nostalgic. He evokes the past with tenderness, but always subjectively. His nostalgia, conceived in lyric purity, should not be confused with the literary nostalgia of the *pasadistas*. Vallejo's nostalgia is not merely retrospective. He does not yearn for the Inca empire in the way that *pasadismo perricholesco* yearns for the

viceroyalty. His nostalgia is a sentimental or a metaphysical protest; a nostalgia of exile, of absence. (Mariátegui 1928)[4]

For Mariátegui, the "experience of exile" described by Vallejo is not that of idyllic withdrawal, through which the poetic voice would remain in harmonious rapport to his rural environs. It rather incarnates a subject dislocated from the domestic space, suspended between the rural and urban contexts, and between his individual destiny and that of humanity as a whole. This "nostalgia of absence" thus characterizes what Alain Sicard (2016) has called "a dialectics of lack" in Vallejo's early poetry, where the concept of "orphanhood" expresses not only familial mourning in relation to the familial unit, the departed brother or the parental dyad, but moreover generalizes *loss* as defining the human condition.[5] Insofar as it remains inscribed in his familial and rural context, Vallejo's nostalgia of absence speaks thus of a past that is never redeemed by manufactured memory, but testifies to a broken rapport in which the subject is defined by a frustrated relationship to the Other. Accordingly, Vallejo's lyric voice is constantly affected by a frustrated relation to his world, to the broken home and his fellow man, provoking a heretical howl against the indolence, or even hatred, of God.

This form of nostalgia, rooted in the immediacy of the domestic scene, yet also defining humanity as traversed by loss, is manifested throughout the poems comprising *The Black Heralds* and *Trilce*. In *To My Brother Miguel*, which is addressed to the departed sibling, Vallejo not only recollects but reenacts the past through memory, as the grief of loss becomes magnified in a temporal reversal: recalling an irresolvable childhood game of hide and seek, Vallejo folds the ubiquity of finitude and mourning back onto the intimacy of the domestic scene, the innocent play between brothers. The poet relives the past of infancy, as the lyric voice becomes disarmed from all eloquence and is reduced to a child's whimpering tremor in the face of desertion.

> Brother, today I sit on the brick bench outside the house,
> where you make a bottomless emptiness.
> I remember we used to play at this hour of the day, and mama
> would calm us: "There now, boys […]"

---

4 Mariátegui 1928, https://www.marxists.org/archive/mariateg/works/7-interpretive-essays/essay07.htm

5 Indeed, Sicard notes that the concept of orphanhood appears in Vallejo's poetry over a year before the death of his mother, as seen in his poem *Bajo los álamos*, published in June 1917 in *La Industria*, Trujillo.

> Now I go hide
> as before, from all these evening
> prayers, and I hope that you will not find me.
> In the parlor, the entrance hall, the corridors.
> Later, you hide, and I do not find you.
> I remember we made each other cry,
> brother, in that game.
>
> Miguel, you hid yourself
> one night in August, nearly at daybreak,
> but instead of laughing when you hid, you were sad.
> And your other heart of those dead afternoons
> is tired of looking and not finding you. And now
> shadows fall on the soul.
>
> Listen, brother, don't be too late
> coming out. All right? Mama might worry.[6] (Vallejo 2007: 155)

The distance that thwarts Vallejo's frustrated recall of the household becomes at the same time sublimated, inscribed without measure in a "bottomless emptiness" that explodes childhood fear into the ubiquitous shadow of human finitude. As the poem closes, Vallejo's nostalgic retrogression becomes concentrated in the arrest of maternal anxiety: "Mama might worry," the poem ends. This desolate cry, however, is already and subtly an act of metaphysical defiance, enabling what time does not allow: its reversal, and thus the reenactment of what has come to pass. Through the unraveling of childhood memory, as Sicard has shown, Vallejo's early poetry produces something akin to a "dialectics of lack," as it "translates this presence of death in the very origin of life"[7] (Sicard 2016: 111, my translation).

The "wound of loss" scarring the poet is but one of the many forms in which Vallejo's poetry attests to a frustrated rapport to the Other. At every scale, from the everydayness of the family bond to the cosmic stand of Man before

---

6 All quotations from Vallejo's poetry are cited from: Vallejo, César. *The Complete Poetry: A Bilingual Edition*, edited and translated by Clayton Eshleman, University of California Press, 2007.
7 Sicard, Alain. "La dialéctica de la carencia en la poesía de César Vallejo," in *Zama*, 2016, p. 111.

> "Vallejo traduce esta presencia de la muerte en el origen mismo de la vida."

God, the poet occupies a dislocated position with regard to his world. This motif is particularly evident throughout *The Black Heralds*, where paternal absence becomes a surrogate for the existential crisis of mankind in the wake of "the death of God" (Girardot 2003): the figure of the dormant Father in *The Distant Footsteps* (*Los pazos lejanos*) reveals the solitude of the unraveling home, while in *The Black Heralds*, the poet, standing for a representative of humanity, is confronted by a scornful and indifferent God. The absence of the divine Father is thus indexed negatively in the annulment of bodily communion, as the "bread is burnt at the oven's door," while the collapse of the familial unit in *The Distant Footsteps* becomes likewise a metonymic symbol for the alienation of Man from his home: "the flight into Egypt, the styptic farewell" ("*la huida a Egipto/el restañante adios*") (Vallejo 2007: 106).

In *The Eternal Dice*, the divine Father's indifferent quietude becomes again negatively correlated to a placid removal from finitude: the motherless, omnipotent force who (pro)creates and gives life but does not lose what it cannot have, for as increate being, existing outside of time, it was "always well." The irony is that the Father's infinite power and disembodied existence deprives him of the singular power of suffering and loss, which is Man's alone. Divine plenitude becomes thus transvalued into a privation, as the *negation of loss*. By the same token, loss becomes transvalued from a negative valence into a vital potency in the face of finitude: only Man can become severed from the Other and from a past, *because he has one*. Alienation, the scarring of time, defines the human subject in its local relation to the Other, but also in relation to the impossible transcendence of divine shelter. In the poem, Vallejo completes the heretical inversion, as divinity is subtracted from paternal indolence and becomes identified with Man's material existence instead:

> My God, had you been a man,
> today you would know how to be God;
> but you, who were always fine,
> feel nothing for your own creation.
> Indeed, man suffers you; God is he! (Vallejo 2007: 99)

As Mariátegui notes, the nostalgia of absence that describes the permanent removal of origins acquires a more elusive and radical form in several poems throughout *Trilce*, unbinding the poetic object from any clear referent or environs, whether of natural, individual or cultural origin. In *Trilce XXXIV*, the poetic voice laments the loss of "the stranger," whose identity is never disclosed, distancing and temporalizing itself as the "ardent evening" descends into the certain night. Vallejo progressively exacerbates the movement of removal until it acquires an apocalyptic scope, undoing the teleological naivety of youth through a stern confrontation with finality that terminates the world without reason: *at the end*, delivered onto death, time annuls all teleological ends or the possibility of restorative closure. The erasure of the "diminutive" tenderness of childhood, indexed in the end of the youthful "holiday," destines the subject to a finality deprived of resolution. The loss of the world becomes an image of the abrupt cessation of human life, where the passing of time afflicts the poet with "unending pain," at once immeasurably intense and yet lacking all finality or purpose.

> That's it for everything at last: the holidays
> your breast-fed obedience, your way
> of asking me not to go out
> and that's it for the diminutive, for
> my coming of age in unending pain
> and our having been born thus for no reason. (Vallejo 2007: 235)

Such nostalgia of absence directly afflicts Vallejo's representation of the rural setting and Indian world. In *Dead Idyll* (*Idilio muerto*), he inscribes the experience of loss in the distance that separates the poet from the rural home. As he contemplatively addresses "his sweet Andean Rita," Vallejo evokes the untamed fertility of the "wild rushes and the wild grape," alongside the sweetness of the "sugar cane brandies of May," contrasting the oppressive urban setting that surrounds him: "suffocating Byzantium," symbol of the capital Lima, from which Vallejo writes (Vallejo 2007: 99).[8] In *Agape*, the exiled, orphaned poetic voice becomes again amplified onto the social scale; the poet speaks as an alienated observer from the mindless tumult of the city populace, as he is rendered woefully invisible: "On this afternoon everybody, everybody passes by / without inquiring or asking me for anything" (Vallejo 2007: 103). In *Imperial Nostalgias* (*Nostalgias imperiales*), Vallejo desecrates the memory of the pre-Hispanic past with melancholic irony, describing the coruscating degeneracy of the rural space in its relentless metamorphosis.[9] He castigates the unbecoming of the folkloric song derived from Incan culture, brutally describing the poverty of the rural present: those "shaggy Incan troubadours," whose existence is journalistically reported by "the poet's exhausted soul" (Vallejo 2007: 51).

---

8 As some commentators have suggested, the figure of Rita may refer to Rita Uceda, mother of the revolutionary guerrilla leader from 1965, Luis de la Puente Uceda.
9 This poem in particular bespeaks the influence of Baudelaire in Vallejo's early works.

Yet observational distance does not lead Vallejo to a repudiation of the modern world or urban space, fleeing from the contradictions of his social environs. He presents Indigenous rituals not as objects of remembrance, but as degenerated morsels of a past stripped from any positive force, amputated from their original locus of significance, swallowed in frustrated process of modernization. Once again refusing the vindication of ancestral grandeur, Vallejo's gaze becomes that of an outsider, whose identity is fractured and suspended; neither the voice of the rural Indian, nor that of the Western, urban mestizo. The impotence of poet's divided identity mirrors the fractured natural and cultural space that he inhabits, in which the defeat of Indigenous imperial glory presents an irremediably torn world, which defines Peru's past and present. As Clayton (2011) argues:

> Vallejo's early writings repeatedly stage an attempted return to the lost idyll of home and Andean ritual, only to discover that the lyric subject is unrelentingly excluded from both, restricted to describing what he witnesses and his own externality to it. [...] Indeed it is striking just how many of the poems in *Los heraldos negros* are structured around images of petrification, paralysis, or emptiness, particularly when they refer to poetic reconstructions of Andean culture; and indeed, those many poems that have been taken as celebrations of the vitality of traditional culture can more pointedly be read [...] as a veiled critique of that culture, of the rituals that made it as static as the urban literary bohemia that implicitly rejected it. (Clayton 2011: 36)

Along the same lines, in the poem *Babel*, Vallejo outstrips the rural scenery of all aesthetic splendor, rendering it ruthlessly "without style," referring to the disarticulated character of its contours through colloquial descriptivism. Linguistic and spatial-architectonic privation of ornamental quality becomes at once the expressive vehicle and the object to which the poet relates:

> Sweet styleless home, built
> from only one blow and of only one piece
> of sunflower wax. And in this home
> she damages and arranges; sometimes says:
> "The poorhouse is nice; quite all right!"
> And other times she begins to cry! (Vallejo 2007: 51)

The poet unravels the figure of the Babylonian tower, Western symbol of hubristic desire, such that the edifice of historical memory is delivered to the intuition of a house cleaner, as she arbitrarily adjudicates the admissible from the inadmissible, with a paradoxical sense of order. Her spontaneous judgment oscillates between inexplicable aesthetic satisfaction and an equally elusive situational abhorrence. But the identification of the banality of domestic labor with the towering Babylonian monument does not revert to a glorification of the household space, any more than it provokes a provincialist affirmation of aesthetic intuition over reflexive knowledge. Rather, in its paradoxical suspension between errant chaos and rational order, the contrivances of sensory immediacy and the familiarity of the domestic appear every bit as inaccessible to understanding, every bit as shrouded in ineffability as absolute erudition. It is thus not only that finitude forecloses omniscience: the poet cannot give cohesion to the banal materiality and everydayness of experience. What proves in any case impossible is overcoming alienation by restorative labor, since loss lingers from the start and until the end.

This resistance to epistemic capture and semantic retrieval warps the poetic language in its attempt to represent the world it perceives and thinks. Vallejo's voice is put continuously in a precarious position, not only in relation to his external environs, but in negotiating with a material reality resistant to narrative or hermeneutic cohesion. Anticipating what will become a prescient motif throughout *Trilce*, in *Prayer on the Road* (*Oración del camino*) he upsets the harmonious association of *modernista* aesthetics with the wellspring of organic productivity, reducing the lyric form to the stench of dead matter. Its aerial symbol (the "singing lark") is subjected to biological decomposition, its majesty overtaken by the enveloping soil; its "saintly gold" mummified and embittered in the valley; the "marble pillars" that consecrate the past (*'consagrados marmoles'*) are ruinously fragmented in shards; a thwarted blossoming or epidemic outbreak ("*brotes*") frustrates all future growth. Under the effects of materiality, language, memory, and even *time itself* decompose, so that cultural corruption and organic decay jointly subordinate the Peruvian landscape and its history. The *stench* of space and time, the putrefaction of living matter, pollutes the "light of gold," and is carried through the expiring power of a "dying sun," whose cessation brings about the end of life itself (Ibid.). The poet's agitated language is thereby no longer the carrier of lyric beauty, but the harbinger of anxiety before a degenerating world. In what is doubtlessly one of Vallejo's most Baudelairean moments, he writes of this putrefaction infiltrating the poetic act itself:

> An odor of time lingers fertilized by verses,
> for the shoots of consecrated marble that would inherit
> the auriferous song
> of the lark rotting in my heart! (Vallejo 2007: 89)

The obsolescence of *modernista* ornamentalism becomes in *Trilce* directly correlated to the unbecoming of Andean cultural heritage, torn beyond repair by the colonial legacy.

In *Trilce XXVI*, the experience of absence is indexed onto the rural Indigenous world as a whole, where death becomes not only a cultural but artistic collective destiny: the "moribund Cuzcos" are coeval with the "moribund alexandrines" of an unraveling *modernista* aesthetics. The rural scene enters the vortex of urbanization and commerce, where the "young alpacas" are morphed into livestock for cloth and coats, reducing the fetishized mystique of the natural setting and tradition to the banal circuit of commodification. This transfiguration of social space under a thwarted modernizing process is expressed in uncanny unison with the visceral properties of the transfigured body, producing the monstrous image of the "coated man" with his "arms morphed into legs," in which dead nature and perverted culture coalesce. Nostalgia here voices not only the poetic exile from the Indian world that it problematically represents, but the destruction of this world, and an implicit act of protest against the horror that the poet witnesses: a symptom of humanity's sickness.

> Undone knot of the sinamayera's
> lacteal gland
> good for brilliant alpacas
> for a coat of useless feather
> - arms more legs than arms! (Vallejo 2007: 217)

The nostalgia for what is to come

In addition to the nostalgia of absence, Mariátegui finds an additional form of nostalgia in Vallejo's poetics, which he characterizes in the *Seven Essays* as the "nostalgia for what is to come" ("*la nostalgia de lo que vendrá*").[10] Unlike the "nostalgia for the future"—that, as Alain Badiou (2014) argues, organizes the "future anterior" of twentieth-century revolutionary poetry—in which the moment of collective triumph is anticipated with solemn melancholy, Vallejo's nostalgic voice celebrates the definitive interruption of suffering through death (Badiou 2014: 104). In *Absent*, Vallejo writes:

---

10 Mariátegui 1928, https://www.marxists.org/archive/mariateg/works/7-interpretive-essays/essay07.htm

Absent! The morning when, like a rueful bird,
I go away to the shore of
the sea of shadow and silent empire,
the white pantheon will be your captivity. (Vallejo 2007: 43)

In these lines, Vallejo submits nostalgia to a unique temporal inversion: the poetic voice is foreclosed from knowledge ("The Mystery," "*El Misterio*," making a clear nod to the esotericism in Darío's *modernista* aesthetics), as time sentences the absent addressee to an abstract captivity, anticipating death. The poet expresses with pathos a vengeful triumph in the prospect of a personal death that at once annuls the experience of loss as it destines its addressee to guilt and mourning. For in death the alienation of the subject from the Other is sublimated into a distance without measure, "more far than far" (Ibid.). At the same time, the absentee, defined by her absolute removal from the poet, paradoxically, can only come closer to him through death, to the point of "captivity," since death is nothing but a kind of absolute absence, the pure and empty form of loss as such, in which the poet now lives only outside of time, in an immemorial capture of the Other. Vallejo conjures the paradoxical affect whereby the poetic voice no longer speaks from a determinate place, but rather retroactively from an anticipated future: a time in which he no longer lives, expressing a rancorous jubilance in the future in which the distance separating the Other from the subject will be definitely erased. The Other then sinks into the black nothingness of the "sea of shadows," as well as into that white nothingness, the "white pantheon" and "penitent lacerated whitenesses" that erase all asymmetry between subject and the whole of time (Ibid.). In this form of nostalgia, existential affliction is no longer specifiable in terms of individual or contingent determinations—not even those of race and culture—but rather exacerbates the tragic condition of human finitude into the warped triumph of the abandoned. The present, punctured by the nostalgia for the future, offers the anticipatory rejoicing of the unrequited at being relieved from alienation, finally, in death.

We now have the template for three kinds of nostalgia addressed in Vallejo's early poetry, specifying three possible relations between the subject, its world and time: (1) *ancestral nostalgia*, as the idealized caricatures of the mestizo imagery that remain caught in the sterile desire for the return of an ideal past or restored rapport with the Other; (2) the *nostalgia of absence* laments loss and absence *in the present*, its irremediably dislocated and forlorn condition as an emblem of protest against the world the poet inhabits; (3) the *nostalgia for what is to come*, finally, condenses the affect for what *will be lost* in an annulled future, enacting a transvaluation of loss into an act of metaphysical protest. This last, "anticipatory nostalgia," Mariátegui tells us, occurs precisely at the point in which the local scope of the poetic voice suddenly acquires a universal dimension: it concentrates the suffering of "three centuries," but also functions as a subversive call, and becomes precisely an act of "metaphysical protest" on behalf of humanity as a whole.

A Materialist Reduction of the Subject: Hermetism, Sexuality and Temporality in *Trilce*

Beyond the three forms of nostalgia that Mariátegui identifies across *The Black Heralds* and *Trilce*, one finds Vallejo grappling with the possibility of a future in which collective engagement is conceived as a means to confront alienation. This problematic, obscure relation to a real future becomes as much a question of existential coping as one about the aesthetic mission of the poetic act, and finally a political question. If the ideal behind *Trilce* constitutes an attempt, as Vallejo tells us, to fulfill "the sacred duty, of man and artist, to be free," then this must not only be understood as a question of formal subversion or as a declaration of the nascent spirit of a new aesthetic avant-garde.[11] Rather, it forms part of an attempt to understand how the living subject can cope in the face of finitude, facing a fractured social bond, accepting the constraints of a decaying materiality without relapsing into a feeble, romantic pathos. In other words, the *formal* experimental tendencies in *Trilce* are to be viewed continuously with an attempt to think *substantively* about a possible horizon for human action and thought that is consistent with and yet defiant of man's alienated condition.

Accordingly, in what follows, I propose to read *Trilce* as part of what recent commentary has called Vallejo's "materialist poetics," which prioritizes the relation of the embodied subject to time and history. More precisely, I argue that the articulation between Vallejo's aesthetic ambition and existential struggle leads to an interrogation concerning the pragmatic conditions for historical change, implying both the tasks of artistic invention and collective emancipation.

---

11 Vallejo, César. *Epistolario general*, Lectorum Pubns, 1982.

"[...] la obligación sacratísima, de hombre y de artista ¡la de ser libre"

The material bases of experience

As we saw, already in *The Black Heralds*, the forms of nostalgia explored by Vallejo imply a tensional negotiation with the ornamental and symbolic tendencies of *modernismo*, upsetting its poetic norms in manifold ways: through the interruption of prosody, neologistic invention, the introduction of the vernacular and the archaic, and so on. Radicalizing this subversive impetus, *Trilce*'s hermetic language exacerbates a discordant rapport between an alienated poetic voice, on the one hand, and an inconsistent, meaningless and fragmentary referent, on the other. As Michelle Clayton (2011) emphasizes, in this collection Vallejo produces a new view of the poetic subject and object while interrogating the problematic relation between the two:

> While mutilating *modernismo* and ripping rhetoric to pieces, *Trilce* also allowed for the emergence of a disconcertingly human, poetically incorrect lyric voice that is audacious and vulnerable at the same time. This voice is no longer the centered and often celebratory voice of romantic poetry but instead belongs to a subject who complains, stutters, and frequently fails to keep hold of his own discourse, who makes spelling mistakes and invents words, who refuses to separate scientific and literary language, who sometimes eschews language altogether in favor of numbers, who reveals himself in moments of the basest physicality—yet who also, paradoxically, soars lyrically. [...] *Trilce*'s voices neither fully articulate a location nor incarnate an identity but rather propose a temporalized, partial, and contingent relationship to place and the lyric speaker's position within it. (Clayton 2011: 69)

For Vallejo, it is only by upsetting the order of commonsense language and the pulchritude of the lyric idiom that this discordant rapport may be thematized, attesting to the "material bases of experience" with authentic realism (Clayton 2014: 99). Vallejo's introduction of the vernacular and archaic in *Trilce* is thereby complemented by the introduction of scientific jargon and mathematical vocabulary, carrying out a reduction of semantic content to syntactic inscription and somatic function. Vallejo thereby undoes the self as a coherent locus of meaning, such that the registers of affect, language and tradition become increasingly ineffectual and precarious throughout *Trilce*. The erudition and majesty of the lyric voice is pulverized into the impotence of an infant's babbling, and eloquence collapses into cacophony. Julio Ortega describes this procedure as the "erosion of the lyric" in *Trilce*, where "the poem sets the scene of a living in babbling" ("*un vivir en balbuceo*") (Ortega

1986: 13).[12] The subject of loss is reduced to banal incarnation, marked by biochemical, libidinal and formal indices that carry no semantic, qualitative or affective specificity.

In particular, Vallejo proposes to reinscribe the experience of alienation and the frustrated rapport to the Other by positively marking those impersonal libidinal processes which underlie the fabric of emotion and human rapport. In doing so, Vallejo does not simply "aestheticize" the material world by interjecting the literal into the literary; instead, as *Trilce IX* expresses, he disassembles the voice of the lyrical subject. As a result, the generational and temporal drama of human life reveals only a primal, meaningless repetition: the reiterative thrust of lust, copulation and procreation, coeval with the iterative multiplication of bodies:

> I sdrive to dddeflect at a blow the blow
> Her two broad leaves, her valve
> opening in succulent reception
> from multiplier to multiplier
> her condition for excellent pleasure
> all readies truth. (Vallejo 2007: 182)

A reduction of the human to its bodily functions operates with visceral violence and even vulgarity throughout *Trilce*. In *Trilce XIII*, Vallejo stages a metonymic play between two subjective positions, in which the singularity of the Other is reduced to its bodily parts, while love is reduced to the transparency of lust. In its prosaic forthrightness, the subject and its expression are voided of depth: the amorous "old feeling" accordingly "degenerates," and the heart becomes "simplified" into "brains," while affect becomes distilled into cold thought:

> I think about your sex.
> My heart simplified, I think about your sex,
> before the ripe daughterloin of day.
> I touch the bud of joy, it is in season.
> And an ancient sentiment dies
> degenerated into brains.[13] (Ibid.: 191)

---

12 Ortega, Julio. *Teoría poética de César Vallejo*. Providence, Del Sol, 1986.
13 "Pienso en tu sexo. Simplificado el corazón, pienso en tu sexo, ante el hijar maduro del día. Palpo el botón de dicha, está en sazón. Y muere un sentimiento antiguo degenerado en seso."

This defiance against humanist sentimentalism is subsequently bound to an extension of the heretical spirit elaborated since *The Black Heralds*, only this time directed against the destructiveness of time. In the second stanza, the allure of the flesh exceeds death in power: a stillborn "begotten by God himself," death is "less harmonious and prolific" than the spatial "grooves" of the body, the "free beast" that "enjoys where it pleases, where it can" (Ibid.). Implicitly subverting Quevedo's romantic triumphalism, it is ultimately sex that is constant and not love, beyond death: the blind productivity of life in its generative prowess. The poem concludes as the libidinal ardor of the poetic voice escalates at the same time as it is disfigured into noise: the "mute thunder" of orgiastic tremor that shatters all eloquence, subjected to syntactic inversion and compression: "*Rednuhtetum!*" (Ibid.).

The act of heresy waged by man in the name of generative materiality is also extended to the familial structure, which punctures the domestic nostalgia of loss in *Los heraldos negros*. In *Trilce V*, Vallejo weaponizes the sexual restlessness of bodies as a means to dispel the parental bond and paternal authority characteristic of his earlier poetry, relegating the relation between begetters and children to the purposelessness of the procreative impulse:

> Dicotyledons group. From it petrels
> overture, propensities for trinity,
> finales that begin, ohs of ayes
> believes to be rhinestoned with heterogeneity. (Vallejo 2007: 233)

In these lines, mankind is first reduced to a biological process in the sexual dyad: a group of *two* "dicotyledons," each coterminous in the other. Through a simple numerical reduction, Vallejo extirpates Man from divine transcendence: the Two of sexed humanity in defiance of the paternal One. The "propensities for trinity" designate thus the self-deification of man in procreation, usurping God of his genetic function, finally reiterating the heretical cry from *The Eternal Dice*: "God is he!" Bereft of support in a demiurge who harbors trinity within himself, the sexed Two thus *are* in themselves "without being more" ("*sin ser más*"); they linger on "without being heard" and "without being seen." The "propensities for trinity," however, mark a possibility beyond the Two of amorous and sexual rapport: subject to the temporal dehiscence of living bodies, the excitations of the flesh lead the climactic consummation of bodies in copulation (the "*ohs of ayes*") to a new life, and the return of the erotic drives, those "finales that begin" (Ibid.). Finally, the Two is simultaneously placed between the silent nothingness of 0, coeval with death and absolute indifference, and the infinite resonance of the wholesome 1, symbol of absolute identity and consistency. The Two remains suspended, split by sexual difference, as "newlyweds in eternity," ultimately defined by their temporal being, and destined to create life from void, condensed in an erectile metaphor: the passage from inexistence to existence, which breeds existence from Zero, "until it wakes the 1, making it stand."

At the same, the reduction of man to his material basis becomes transvalued into a latent potency for a kind of subversion: no longer a negative "cry of protest," the heretical act in *Trilce* acquires a measure of confidence, pitting the human animal against the voice and the divine power, at once. In *Trilce XXXVI*, Vallejo thus again channels the reproductive drive against divinity through pure mathematical operations, in which the divided sexed become interwoven in the act:

> Female is continued the male, on the basis
> of probable breasts, and precisely
> on the basis of how much does not flower! (Ibid.: 239)

Continuity, probability, division: mathematical concepts register more than an empty formal symbolism, becoming a medium that captures the creative furor of desiring bodies. The mutual arrest of the sexes is thus "rooted" (*a raiz*), operating not over abstract quantities but mapping their measurable material contingency, assigning a probabilistic index that "holds in" an uncertain future, giving birth to a "standing imperfection." At the end, the poem enacts a transvaluation of orphanhood: the splitting of the evenness of the Two into the *oddness* of the newborn life, those "propensions for trinity" whose anonymity signals the promise of the future:

> Make way for the new odd number
> potent with orphanhood! (Ibid.)

But libidinal defiance also goes beyond the nucleus of the sexed couple in *Trilce*, acquiring a properly socioeconomic dimension. Paradigmatically, in *Trilce XLVIII*, Vallejo sexualizes arithmetic succession, drawing an analogy between the orgiastic ascent of libido and monetary accumulation, projected into the austere coins that make up the poet's "70 Peruvian soles." The poetic voice then enters an escalating vector, as the poet grabs the "penultimate coin" that suddenly stacks up into another, and so on onto infinity: "This coin, being 69, bumps into 70, then scales 71, bounces on 72," "vibrating and struggling," augmenting as it screams ("letting out yelllls"). In this way, the infinity unleashed in the monetary accumulation provides a surplus enjoyment, sublimated until it becomes indiscernible from life itself: "all numbers / the whole of life."[14]

The collective subject to come: Materiality, animality and history

Attesting to a temporal prison with no escape, and tethered to the fatal dehiscence of the body, we might ask: Does not the poetic freedom belabored in *Trilce* coincide with the denial of all agency, leaving no subject to issue an address, nor the consistency of an object to be addressed, thereby reducing the relation between the poet and world to the degeneration of temporalized matter, and the corruption of capitalist accumulation? If so, then Vallejo's "materialist poetics" would entail a kind of antihumanist nihilism, in which the future becomes definitively voided of significance, despite the endless copulative generation of new life beyond the present.

But this would be an overly hasty interpretation; for Vallejo also ventures to conceive of a new subject that enacts a subversion of finitude, beyond the constraints of bare animality, in which the time of individual bodies is superseded in collective becoming. In this regard, William Rowe (2013) calls attention to *Trilce XXXVIII*, where Vallejo evokes the tension between societal complacency and the emergent promise for historical change. The poem's central metaphor—that of the abstract "crystal"—condenses a still-unrealized time, a nameless, virtual materiality that resists the voice that interdicts it, awaiting incarnation. Rowe describes this as "the material un-named and waiting to be re-named [...] not precisely undetermined, or a-historical, or simply natural. It is not some sort of pure substance as such."[15] The crystal is first defined by its geometrical integrity and resilience, anticipating a process of temporalization: it does not "surrender through any of its sides" ("*no dase por ninguno de sus costados*"). It harbors a dormant power identified with coming incarnation (the "bread yet to come"), as it awaits being "sipped in the rough" ("*sorbido en bruto*") by a "future mouth without teeth" ("*la boca venidera/sin dientes*").

---

14 "todos los guarismos, / la vida entera."
15 Rowe, William, "The Political in *Trilce*," in Politics, Poetics, Affect: Re-visioning César Vallejo, edited by Stephen M. Hart, Cambridge, 2013, pp. 8.

Entering this body with its ideal integrity intact, the crystal becomes an embodied form, an internalized idea resisting decomposition, clearly contrasting the stillborn arrival of the "burnt bread" and thwarted productivity from *The Black Heralds*. As it becomes observed and interjected, the crystal stoically rejects the attempt to "humanize it" back into the voice that addresses it. Lacking "animal affections" (*"cariños animales"*), colorless, the crystal "will be sent for love and for a future," as its abstract existence enters a new collective being; it grabs hold of the "sugar mold for names" (*"horna de los sustantivos"*), and while refusing "animal affections" it goes on "to form new lefts," named also the "new Less" (*"los nuevos menos"*) (Vallejo 2007: 243, translation modified).

The becoming incarnate of the crystal is thereby identified with a kind of minoritarian struggle, signaled in the numerical figure of the negative: neither the mere positivity of the "animal order" which determines individual being, nor the crystalline zero of the abstract Idea. The "new Less" comes into existence as the Idea becomes materialized, structurally becoming potentiated from void to plenitude, corresponding to what Alain Badiou (2009) names a *strong singularity* or *event*, where "the inexistent of a world" springs forth from the void and into the world, enjoying existential plenitude. More precisely, for Badiou, the event signals a historical process of intensification and subjectivation, by virtue of which a nameless multiplicity or inexistence with no force suddenly appears with "maximal intensity," becoming a "strong singularity," reorganizing the distribution of bodies and languages in a world[16] (Badiou

---

16 In negotiating the poetics of *Trilce* with a nascent concept of temporality and history, Rowe goes on to suggest three possible readings of the relation between "the Subject, politics, and number," favoring a reading he identifies with Badiou's mature theory of subjectivation and of the event, as a rupture in the temporal fabric in moments of invention:

> The third [interpretational orientation] would be to follow Badiou's later book *Being and Event*, and to hypothesize that the Subject of *Trilce* is the subject of an event, where the event is taken to be a "creation ex nihilo, a chance to begin again from scratch, to interrupt the order of continuity and inevitability," and where "what is encountered through an event is precisely the void of the situation, that aspect of the situation that has absolutely no interest in preserving the status quo as such." [...] Event, in this context, should be taken in the strong sense of an epochal change which breaks with the order of the status quo, i.e. breaks the order of what can be numerated in the situation. [...] If the event in this sense opens the possibility of a universal truth, and it's in that truth that the Subject finds its existence, then the problem with this third stance, which is the most difficult one to work out, is the question what would be the event in Trilce? In other words, one can speak of an event in the later poems, especially of course those of *España, aparta de mí esta cáliz*, but that's not the case with *Trilce*. (Hart 2013: 12)

2009: 322). The passage from Vallejo's crystalline being into the collective body of the "the new Less" anticipates thus the rise of a nameless, collective subject, defined by the unqualified pursuit of "love and a future," and resisting the allure of "animal affections." In this way, Vallejo's materialist poetics anticipates a different production than the procreative circuit of sexed bodies, where the "sacred duty to be free" coordinates aesthetic subversion to "political agitation," in a gesture that, like Mariátegui, Vallejo conceived as the lasting subversive heart of the Romantic tradition. As he had already written in his 1815 thesis:

> The principles of literary freedom were, after all, genuine manifestations of the free, confused and complex social and political agitation of the epoch. And so the lemma of the disciples of forward-thinking Romantics was the renovation of style and of the metric in molds of greater free spontaneity, for the purposes of enveloping in them the new practices of the century.[17]

The question that follows, which takes us beyond the embryonic historical musings found fragmentarily in *Trilce* and into Vallejo's work since his exile in Europe, remains the question prefigured in *Trilce*: How to reconcile the experience of loss and deliverance onto death that destines the material basis of living bodies to the sundering of time, with a productive, *concrete* notion of historicity and collective subjectivity which defies mere repetition and brings about a real future?

The Paris Years—Vallejo's Aesthetics of Transmutation in *El Arte y la Revolución*[18]

A closer look at Vallejo's intellectual production after his exile to Europe in 1923, during the so-called Paris years, reveals how the experience of alienation opened a collective horizon underwritten by inventive passion. The critical appropriation of Marxist–Leninist thought since 1927 allowed him to clarify the role of the subject, which in *Trilce* remained but an abstract figure of minoritarian struggle, and the role that the poetic act plays in

---

17 Cited in Clayton 2014, p. 49.
18 All translations from *El arte y la revolución* in what follows are my own. The entirety of the original text and the references are available at: https://edisciplinas.usp.br/pluginfile.php/352721/mod_resource/content/1/Vallejo.%20El%20arte%20y%20la%20revoluci%C3%B3n.pdf

relation to possible emancipatory-political ends. In this regard, we must understand Vallejo's involvement with socialism as an attempt to interrogate the nature and possibilities of human liberty, and only secondarily as entailing affinity with a particular kind of politics. In a letter to Pablo Abril dated 27 December 1928, Vallejo writes of his progressive immersion in revolutionary thought as part of a vital, personal development, as opposed to a doctrinal alignment or theoretical instruction: "I am beginning to develop a revolutionary feeling, through my lived experience more than through learned ideas"[19] (Vallejo 1928).

Like Mariátegui, throughout his time in Europe Vallejo would progressively see socialism not as a fixed normative core to be blindly copied, but as a historical and dynamic mode of thinking whose central tenet was creative experimentation. But, unlike Mariátegui, for Vallejo, the spirit of socialism was not conceived in terms of a nationalist program for social integration, adapting the tenets of Marxism to a local situation; rather, he emphasizes the internationalist and *universal* project of human liberation latent in the socialist view, which expressed at once an aesthetic and social mission that dissolved national boundaries and contingent partisan affiliations.

While celebrating the defiant and triumphant spirit of the Soviet revolution, it is striking that Vallejo's paradigmatic referent for a social model becomes rather the collaborative and internationalist Parisian intellectual milieu, exemplifying a universal dimension that launched "a vital and human exploration, that is, generous and uncorrupted."[20] In a chronicle written in November 1926 titled *The Twilight of the Eagles* (*El crepúsculo de las águilas*), published in *Mundial*, Vallejo speaks of his "becoming-Parisian" as a process of *universalization*: more than a site for multicultural encounters, he affirms Paris as a "cosmic city," enabling the free association between members of multiple origins, ideals and identities, guided only by creative desire for "coexistence"

---

19 Cited in Clayton 2014, p. 144.
20 Ibid.: 167. Clayton translates Vallejo's "acendrada" as "deep rooted," which changes crucially the meaning of the sentence. For Vallejo, Paris is not a site where a deep-rooted identity becomes expressed, but rather where individuals are *uprooted* from their national determinations in sight of a new collective form of pragmatic and intellectual exchange. Vallejo's designation of "acendrada," taken to mean an "uncorrupted" expression, conveys how corruption involves the compromising of universality in sight of individual interests.

("*convivencia*"; more literally "living-with"). As he writes: "Paris is New York, Berlin, London, Rome, Vienna, Moscow and, also, Paris."[21]

The affirmation of Paris as a universalist model for transnational cultural activity would find poetic expression in the *Human Poems* (*Poemas humanos*), intercalating the poet's solitude in exile, as he faces the cyclical ubiquity of time, with a celebratory proclamation of human creation, divided between Spanish and French. Beyond the circularity of the passing of seasons and the solitary confinement of the individual within a temporal prison, Paris is named the "kingdom of the world": "*¡c'est Paris, reine du monde!*" Affirming life in a double negation, or the death of death itself (*C'est la vie, mort de la Mort*), the poem anticipates the celebratory universalism that would take shape in *Spain, Take Away from Me This Cup*, where rejoined humanity opens a future in which "only death will die":

> Heat, París, Autumn, so much summer
> In the midst of the heat and of the city!
> ¡C'est la vie, mort de la Mort!
> It's as if they had counted my steps. (Vallejo 2007: 436)

The universalist ideal would guide Vallejo's articulation of art and politics toward a critical stance with regard to Soviet Marxism, while informing his subsequent figurations of the revolutionary subject. This implied, first, defining the role of the revolutionary subject in terms of a fidelity to creation and unqualified human solidarity. As with Mariátegui's appropriation of religious notions, inspired by Barbusse and Sorel, Vallejo secularizes theological-religious vocabulary in order to define the distinctiveness of the revolutionary spirit, reinscribing the heretical cry of protest and materialist poetics in an affirmative register. In a piece also published in *Mundial* in 31 August 1928, titled *The Communist Spirit and Fact* (*El espíritu y hecho comunista*), Vallejo highlights the incipient promise of "an authentic and virginal political movement that, if you want, may be assimilated into a new religious liturgy."[22] And in his polemical text *Russia in 1931* (*Rusia en 1931*), he echoes Mariátegui in identifying socialism with "the birth of a new myth," and even a new dogma: "we can neither ignore the existence

---

21 Vallejo, César. "El crepúsculo de las águilas," in *Mundial*, December 17, 1926, my translation.

  "París es Nueva York, Berlín, Londres, Roma, Viena, Moscú y, además, París."

22 Vallejo, César. "El espíritu y hecho comunista," in *Mundial* no. 429, August 31, 1928, my translation.

in the socialist revolution of a new myth and a new dogma. But this myth and dogma are equally of materialist essence and Structure: which is to say, economic"[23] (Vallejo 2014: 106). And just like Mariátegui, short of promoting blind attachment to doctrinal principles, the "faith" and "dogmatism" in question takes as its nonnegotiable basis the necessity of creative transformation, tying formal experimentalism with a substantive existential mission for humanity as a whole.

Several of the texts compiled under the title *Art and Revolution* (*El arte y la revolución*), written between the late 1920s and early 1930s, stage an explicit refusal of fanatical dogmatism. In *The Lessons of Marxism* (*Las lecciones del Marxismo*), written 19 January 1929, Vallejo castigates the crass projection of Marxist categories onto the life of communities as the "human calumny" of "forcing social reality to prove the principles of historical materialism, literally and faithfully."[24] And in his essay *The Doctors of Marxism* (*Los doctores del Marxismo*), explicitly targeting Plekhanov and Bukharin, Vallejo derides those who have "ossified Marxism" so as to constrain socialism into an "iron shoe" ("*zapato de hierro*") (Vallejo 1973: 64).[25] He mocks the intellectual rigidity of those "rigorous Marxists, fanatical Marxists, grammatical Marxists, who pursue its realization by the letter [...] even denaturalizing facts and disfiguring the meaning of events" (Ibid.). Against the "weighty mediocrity" of "Bolshevik partisans," he lauds Marx and Lenin for their relentless critical and creative spirit. Like Mariátegui, Vallejo conceives of Marxism as a self-correcting enterprise, following "closely the changes in life and the transformations in reality to rectify doctrine and correct it" (Ibid.: 65). According to Marx, Vallejo argues, the dialectical materialist "science of history" was a dynamic creature, at once "reflexive, conscious, technical." In *The Revolutionary Function*

---

23 Vallejo, César. *Rusia en 1931*, Lingkua Digital, 2014, p. 106. my translation.

"Tampoco hay que desconocer la existencia en la revolución socialista de una nueva mítica y esta dogmática son igualmente de esencia y estructura materialistas, es decir, económicas."

24 Vallejo, César. "Las lecciones del Marxismo," in V*ariedades*, no. 1090, Lima, January 19, 1929, my translation.

"Los marxistas rigurosos, los marxistas fanáticos, los marxistas gramaticales, que persiguen la realización del marxismo al pie de la letra, obligando a la realidad social a comprobar literal y fielmente la teoría del materialismo histórico."

25 "A fuerza de querer ver en esta doctrina la certeza por excelencia, la verdad definitiva, inapelable y sagrada, una e inmutable, la han convertido en un zapato de hierro."

of Thought (*Función revolucionaria del pensamiento*), Vallejo defines socialism thus as a "constructive faith," echoing Mariátegui's "creative antagonism":

> Our tactics, critical and destructive, must march united inseparably from the profession of a constructive faith, derived scientifically and objectively from history. Out struggle against the reigning order harbors, according to the materialist dialectic, a Movement, tacit and necessary, towards the substitution of that order by a new one. Revolutionarily, the concepts of destruction and construction are inseparable. (Ibid.: 16)

These scattered musings on the universal and creative essence of socialist thought and practice naturally inform Vallejo's understanding of the tasks of a revolutionary poetry and art. Throughout *El arte y la revolución*, he schematically outlines the grounds of an aesthetic theory in which the experimental spirit of the European avant-garde complements theoretical revision at the philosophical level. In the text *What Is a Revolutionary Artist?* (*¿Qué es un artista revolucionario?*), Vallejo provides a schematic typology of artistic orientations, synchronically distinguishing between a *bourgeois art*, a *Bolshevik art* and a *socialist art*. In short, if bourgeois art serves primarily an ideologically, reactive function that is essentially *repetitive*, and if Bolshevik art is a mimetic and sterile effort beholden to an intransigent orthodoxy, socialist art is defined by its ruthless capacity to subvert all normative and ideological strictures in its inventive pursuit: its primary purpose is neither formal subversion, nor to forge a "national consciousness," but to incarnate a *universal consciousness* that subverts all human limitation.

Occupying an ambiguous, intermediary position, Bolshevik art designates Soviet artistic production after the October revolution, which Vallejo scolds for relapsing into a monotonous propagandistic function.[26] He claims that Bolshevik art remains caught in an "aesthetics of reflection," which produces an analytical conception of socialist artistic practice, bound to a descriptive empiricism that betrays the transformative kernel of socialism. The function of art was, under this framework, modeled in analogy to the representational

---

26 In his short text *The Execution of Bolshevik Art* (*La ejecución del arte Bolchevique*) and in his notoriously polemical *The Maiakovski Case* (*El caso Maiakovski*), Vallejo reiterates thus that Soviet socialism threatened to reduce the literary revolutionary spirit to mere "propaganda and agitation." In Maiakovski's texts, in particular, Vallejo finds not the expression of lived struggle, but a stale reiteration of Soviet tropes, which led to an "an art based on formulas and not in the affective and personal sincerity" and engendered "verses devoid of any laudable warmth and feeling, evoked by mechanical and exterior traction, by artificial heat" (Ibid.: 109).

function of scientific knowledge: art had to *report* on the glorious upsurge of the proletariat masses in a gesture of commemorative mimesis, recognizing the party as its organizing core and its leadership as its spiritual anchor. And yet only in descending from their ideological stupefaction to a "worldly plane," Vallejo argues, will Soviet artists escape the fate of producing mere "apostrophes of struggle," that is, waning echoes of revolutionary combative furor, when the moment of "labor of harvest or sowing" has finally arrived.

> Bolshevik art serves a periodic vicissitude in society. Once this transformation or Marxist "leap" has taken place, the harangues, the proclamations, and admonitions lose all their aesthetic relevance and, should they continue, it would be as if in the midst of the labor of harvest or sowing, one heard hymns of war, apostrophes of struggle. (Ibid.: 26)

This ambivalence toward the Soviet revolution and the mimetic spirit of Bolshevik art finds a unique poetic expression in *Angelic Salutation* (*Salutación angélica*) from *Human Poems* (*Poemas humanos*), where Vallejo celebrates revolutionary enthusiasm while cautiously suggesting that insurrectionary *destruction* must be overcome. The "time of war," of affective upsurge and violent struggle, thus anticipates the "the time of harvest," guided by collective creation and no longer by destruction. And so, the Bolshevik's "doctrinal warmth" threatens to be amputated from its productive counterpart, becoming "the vehicle of death." A "growing pleasure" drawn from the anarchic desire for destruction corrupts it; "weed[s]" grow in the "nouns" of its disfigured language, whose violence injures the generic being of "common man," with whom the poet identifies. The mutilated poet remains thus "silent and half one-eyed" (Vallejo 2007: 382, translation modified).

Above all, Vallejo sees that once the "dictatorship of the proletariat" relapses into mere ideological veneration, the revolutionary process tips over into a repressive, brutal form of state politics, and its art falls short of achieving a universal dimension. Accordingly, the distinction between Bolshevik and socialist art is also the distinction between a nationally and institutionally bound conception of revolutionary practice, centered on antagonism, and its authentic universalist expression, oriented toward unbound creation. The poetic act must be untethered from doctrinal and partisan alignments, becoming the expression of the generic "human function of sensibility" and suggesting a *universal aesthetics*: "For the socialist poet, the poem is not, then, a spectacular trance, provoked at will and to the preconceived service of a creed or political propaganda, but it is a natural and simply human function of sensibility" (Ibid.). The erasure of authorship in the poetic act mirrors the erasure of political idolatry characterizing the "great leaders" of the socialist revolution, as they are effaced as individuals and become emblems of the "collective will":

> Politically, the great men (Lenin, Trotsky, etc.) are not objects of individualist and deifying idolatry enjoyed by the great bourgeois rulers of capitalist countries. [...] Stalin and Trotsky do not exist and are interesting to no one. What exists and is interesting to everyone is the theory and practice of each in function of the revolutionary interest. [...] Lenin is an idea, not a person. (Vallejo 2014: 82)[27]

However controversial the attribution of such "impersonality" may be, the essential point is that for Vallejo socialist practice must view its individual figures, as much as its contingent manifestations across the party, as provisional mediators of the universalist communist goal, of its fundamental productive horizon.[28]

Nevertheless, we should be wary of allowing the analogy between the artistic avant-garde and revolutionary politics to blur the distinction between the two domains. For Vallejo, the asymmetry concerns the different relation that art and politics bear to the economic basis of socialist thought: while politics must remain *analytically* grounded in science to *represent* socioeconomic structures (the "dogmatism" of historical materialism) so as to eventually transform this reality, the revolutionary aesthetic is not *representational* or analytic, even if it too aims toward the liberation of human expression.

Seen in this light, the real problem that Vallejo found in Bolshevik art was that its commitment to an "aesthetics of reflection" erroneously transposed the scientific condition and analytic function of emancipatory politics into

---

27 "Políticamente, los grandes hombres (Lenin, Trotsky, etc.) no son objeto de esa idolatría individualista y endiosadora de que gozan los buenazos gobernantes burgueses de los países capitalistas. [...] Stalin y Trotsky no existen ni interesan a nadie. Lo que existe e interesa a todos es la teoría y la acción de cada uno en función del interés revolucionario."

28 And it is perhaps in sight of this felt divergence from the "official" poetic norms of "Bolshevik" art which led Vallejo to leave the Paris poems unpublished, exercising caution against potential charges of being a reactive dissident to the Soviet cause. After all, as Flores Galindo shows, dissent from the official line of *Komintern* had already caused Mariátegui no shortage of opprobrium from his fellow Latin American Soviet representatives (cf. Chapter I).

artistic practice, binding poetic liberty to the *local* representations of struggle and its mediating institutions. In contrast, in *The Work of Art and the Social Medium* (*La obra de arte y el medio social*), Vallejo proposes an *aesthetics of transmutation* corresponding to the socialist spirit, which concentrates the anxiety of the individual before an unraveling society, and transforms this anxiety into a productive, collective power:

> The artist absorbs and concatenates the surrounding social anxieties as well as his own individual ones, not to return them such as he absorbed them [...] but to transform them, within his spirit, into other essences, different in form yet identical in substance, to the primary matters thus absorbed. (Ibid.: 48)

This process of transforming destructive affect into a creative potential is precisely what Alain Badiou (2011) crystallizes, theoretically, as the passage from *anxiety* to *courage*, and from *destruction* to *recomposition*, which defines the revolutionary subject: the *fortitude* through which the subject traverses the negation of the "symbolic order" within which individuals and collectives are unequally distributed, and draws from it a positive, transformative act which is also a new logic of placement:

> Courage is insubordination to the symbolic order at the urging of the dissolutive injunction of the real. [...] Courage positively carries out the disorder of the symbolic, the breakdown of communication, whereas anxiety calls for its death. [...] This makes clear why a political subject comes into being only by tying the revolt to a revolutionary consistency, and destruction to a recomposition. (Badiou 2011: 160)

In the end, while reiterating Mariátegui's integration of intellectual and manual labor, and between art and politics, through creative synthesis, Vallejo also contemplates the possibility that a revolutionary art might occur independently of revolutionary politics. More radically, he surmises that a revolutionary art obtains only in freeing itself from the reflexive cognition that grounds socialist "scientific" understanding and political action.

This is the case even if, as Vallejo argues, "the complete artist" is one who is *also* a revolutionary in political matters:

1. An artist may be a political revolutionary and not be a revolutionary, as much as he may want to consciously and politically, in what concerns art.
2. And vice versa, an artist may be, consciously or subconsciously, revolutionary in art and not in politics.

3. There are cases, very exceptional, in which an artist is a revolutionary in art and in politics. The case of the complete artist.
4. Political activity is always the result of a conscious will, freed and reasoned, while the work of art escapes, the more authentic and grander it is, the conscious springs, reasoned, preconceived at will. (Vallejo 1973: 34–35)

This contrast suggests a primitive distinction between a *rational* enterprise, related to revolutionary politics in its representational and creative functions, and the labor of an aesthetics of transmutation guiding revolutionary art and oriented toward capturing the function of "human sensibility." This distinct commitment to universal humanity leads Vallejo to unbind socialist art from any particular place and time: it may emerge and has emerged in history across different contexts, often independently of specific political commitments, or overt affiliations. Indeed, the historical present of revolutionary politics, for Vallejo, lagged behind its accomplishments in art, precisely because the former remained, under the aegis of the Bolshevik sequence, overly bound to dogmatic partisanship and a representational mode.

In *Does a Socialist Art Exist?* (*¿Existe el arte socialista?*), Vallejo notes that while a genuine socialist community is yet to exist, exemplars of a socialist art do exist and have existed. He refers to figures that sublimated their individual destinies to inaugurate unprecedented historical forms, proper to a sensibility that applies to "every man without exception":

Socialist art exists. Examples: Beethoven, many Renaissance fabrics, the pyramids of Egypt, Assyrian statuary, some of Chaplin's movies, Bach himself. [...] Why do these works correspond to the notion and content of a socialist art? *Because, in our estimation, they respond to a universal concept of mass and of sentiment, thinking common interests [...] of every man without exception.* Who constitutes every man without exception? In this denomination are included individuals whose life is characterized by the preponderance of human values over the values of the beast. [...] When a work of art serves and cooperates towards this human unity, underlying the diversity of historical and geographical sites in which it is rehearsed and realized, it is socialist. (Ibid.: 37, my emphasis)

The freedom aspired to by poetry, and its obligation toward the "human function of sensibility," becomes thereby conceived in terms of the task to construct a "universal language," which he defines and anticipates in *The Universality of Verse for the Unity of Languages* (*Universalidad del verso por la unidad de las lenguas*) by attesting to the historical, living nature of poetry as an evolving enterprise. In what appears to be an overt flirtation with a kind of *textual vitalism*, Vallejo inflects poetry to organic productivity (what Bergson named "creative evolution") and describes it as follows:

> A poem is a vital entity, far more organic than a natural organic being. An animal's limbs may be amputated and it may live on. A vegetable's branch may be cut and it lives on. But if a verse is amputated from a poem, a word, an orthographic sign, it dies. Like the poem, upon translation, it cannot preserve its absolute and living integrity, it must be read in its original language, and this, naturally, limits for now the universality of its emotion. But one must not forget that this universality will only be possible the day in which all languages are unified and melt, through socialism, in a singular socialism, in a unique universal idiom. (Vallejo 1973: 62)

The impersonality demanded for such revolutionary agency would become subsequently sketched not only in Vallejo's poetics, but also in his works in prose. In the sections that follow, I trace figurations of the revolutionary subject in Vallejo's literary works during his socialist period, in his progressive attempt to give shape to the universalist ideal that orients his "aesthetics of transmutation." I first focus on his projection of the proletariat Indigenous subject in his play, *Pedro Yunque*, and his short novel, *El Tungsteno*, before assessing the manifestation of the global proletariat and revolutionary spirit in some key works comprising the Paris poems.

The National and the Global: El *Tungsteno* and the Militant Indian Proletariat Subject

In the course of his theoretical negotiations with socialism, Vallejo's depiction of the Peruvian context and the reality of the rural Indian would progressively shift away from the problematic relation separating the subject and world. In place of nostalgia or carnal fixation, Vallejo's works during the Paris Years progressively integrate existential alienation into the context of specific geopolitical circumstances binding the destiny of Peruvian society to its geopolitical context. In the early 1930s, Vallejo's works in prose reveal the extent to which, under the socialist imaginary, it became necessary to understand the tragic reality of the rural Indian as bound to the imperialist venture of the rising economic powers in Latin America. Indeed, the intensified brutality against rural communities by the extractive industries in the Andean regions had established a predatory relation, through which the exploitation and subjugation of Indian labor was carried out with impunity, suspending the order of law in complicity with an emerging national capitalist class. Attesting to this complicity, which perpetuated the instrumentalization of rural labor in the absence of an industrial proletariat, Vallejo would write years later, in 1937, that Peru's thwarted modernization was correlated to its exploitation and expropriation by foreign imperialist forces:

> Peru's economic life rests entirely on agriculture and mining. There are no transformational industries to speak of, and even less heavy industry. Al most all explorations are carried out by foreign firms whose only activity in the country, as a source of work and wealth, consists in the pure and simple extraction of minerals and their bulk exportation overseas.[29]

Beyond this crude diagnosis, Vallejo's socialist views begin to take more precise shape in his literary works after the early 1930s. The growing intrusion of foreign capitalist economic interests into the nation creates, he argues, a sinuous synergy between the state authorities and the rural economy, exacerbating inequality between the mestizo oligarchy and the rural Indian. It permeates educational institutions, determining the privileges and exclusions between the children of the *gamonales* and the Indians, sentencing the latter's future to repeating that of their parents. In Vallejo's short story *Paco Yunque*—composed shortly after his novel *Tungsten (El tungsteno)* in Madrid in 1931, but first published in 1951—the author describes how class inequality infiltrates even the primitive educational system in the rural provinces, echoing Mariátegui's skepticism with regard to the idea that schooling and capitalist modernization is the key to the Indian's emancipation. In the story, the ensuing exploitation of the Indian is indexed to the corruption that permeates the microcosm of the rural primary school system, where a system of privileges and exclusions already predetermines the relationship between students since early childhood. Set in an anonymous town in the southern Peruvian highlands, the story narrates how the young protagonist, Paco Yunque, is bullied and plagiarized in school by the son of the town mayor and railway manager, Dorian Grieve. The relation between the Grieve and Yunque families represents the generational transmission of both political and economic disparity: Paco's father works for and is exploited by Dorian's enterprise, just as Paco's labor power in the school

---

29 Cited in Clayton 2014, pp. 113–114.

"La vida económica peruana descansa enteramente en la agricultura y en la minería. No existen por decirlo así, industrias de transformación y menos aún, por supuesto, industrias pesadas. Casi todas estas explotaciones pertenecen a empresas extranjeras cuya única actividad en el país, en cuanto fuente de trabajo y de riqueza, consiste en la pura y simple extracción del mineral y en su exportación en bruto al extranjero."

is stolen with impunity by Humberto. The melancholic frustration at the end of the story indicates the perpetuation of class privilege, jeopardizing both the liberal pedagogical solution and the dream of urban modernization as a means for the emancipation of the Indian. The disposition of the Indian to learn and work will remain insufficient as long as physical and intellectual labor can be stolen and appropriated with impunity.[30]

But it is noteworthy that, in Vallejo's story, the primary enemy is not the local authorities or the rural oligarchy, but the emerging national capitalist class and the international influence that brings capitalist "modernity" to the nation, while perpetuating the historic inequality that subordinates the Indian workers, surrendering the sovereignty of the nation to foreign interests. Without doubt, the decisive effort to understand Peru's position in the context of global capitalism remains his 1931 short novel, *Tungsten* (*El Tungsteno*). The story describes the ruthless but asymmetrical complicity between the "Marino Brothers" ("*Marino Hermanos*") in their servile association with the North American Mining Society, as they carry out the systematic exploitation and ravaging of the rural community of Quivilca, in the southern province of Cuzco, at the same time surrendering the nation to the interests of international capitalism. Pressured by the military demands of the First World War, Indigenous communities are forced into deplorable working conditions as their lands and labor become usurped in acts of arbitrary appropriation and abuse. Vallejo explores the creeping degeneration of capitalist modernization and commercial life as it functions to corrupt the Indian in a vortex of greed, violence and debauchery. He alludes to a different "trinity of evil" than that outlined by González Prada and transposed into a literary register by Matto de Turner, reflecting the primacy of class contradiction and socioeconomic role in relation to institutional rank or ethical corruption: first, the international capitalists who promote their imperial agenda as they serve wartime needs; second, the corrupt emergent national capital class and business owners and third, the corrupt state officials who surrender the sovereignty of the nation in complicity with North American capital.[31] This trinity concentrates not only the tension between the rural Indian and the mestizo/creole, but the fundamental crisis of sovereignty of the nation before

---

30 The story was first published in the magazine *Apuntes del hombre*, Lima, July 1951, Year 1, #1.

31 The writing and publication of the novel chronologically coincides with Vallejo's "approximation to Stalinism," inspired not only by Mariátegui's call for a socialist literature, but above all by his visit to the Soviet Union in 1931, as detailed in his series of reflections compiled under title *Russia in 1931* (*Rusia en 1931*).

imperialist capitalism. The destiny of class struggle which will decide the fate of the Peruvian nation becomes inextricable from the destiny of the proletariat revolution, in its internationalist scope, to resist the growth of imperial capital across the globe.

In defiance against this "trinity of evil," Vallejo again resists projecting the figure of enlightened mestizo/creole who would assist the Indian masses. The educated but moderate liberal, Leonidas Benites, whose guiding imperative is "to work and save money," is depicted as the silent accomplice to the hegemonic complicity between mestizos and foreigners, promoting a quietist pacifism in the face of injustice. By the same token, the Indian commoners are not idealized as innocent victims, whose dignity lies in awaiting an educational or professional venture to the city. The Indian masses appear ruthlessly deprived of all dignity and spiritual depth, dehumanized in the eyes of an uneducated and barbaric oligarchy, disarmed from all intellectual or practical power in their material reality.

In contrast to figures of the liberal Benites and the derelict Indian commoners, Vallejo anticipates the coming subversion of the rural Indian, given voice through the solitary figure of the blacksmith, Servando Huanca: a "pure Indian," who emerges from the protesting masses, defying the authority of the town's mayor and the local police:

> A man rose from the people among the crowd and, throwing himself against the mayor Parga, emotionally but energetically said:
> The people, sir, demands that justice be made!
> Yes! [...] Yes!-[...] Yes! [...] chanted the multitude—Justice! Justice against those who have been struck! Justice against murderers!
> The mayor turned pale.[32]

In this passage, the work of "endless metonymy" which Michelle Clayton describes as organizing Vallejo's poetic *oeuvre* acquires a concrete political dimension, rising from the cacophonous vituperation of the masses whose clamor is ambiguously described as *from* "the village" and *of* "the people" (*"del pueblo"*). Huanca *emerges from* the tumult as a singular exception, while his

---

32 Vallejo. César. *El tungsteno*, Edición Cultura Universitaria, 1932. pp. 91. my translation. The complete original text corresponding to this edition can be found at: https://archive.org/stream/eltungstenonovel00vall/eltungstenonovel00vall_djvu.txt

voice *belongs to* the oppressed Indian workers as a whole, shaping the "obscure and vague" indignation of collective vituperation in a concrete demand.

> The most abominable and scandalous abuse of authority did not arouse in the people but an obscure vague and diffuse sentimental malaise. Impunity was, in the history of administrative and communal crime, a traditional and common affair in the province. But here, now something new and unprecedented happened. The case of Yepez and Conchucos stirred violently the popular masses, and a man arising from the latter dared to raise his voice, asking for justice and defying the wrath and vengeance of the authorities. Who was, then, this man? He was Servando Huanca, the blacksmith. (Ibid.)

The absence of details about Huanca's past and his lack of interpersonal relations in the story transform him into a symbolic presence: he does not speak as an individual, giving cohesion and a practical horizon to the otherwise inarticulate masses. Unflinchingly, he issues a blunt response to "the injustice of men," as he feels

> a growing pain and rage against the injustice of men. Huanca believes that in this pain and, in this rage, there were not but little personal interests involved. [...] He was convinced that one ought to protest always and vigorously against injustice, no matter where it may manifest itself. Already then, his spirit, re-concentrated and wounded, ruminated day and night on these ideas and will for rebellion. Did Servando Huanca already possess a class consciousness? Was he aware of it? His only combative tactics boiled down to two very simple things: the unification of those who suffer social injustice, and the practical action of the masses. (Ibid.: 92–93)

Speaking on behalf of the desolate Yepez, whose silence echoes the invisibility of the common Indian worker, Huanca protests to the local authorities with clarity: "This man is a poor, ignorant Indian. You stand before him. He is an illiterate. An unconscious man. A disgraced man. He ignores his own age. He ignores whether he is inscribed in the military service. He ignores everything, everything" (Ibid.: 97). Actively dispossessed of practical and theoretical resources, the rural Indian is not merely "misrepresented" as bereft of all social substance by a racist ruling class, but is *objectively* deprived and alienated, kept in subjugation without a future. Their incapacity to read or speak in the language into which they are interjected excludes them, de facto, from political agency within the legal and state apparatus, so that emancipatory politics must then come to grips with the real effects of socioeconomic exploitation and the necessity of subversion.

Huanca's imperative cry is progressively amplified in its scope and intensity, situated against not only the local authorities but also as part of the international proletariat movement. In the closing dialogues with Leonidas Benites, Huanca integrates the local struggle of the Peruvian rural Indian into the horizon of global socialist revolution. As the heated dialogue ensues, Huanca disavows the idea, defended by the pacifism of his interlocutor, that emancipation ought to "trickle down" from the educated elite to the poor masses (cf. Chapter I). Dispelling the idea that an educated elite naturally serves the development of the rural masses, Huanca argues with combative skepticism that the ministers, lawyers and priests are equally indifferent to the interests of the workers, operating as the accomplices or direct perpetrators of their tragic fate.

Nevertheless, the dialogue also expresses cautionary ambivalence: though moved by Huanca's uncompromising demand for justice, Benites worries that the revolutionary call for insurrectionary violence promotes a hatred of educated mestizos, thwarting the possibility of a coalition or reconciliation. In response, Huanca does not deny in principle the ideal of cooperation, but affirms that any coalition would have to imply the immediate subordination of the interests of mestizo intellectuals and activists to the interests of Indian workers: only when this class asymmetry between the urban mestizo and the rural Indian obtains, he claims, will it be possible to "work, later, together and in harmony, as true brothers. [...] Make a choice, Mr. Benites. [...] Make a choice." The militant hero becomes a figure of martyrdom, awakening class consciousness within the Indian masses, preparing the national upsurge against imperial capital, finally guiding the transition from *myth* to *history*: the moment where the Indian subject becomes the transitionary figure who brings into existence the nation to come.

As we shall see in the next section, this internationalist scope of the proletarian struggle, binding the individual and local to the collective and the global, is progressively developed across Vallejo's Paris Poems, leading to the formation of a "global proletariat subject."

The Time of Harvest: The Global Proletariat Subject in *Poemas humanos*

Across many of the poems in *Human Poems* (*Poemas humanos*), Vallejo revels in announcing the advent of *the global proletariat subject*, not only as the insurrectionary force of the "coming tempest" against the hegemonic powers of his time, but as the bringer of what the poet calls "the time of harvest." Following his verdict in his critical essays on Bolshevism and his avowal of a "socialist art" driven by an aesthetics of transmutation, Vallejo's Paris Poems give expression to the ideal of a creative universal humanity beyond insurrectionary furor. Accordingly, after the moment of war and defiant militancy, Vallejo imagines a utopia in which the experience of alienation that severed the poetic voice between the urban and rural worlds becomes tethered not to a lost past and derelict present, but to a radiant future, woven by collective labor. The individuality of the poet is suddenly trivialized, measuring itself not against the impersonal undercurrents of libidinal matter in its finitude, but against the grandeur of humanity as a whole.

In *It Was Sunday in the Bright Ears of My Donkey* (*Fue domingo en las claras orejas de mi burro*), Vallejo invokes a colloquial sadness for his "Peruvian donkey in Peru," both spatially separated and temporally disjoint from the European evening of "his personal experience" (Vallejo 2007: 386). With a taint of apologetic embarrassment, this recollective pronouncement defines the poet's identity at the core of his "microbial cycle" ("*ciclo microbiano*") and "patriotic hairstyle" ("*patriótico peinado*"). He feels not only alienated in relation to his European ambience, separated in exile from home, but becomes jubilant in commemorative memory: the Andean world is celebrated in its holistic articulation, from those "inorganic bodies" that compose its natural landscape, to mankind's generational descent, as the latter is no longer reduced to the procreative multiplication of animal bodies. The nostalgic sentiment for the lost home is in this way characterized with a positive, fertile productivity, through which the memory of the past rekindles life in the present and toward a future, "painted with belief":

> So do I see the portrayed hills of my country
> rich in jackasses, sons of jackasses, parents today in sight
> that now return painted with beliefs
> the horizontal hills of my sorrows. (Ibid.)

The conflicted relationship toward the Andean world becomes the lever to introduce a celebratory integration of the nation into a global destiny, in continuity with Mariátegui's vision, in which rural Indigenous cooperativism emerges as an expression of the internationalist spirit of socialism. In an exacerbated metonymic play, in the poem *Telluric and Magnetic* (*Telurica y magnetica*), the local world and the poet's relation to the past give way to a generative rather than destructive temporality, where the singular details of the rural landscape, its mountain slopes, flora and fauna are sutured first to the national scale, and finally to the worldly "orb":

> Oh human fields!
> Solar and nutritious absence of the sea,
> and oceanic feeling for everything!
> Oh climates found within gold, ready!
> Oh intellectual field of cordilleras,
> with religion, with fields, with ducklings!
>
> Tearful auchenia, my own souls!
> Sierra of my Peru, Peru of the world
> and Peru at the base of the orb;
> I adhere. (Vallejo 2007: 332)

In these verses, Vallejo anthropomorphizes natural scenery as the expression of a productive prowess, at the same time as he flattens the human onto nature, rendering divergent ontological strata porous. The "human fields" of collective labor, in which the social bond itself grows, are situated at a safe distance from the devouring ocean, as the Andean mountains concentrate knowledge and labor as "intellectual fields." The cyclic temporality of the seasons becomes in turn coterminous with and enabling of the time of labor; the soil provides both its "theoretical and practical ground," entwining cultural and natural history as an integral system. Human productivity forges labor from the inexhaustible heterogeneity of nature and its elements, articulating "an astonishing hierarchy of tools." The absence of the Father and the identification of Man with God's divine creative power in Vallejo's heretical cry of protest are now identified with the Promethean prowess of the hand, which masters the "technics of the Heavens" (*"tecnica del cielo"*; both "sky" and "Heaven") and binds inorganic matter and organic productivity to human labor: the "abrupt" molecule in its deviant motion, the "judicial" mice in its survivalist skepticism, the "poultry-yard" of angelic roosters and the "patriotic asses" of the poet's life all join the universal struggle of common man:

> Quarterly maize, with opposed birthdays!
> I hear through my feet how they move away;
> I smell them return when the earth
> Clashes with the technics of the Heavens!
> Abruptly molecule! Terse atom!
> Oh human fields!
> Solar and nutritious absence of the sea,
> Oh climates found within gold, ready!

Oh intellectual fields of cordilleras,
With religion, with fields, with ducklings! (Ibid.: translation modified)

The redoubling effect of light, reflecting the poet's self-image in the mirror's surface, is disseminated as it "climbs in," filtered through the mind, animating the skeletal dust of the body and taking it beyond the inert shadow of representation into the movement of the living idea: "Oh light hardly a mirror [away] from shadow, which is life with the period and, with the line, dust, and that is why I revere [it], climbing through the idea to my skeleton!" (Ibid.). The poet systematically reiterates the unity of theory and practice, as the imperatival force of the idea now subjectivizes the body, animating it: the "crystalline" body that characterized *Trilce*'s timid insinuation for the future as abstract principle becomes incarnate and set in motion, that is, *to work*.

In *The Miners Came Out of the Mine* (*Los mineros salieron de la mina*), Vallejo sketches the contours of a qualified vitalism, characterizing how the "bottomless depths" of human suffering are transvalued through labor rather than through aesthetic allure or bare affect. The manual productivity of the miners' strife speaks to a spiritual prowess; they are honored as those "creators of profundity" in which the depth of cooperative labor shines forth (Ibid.: 336). Similarly, in *Glebe* (*Gleba*), the worker's strife reintegrates the poet's fragmented body and the complexity of its organic functions, not into a reconstituted individual, but into a multiple collective body woven from humanity as a whole: it gives shape to the "global effect" of a "brightening candle" that incorporates the phallic "foreskin," the worker's "beaten bodies" and their extremities, into a new energy, an integral, collective mass of "functional laborers." Subtracted from the time of the flesh, the laborers "lack clocks"; in their immortal productivity, they "never gloat to breathe," but carry on with impersonal diligence:

> They own heads, their trunks, their extremities,
> They own their pants, their metacarpal fingers and a little staff
> To eat they dressed themselves in height
> And they wash their faces caressing them with solid doves
> Have their head, their torso, their extremities
>
> Their pants, their metacarpous fingers and a Little stick
> To eat dressed in tallness
> And wash their faces caressed with solid doves. (Ibid.: 390)

The universality of the idea that guides the collective transcends every localized manifestation and is ultimately resistant of the finitude which afflicts mankind as the bearer of contingent biological, economic and cultural determinations.

In *There Is a Man Mutilated* (*Existe un mutilado*)—written apropos the historical figure of a certain French coronel named Piccot, dismembered in 1914 during the war—Vallejo reiterates the integrity of Man over the disparate function of bodily parts, persisting even when its supporting organs are removed and the body is ravaged:

> There is a man mutilated not from combat but from an embrace, not from war but from peace. [...] Face mutilated, face covered, face closed, this man, nevertheless, is whole and lacks nothing. He has no eyes and he sees and cries. He has no nose and he smells and breathes. He has no ears and he listens. No forehead and he thinks and withdraws to himself. No chin and he desires and subsists. Jesus knew the man whose mutilation left him functionless, who had eyes and could not see and had ears and could not hear. I know the man whose mutilation left him organless, who sees without eyes and hears without ears. (Vallejo 2007: 353)

The inversion is palpable; as man becomes unbound from his bodily supports, and as his own face is erased, he rises to the universal in an act of martyrdom, driven by the integrity of the idea. In *There Is No One Left in the House* (*No hay nadie ya en la casa*), Vallejo transforms impotence before alienation within the domestic space into a power of transformation. The subject appears as the "agent of the gerund," noun turned verb, a pure historical agency whose unity is incorruptible. The circle, once the image of the ubiquity and cyclical unrest of repetition, weaves together the amputated body, constructing a functional system that remains irreducible to its biological parts; the heart, the lips and feet are trivial in themselves, but jointly generate ceaseless creativity and labor. What persists in time, beyond the time of loss and the disintegration of the finite body, is "the subject of the act":

> When somebody leaves, somebody remains. [...] What continues in the house is the organ, the agent of the gerund and in circle. [...] What continues in the house is the foot, the lips, the eyes, the heart. [...] What continues in the house, is the subject of the act. (Ibid.: 347)

As we mentioned, this reintegrative function, achieved through labor, not only overcomes the bodily constraints of individual being but also the wealth of determinations that dissolve universality into the specificity of biological and cultural determinations. In *I am Going to Speak of Hope* (*Voy a hablar de la esperanza*), Vallejo erases the name and individual identity of the self, taking the form of an empty "I" defined by a "simple" suffering without further qualification: "I do not suffer this pain as César Vallejo. I do not ache now as an artist, as a man or even as a simple living being. I do not suffer this pain as a Catholic, as a [Muslim] or as an atheist. Today I simply suffer" (Ibid.: 343). The poem unravels the entire fabric of nouns and predicates that split Man from within by contingent differentiations. The self-effacement of the authorial voice unveils then a nameless subject: a dismembered, generic being, voided of particularity, an anonymous Man who "simply suffers" on behalf of mankind as a whole.

In the end, the subject of socialist art does not suspend representation by interrupting the mimetic dependence on foreign forms or by bringing forth a self-portraying autochthonous subject. Rather, it announces the necessity of poetry to partake in the construction of a new collective subject, defined only by cooperative labor and unbound inventive freedom. This *hymnal poetics*, which captures the spirit and language of a universal humanity, announces the agency of a delocalized subject, neither dispersed in the lived experience of the suffering body nor reducible to determinations of nation, class, race or political determinations.

Nostalgia for the Future: The World of Justice and the Generic Human Subject

Although the universalist ideal in Vallejo's poetry is clearly discernible across his work during the Paris years, it doubtlessly finds its apotheosis in his last poetic collection (1939), *Spain, Take Away from Me This Cup* (*España aparta de mi este cáliz*). In these poems, a particular historical event becomes the surrogate for the universal destiny of mankind, which outlives and exceeds its contextual specificity. Thus, while the Parisian "cosmic city" was the site for a free association of intellectuals, the Spanish territory, caught in the midst of civil war, becomes the site for internationalist militant resistance against social oppression. As Alain Badiou (2014) argues, the unique internationalist quality of the Spanish Civil War resulted in an immeasurably rich sequence of artistic and intellectual production, harmonizing divergent and even incompatible ideological orientations:

> Let us observe that the Spanish civil war is certainly the historic event that has most intensely mobilized all the artists and intellectuals of the world. On one hand, the personal commitment of writers from all ideological tendencies on the side of the republicans, including therefore the

communists, is remarkable: whether we are dealing with organized communists, social democrats, mere liberals, or even fervent Catholics, such as the French writer Georges Bernanos, the list is extraordinary if we gather all those who publicly spoke out, who went to Spain in the midst of the war, or even entered into combat on the side of the republican forces. On the other hand, the number of masterpieces produced on this occasion is no less astonishing. We already announced as much for poetry. But let us also think of the splendid painting by Pablo Picasso that is titled *Guernica*; let us think of two of the greatest novels in their genre: *Man's Hope* by François Malraux and *For Whom the Bell Tolls* by the American Ernest Hemingway. The frightening and bloody civil war in Spain has illuminated the art of the world for several years. (Badiou 2014: 96)

In the collection's opening poem, titled *Hymn to the Volunteers of the Republic* (*Himno a los voluntarios de la república*), Vallejo reiterates the fraternal celebration of labor found throughout *Human Poems*, as he pays homage to those who congregate from all corners of the world to fight in the Spanish soil in the name of unqualified humanity. Overwhelmed as he witnesses the collective martyrdom but also the jubilance of the volunteers who "march to kill" with their "world-wide-agony," the poetic voice is at first moved to the point of impotence. The collapse of poetic eloquence, however, progressively becomes reconstituted, recognizing a universal passion to which the poet humbly incorporates himself, bearing his "impersonal forehead." Alienation becomes overturned into the qualitative fullness of a historical, "long ecstatic movement" and "double-edged speed" that the poet is incapable of "retaining in his hands":

For my hands won't hold your long ecstatic moment
and I smash against your double-edged speed
my smallness dressed up in grandeur. (Vallejo 2007: 569)

The nostalgia "for what is to come," which signaled the anticipation of a death without redemption in The Black Heralds, now incarnates universal struggle, giving a concrete historical presence to what was but an abstract ideal in *Trilce*. The "inexistent" being of the "crystalline idea," which abstractly prefigured the minoritarian upsurge of the "new Less" as a latent historical potency, is here given concrete measure: the poet, witnessing the materialization of a global humanity in the Spanish soil, conveys what Badiou names a distinct "nostalgia for a grandeur," whose projective "future anterior" inscribes the collective hope for the coming humanity: "[T]he nostalgia for a grandeur and a beauty that nevertheless have not yet been created. Communism here works in the future anterior: we experience a kind of poetic regret for what we imagine the world will have been, when communism will have come" (Badiou 2014: 104).

As the poem proceeds, Vallejo goes on to ponder, in a protracted history of "Spanish affairs," the inventive prowess of the great artists across the history of Spain, from Calderon to Cervantes, from Goya to Quevedo, from Cajal to Odena. This litany, which Vallejo "brings to the balance" sheet of history, attests to the spirit of a socialist art that, although produced in a singular time and place, was also universal as an expression of human creative liberty. And in the same way that Paris is more than "just Paris," but the site for intellectual cooperation between thinkers from around the world, the "volunteer of Spain" is not *only* Spanish, but a collective body that ignites a "captive matchstick" with "choleric gold," through which the "sorrows of common people" carry "the hopes of men" ("*Dolores de pueblos con esperanzas de hombres*") (Vallejo 2007: 569).

The subject dies not in individual solitude, but rather of the universality that afflicts it: the martyr "proletariat that dies of universe" in a "methodical chaos," at once "theoretical and practical." This violent upsurge and negative movement against the present is then matched by egalitarian ambition: that "Dantesque desire" in which the "fallen farmer" is vitally enveloped by the "green foliage" of fertile lands, to be sown in cooperative labor (Vallejo 2007: 569). The Dantean descent to "the form of the soul" tracks this expansive movement, such that the individual rises to the universal and the body becomes incorporated to the integrity of the universal idea, "without track to his body" (Ibid.). As Badiou writes, reiterating the passage from anxiety to courage that defines the creative transformation of destructive furor in the revolutionary subject: "This unknown liberty is precisely that of the reversal of misery into heroism, the reversal of a particular anxiety-ridden situation into a universal promise of emancipation" (Badiou 2014: 98).

Echoing the universalist spirit of Whitman, the sacrifice of the proletariat binds disciplines and modalities of labor: the militiamen express themselves horizontally and uniformly, as incessant "blades of grass." The proletariat are "Builders, agricultural, civilian, and military," makers of "light" and "eternity" (Ibid.). The violence that the militiaman inflicts, rather than meeting its end at the borders of the flesh, opens the horizon of "the time of harvest," when the collective body of the collective subject incorporates disparate individualities ("your creature") and "rises to the weak" (Ibid.). Only then, reaching the apotheosis of the universalist clamor, does Vallejo's voice become void of all melancholy, yet prophetic in sight of the future, erupting into a hymnal celebration of a generic humanity to come:

> All men will love one another
> and will eat holding the corners of your sad handkerchiefs
> and will drink in the name
> of your ill-fated throats!
> They'll rest walking at the foot of this run
> and they'll weep thinking of your orbits, happy
> they'll be and to the sound
> of your return, atrocious, flourishing, innate,
> tomorrow they'll adjust their chores, the figures they've dreamt and sung!
> The same shoes will fit him who ascends
> without track to his body
> and him who descends to the form of his soul! (Ibid.)

These lines progressively reinscribe the Christian dialectic of death and resurrection, of individual martyrdom and heavenly redemption, in the transition from to eternity and brotherhood. The revered militiaman imparts the joyous return to fraternal embrace, and the severed link to the Other which defined subjective alienation is restored in collective synergy. A world transfixed by the idea of justice is affirmed, while Vallejo's desire for uncompromising inclusiveness defies the laws of men, nature and the divine all the same.

At its apex, the universal voice not only demands but prophesizes the imminent advent of redemption for the human and nonhuman, vindicating the living and the dead in an act not of metaphysical protest or heresy, but of productive transgression:

> Embracing, the dumb will speak, the lame will walk!
> The returning blind will see
> and, quivering, the deaf will hear!
> The ignorant will be wise, the wise ignorant!
> Given will be the kisses you couldn't give!
> Only death will die! The ant
> will bring scraps of bread to the elephant fettered
> to its brutal delicacy; aborted children
> will be born again, perfect, spatial,
> and all men will work,
> all men will procreate,
> all men will understand! (Ibid.)

The reiterated totality of "all men," overcoming all loss and suffering, culminates in the assignation of three basic determinations that define a new subject: the universal community to come jointly enjoys the fruits of *labor*, of *love* and of *understanding*, an immanent trinity of practice, affect and thought. All living beings are to relate freely, and the departed return in a creative joy, with enthusiasm that knows no boundaries: species assist one another irrespective of size or might, procreation becomes absolutely unbound from the divisions among beings, while the unjustly damned return to celebrate with the living. If, as we saw in the *Poemas humanos*, man and nature had already been identified with the productive temporality of life and labor, here Vallejo dares to imagine a positive overcoming of the disjunction between life and death itself: as individuals are effaced in their alienated, bounded existence, they also "cease to die," and bodily erasure is vindicated retroactively from the future anterior. The aborted children that were deprived of life, covered in glory, under the glare of a promise for eternity, now return, exempt from the destructive verdict of time, as purely "spatial" beings.

More than any identifiable "Marxist" utopia, Vallejo's delirious jubilation forges a standard for justice, a measure not only situated beyond the confines of individual identities, ethnicities, nations or languages, but even beyond the order of matter and temporal finitude. In its uncompromising affirmative grandeur, extending its universal clamor to the dead as much as the living, his address approximates what the French philosopher Quentin Meillassoux names the "world of justice," which traverses all ontological strata, from the inorganic to the cultural.[33] For Meillassoux, as for Vallejo, the clamor for universality results in an "irreligious" avowal of resurrection, in which revolutionary hope retrieves bodies subjected to an untimely death. In the course of deploying the untamable, absolute power of "absolute contingency" to disrupt the lawful continuities in the orders of Matter, Life and Thought (the "three worlds" which have come to pass as moments of historical, ontological rupture in history until now), Meillassoux anticipates the advent of a world of Justice, which he names a "pure object of hope" (Ibid.). It transfixes the living, in the present, with the idea of a future in which the limitations of nature and culture are superseded and transgressed, announcing "the World of the rebirth of humans that makes universal justice possible, by erasing even the injustice of shattered lives."[34] As an "object of hope," the world of justice is

---

33 Meillassoux, Quentin, *The Divine Inexistence*, in Graham Harman. "Quentin Meillassoux: Philosophy in the Making", Edinburgh University Press, 2011, p. 190.
34 Ibid., p. 190.

but the egalitarian future carried by what Vallejo names "the hopes of men," leading joyously toward a future in which not even death can constrain the clamor for the Good:

> The more one denounces the requirement of universal justice as a pure illusion belonging to the imaginary realm of the human, the more one emphasizes that with the advent of such a chimerical requirement, becoming displays its capacity for producing something that previously did not exist at all. Namely, it is an imaginary Good, aimed at by an illusion for which only thinking beings are equipped. It is a Good at which one aims, perfectly inexistent in the world that precedes the rise of humanity. And it manifestly exceeds the capacities of matter, in whose midst it has nonetheless emerged in the form of an obstinate hope. Thus, one emphasizes all the more the capacity of time to transgress even its own laws toward the objective advent of justice. (Ibid.: 205)

As the clamor for justice traverses the memory of past injustices with ruthless affirmation, the future becomes at once redemptive and inventive; Meillassoux describes as follows the premonitory knowledge that elides contingent differences and actualizes the universal:

> The eternal truths to which our condition grants access are in fact indifferent to differences, to the innumerable and necessary differences between individual thinkers. The differences are necessary because humans, as simple existents, are contingent and particular beings indefinitely differentiable from other humans. [...] Justice can survive only as an idea of existent and irreparable wrongs, and we owe the dead nothing less. When the requirement of justice actually transfixes us, it also summons our refusal of injustice for the dead, for recent or ancient deaths, for known and unknown deaths. For the universal is universal only when it makes no exceptions. (Ibid.: 192)

Affirming the promise of rebirth, Vallejo's late, hymnal poetry subtracts heresy from the protest against an absent deity, directing it against the very "material bases" of experience, transforming these into contingent constraints and supports for the universal Idea.

This impetus finds pristine expression in the poem *Masses* (*Masa*), where the figure of the "dying militiaman," nameless and anonymous, without rank or nationality, rises at the precise moment in which all of humanity congregates and unity becomes exceptionless:

> Then all the inhabitants of the earth
> surrounded him; the corpse looked at them sadly, deeply moved;
> he got up slowly
> embraced the first man; started to walk. (Vallejo 2007: 611)

Across the entire collection, in fact, Vallejo indulges in unrestrained affirmation against all normative orders, while avoiding a relapse into religious or "spiritualist ecstasies." In *Battles* (*Batallas*), Vallejo celebrates the resilience of the militant subject, immortalized through collective struggle: those "immortal dead" that overcome finitude by conjoining themselves with history, eventually "finished weeping, finished / hoping, finished / aching, finished living /, finally being mortals." And in the commemorative poem to the deceased militant Pedro Rojas, the individual body of the proletarian militant becomes the immortal carrier of the universalist dream after death: "His body was full of the world" (Ibid.).

Finally, in the untitled second poem to the collection, the thwarted "oven" which offered those "burnt breads" in the familial space of *The Distant Steps*, haunted by the absent Father, are now themselves lost, erasing the locality of the event of birth within a timeless horizon, erupting from the region of Malaga and encompassing the entirety of human history: "Malaga, without father or mother / no pebble, nor oven, nor white dog! Malaga defenseless, where my death was born taking steps and out of passion died my birth" (Ibid.). The "flight to Egypt" no longer designates the point of alienation and the absent, transcendent Father, but sings the incorporation of the particular life into universal history, that "innate orb" immanently expressed in the Spanish soil:

> Malaga, literal and from Malaga
> Escaping to Egypt, since you are stuck
> Widening in suffering identical to your dance
> Resolving in you the volume of the sphere. (Ibid.)

In the last instance, Vallejo produces a genetic subject not only unbound from ethnic or cultural determinations, but also from the material and economic ambitions of socialism, modulating its emancipatory dreams in the pursuit of national expression, as imagined originally by Mariátegui. Its universality is unapologetically hyperbolic; its sense of justice is "exorbitant," abjuring any semblance of programmatic imagination and reducing the future to an inchoate promise for egalitarian fraternity.

Chapter 3

THE LIGHT WITHIN THE WORLD: JOSÉ MARÍA ARGUEDAS AND THE LIMITS OF TRANSCULTURATION

Introduction: The Limits of the Integrative Dream

In this chapter I propose to read José María Arguedas's literary works as the culmination of the historical sequence of *indigenismo* that follows from Mariátegui's integrative socialist project, which in essence conceived of the possibility of constructive mediations between the urban mestizo and the rural Indian through the agency of a new revolutionary subject.

In the first section, I consider the polemics between Arguedas and Julio Cortázar, in which the tension between regionalism and universalism emerges in the context of clarifying how intellectual labor relates to social imperatives. I show that Arguedas is led to conceive of a new universalism that would be not the opposite but the obverse of regionalism. In searching for novel possibilities of mediation between Western and indigenous forms, such a view also, like Mariátegui's own project, imagines a collective identity for the Peruvian nation. In the second section, I trace how Arguedas aims to extend Mariátegui's ideal of appropriating Indigenous cooperativist productive modalities, while refusing the derision of cultural concerns as proper to a residual romanticist nostalgia. In doing so, I show how he underscores the indissociable link between subjective cultural–normative factors and objective economic-productive determinations. In the third and fourth sections, I trace how an anthropologically informed conception of the indigenous world in its relation to the West mediates this correction, as cultural determination becomes part of the scientific ideal of socialism. Following Ángel Rama, I show how "transculturation" becomes the lever through which Arguedas begins to think of a possible reconciliation between what he calls the "magical and rational" conceptions of the world. This leads Arguedas, like Vallejo, to search for a new language in what he calls a "superior universalism," a "more absolute act of creation" that would preserve and potentiate the *ethos* of labor present in Indigenous culture. In the fifth section, I begin to assess the way in which Arguedas progressively develops the search for a new language commensurate to this "superior universalism" by thinking different forms of *revolutionary transcultural subjectivity*, starting from the figure of the *militant Indian subject* who returns from the city, as depicted in his short story *Agua*. In the sixth section, I focus on the figure of the *collective Indian subject* depicted in his first novel, *Yawar Fiesta*, in which Arguedas transforms the subject into a collective voice whose agency proceeds without a central protagonist. In the seventh section, I assess the culmination of the transcultural search for a new integrative consciousness under the figure of the *post-Indigenous transcultural subject*, elaborated in Arguedas's 1964 novel *Todas las sangres*. In this work, the consolidation of a transcultural subjectivity serves as a strategic mediator who integrates the collectivist values upheld by Indigenous *ayllu*, the elegiac repentance of the waning landlord oligarchy set in the path of Christian martyrdom, and the rational and pragmatic thrust of the new capitalist urban class, all jointly endangered by the mantle of international capital. In the eighth and final section, I show how the years leading to Arguedas's last, truncated 1972 novel, *The Fox from Up Above, The Fox from Down Below* (The Foxes), attests to the collapse of the transcultural subject and the appropriative productivist dream, in the wake of changes in Peruvian society and its economy after the 1968 agrarian reform and the abolition of the latifundio.

This arc leads to the apotheosis of the dream of alternative modernity that guides *indigenista* narratives, leading to the collapse of the integrative socialist project. For Arguedas witnesses the effects of a thwarted modernity in the urban space, where the mass migration of disenfranchised Indigenous masses into the city pulverized the collective bond and perpetrated their subjugation. Facing the deterioration of the hopes of potentiating the cooperativist ethos of the rural Indian world, however, in *The Foxes*, Arguedas tantalizingly conceives of the figure of a *generic post-cultural subject*, woven from the "rabble of culture" composing the inconsistent individualities and collectivities in the urban space.

The Tasks of the Intellectual: Between Regionalism and Universalism

In his polemical 1967 letter to Roberto Fernández Retamar—published in no. 45 of *Casa de las Américas*, and questioning "the place of the Latin American intellectual" in global culture—Julio Cortázar criticized the "telluric" fetish of those Latin American writers who isolated themselves from a global horizon of literary production in the name of their native traditions. Guilty of promoting a "parochial and villagey" localism, and inspiring a politically dubious nationalist allergy to foreign cultural forms, such a "regionalist" orientation was indicted for relying on a totalizing conception of culture, and for positing a problematic contrariety between *country* and *world*.

> The tellurism, as one might understand for example Samuel Feijao, appears to me as profoundly alien because it is narrow, parochial and I would even say "villagey" (*aldeano*); I can comprehend it and admire it in those who don't reach, for different reasons, a totalizing vision of culture and history, and concentrate all of their talent in the labor "of the zone," (*de zona*) but I see it as a preamble to the worst advances of the negative nationalism when it becomes the creed of writers that, almost always for reasons of cultural misconceptions, obstinately exalt the values of the plot against values as a whole, the country against the world.[1] (Cortazar 1967)

Defying such regionalist isolationism, what Cortázar names the "contemporary intellectual" is defined by the will to enter an expansive horizon of intellectual production, in which all nations participate in sight of the universal ideals of "global peace" and "social justice," forging "conjunctions and syntheses," thereby occupying a "planetary" perspective:

> The problem of the contemporary intellectual is one alone: that of a peace grounded in the social justice such that the national belonging of each individual only subdivides the issue without taking its basic character away. But it is here that the writer distanced from his country is situated by force in a different perspective: the sentiment of the human process becomes in a way more planetary, it operates by conjunctions and by syntheses, and if it loses the force concentrated in an immediate

---

1 Cortázar, Julio. "Letter to Fernández Retamar," in *Casa de las Américas*, no. 45, 1967, my translation, here and below. http://www.mundolatino.org/cultura/juliocortázar/cortázar_3.htm

> "El telurismo, como entiende entre ustedes un Samuel Feijoo, por ejemplo, me es profundamente ajeno por estrecho, parroquial y hasta diría aldeano; puedo comprenderlo y admirarlo en quienes no alcanzan, por razones múltiples, una visión totalizadora de la cultura y de la historia, y concentran todo su talento en una labor 'de zona,' pero me parece un preámbulo a los peores avances del nacionalismo negativo cuando se convierte en el credo de escritores que, casi siempre por falencias culturales se obstinan en exaltar los valores del terruño contra los valores a secas, el país contra el mundo."

context, it achieves in turn an almost unbearable but always clarifying lucidity.[2] (Ibid.)

This internationalist aspiration was not, however, supposed to entail a disavowal of native traditions: on the contrary, Cortázar argues that by folding his own production into the planetary sphere, his own Argentine identity had been incorporated into "an infinitely wider and richer path":

> The Argentine quality of my work has gained rather than lost as a result of that spiritual osmosis in which the writer does not relinquish anything, does not betray anything, but rather situates its vision in a plane where original values become inserted into an infinitely wider and richer path [...] situating oneself in the more universal perspective of the old world [...] so as to little by little discover the true roots of Latin America. (Cortazar 1968)[3]

In response to Cortázar's verdict—and initiating a fierce polemics that would extend over the course of several publications, until 1969—José María Arguedas questioned the "solemn conviction" of his contemporary that would allegedly allow Latin American writers to understand themselves *only from without*.[4] On the contrary, if there was a danger in the self-perceived role of Latin American writers within the horizon of international culture, he argued, it was precisely the belief that exposure to and involvement in the foreign was sufficient for an understanding of regional traditions. In short, Arguedas notes that alertness to the threat of a myopic *provincialism* that disavows involvement with the global must not make us blind to the opposite threat of an eurocentrism that disavows the intricacies of the local in the name of planetary "integration."

---

[2] "[E]l problema del intelectual contemporáneo es uno solo, el de la paz fundada en la justicia social que las pertenencias nacionales de cada uno sólo subdividen la cuestión sin quitarle su carácter básico. Pero es aqui en dónde el escritor alejado de su país se sitúa forzosamente en una perspectiva diferente [el] sentimiento del proceso humano se vuelve por decirlo así más planetario, opera por conjuntos y por síntesis, y si pierde la fuerza concentrada en un contexto inmediato, alcanza en cambio una lucidez a veces insoportable pero siempre esclarecedora."

[3] Cortázar, Julio. "Carta Abierta a Roberto Fernández Retamar," in *SIMO, Ana María. Cinco miradas sobre Cortázar*. Tiempo Contemporáneo, 1968, my translation.

[4] Arguedas, José María. "Primer diario," in *Amaru*, no. 6, April–June 1968—(later included in his posthumous novel, *El zorro de arriba y el zorro de abajo*).

According to Arguedas, Cortázar's "contemporary intellectual" promoted not a genuine universal perspective, but rather the Westernized elitism of the "professional writer," who sought to "sting with his 'genius,' in the solemn conviction in that one better understands the essence of the national from the high spheres of the supranational"[5] (Arguedas 1968). Turning the argument on its head, Arguedas attributes to Cortázar a culturalist bias that vitiates the alleged claim to a universal stance. For if it is only through integration into an international horizon that the provincial writer escapes provincialism, then for Arguedas it must be equally true that only from an intimate knowledge of and immersion in the local can the universal aspiration become something other than the reification of abstract platitudes. He argues that every writer is always a "provincial writer" who is also, however, part of a universal *continuum*: the normative horizon of "value-in-itself" that folds the local into the global: "We are not different in what I was thinking of in speaking of provincials. We are all provincial, don Julio. Provincials of nations and provincials of the supranational which is, also, a sphere, a well-closed stratum, that of 'value-in-itself,' as you point out with great joy" (Arguedas 1968).[6]

In the end, while agreeing with Arguedas's rejoinder, Cortázar responds by insisting on the importance of distinguishing between provincialist fetishism and the trivial fact that we are all determined by certain native-regional traditions.

> We are all provincial, provincial of the nations and provincial of the supranational. Agreed; but there is an enormous difference between being provincial in the way that someone like Lezama Lima is, who precisely knows more about Ulises than Penelope herself, and the provincials of folk obedience for whom the music of this world begins and ends in the five notes of a quena.

Arguedas's response notes the disavowed occidentalism that makes itself explicit in a caricature of Andean folklore, ironically mocking Cortázar when letting him know that modern *quenas* and the *jaylli* Queuchua enjoyed more than "five notes."

---

5 "[...] aguijonear con su 'genialidad,' con sus solemnes convicciones de que mejor se entiende la esencia de lo nacional desde las altas esferas de lo supranacional."
6 "No somos diferentes en lo que estaba pensando al hablar de provincianos. Todos somos provincianos, don Julio (Cortázar). Provincianos de las naciones y provincianos de lo supranacional que es también, una esfera, un estrato bien cerrado, el del 'valor en sí,' como usted con mucha felicidad señala."

I now begin to suspect that the only one in some way "exiled" is you, Cortázar, and that is why you are so conceited by the glorification, so folkloric of those of us who work *in situ* and like to call ourselves, to your dismay, provincials of our peoples of this world, where, as you say, jets have already been tried and operated very efficiently, a marvelous device to which I dedicated a Quechua *jaylli*, a bilingual hymn of more than five notes as happily our modern quenas *enjoy*.

As we have seen, Mariátegui defines the core of *indigenista* literature in terms of its simultaneous aspiration toward a *modern* approximation to global currents in culture, and a *realist* approximation to the Andean world, where formal experimentation serves to resist idealization or nostalgic fetishization. Seen in this light, Arguedas's literary works can be said to elaborate on the posited complementarity between the specificity of local tradition and the general reach of universalism, tracking not only the mediations between the urban mestizo and rural Indian, but between Western and Indigenous culture more broadly. In the next section, I show how this task involved a methodological rejoinder to the economism that runs throughout Mariátegui's socialist project, emphasizing cultural determinations when satisfying the ideal of appropriative integration.

The Rehabilitation of Culture against Economism

In his 1950 essay *The Novel and the Problem of Literary Expression in Peru* (*La novela y el problema de la expresion literaria en el Perú*), Arguedas rejects the identification of his work with the label "indigenismo," insofar as he conceived of his own project not as addressing the reality of the rural Indian as an isolated group, but as part of an integral narrative binding the Andean world to a national and ultimately global context.[7] He draws a distinction between a literature that takes the rural Indian as its central subject matter, and one which aims to apprehend the complexities of the *Andean world*, in which the rural Indian appears as an element of a broader system:

> One speaks thus of the *indigenista* novel; and it has been said that my works *Agua* and *Yawar Fiesta* are *indigenista* or Indian. And that is not true. These are novels in which the Peruvian Andes appear in all of

---

7 Arguedas. José María. "La Novela y el Problema de la Expresión Literaria en el Perú," in *Qepa Wiñaq [...] Siempre Literatura y antropología*, edited by Dora Sales, Iberoamericana, 2009.

their elements, in their disquieting and confused human reality, in which the Indian is but one among many and different characters.[8] (Arguedas 2009: 153, my translation here and below)

If *indigenista* narratives continued to miss the complex reality of the Andean "world" in relation to its national and global exterior, it is because they failed to account for the way in which productive factors remain linked to cultural ones. Arguedas's holistic vision thus conceives of the identity and placement of the rural Indian as only intelligible not only as part of a socioeconomic context, but also in the rift between different cultures and normative systems.[9]

Following Mariátegui, this meant that the political–normative horizon for the rural Indian could not be restoration or vindication, but had to imply a kind of *preservative transformation*, one which would retain its distinctive character while nevertheless accommodating the demands of modernity. Such a transformation, however, could not only consist of reconciling cooperativist economic-productive modalities into a new modernizing project; it had to also conceive of a new cultural bond that would mediate between the Indigenous and Western worlds. As he would express years later in a retrospective assessment, Arguedas endorsed what we can name a *principle of reconciliation*, between the "rational" and "magical" conceptions of the world, associated with the Western world and the Indian world, respectively. As he would state in the infamous 1964 roundtable about *Todas las sangres*, such a principle condensed the hope of overcoming the contradiction between Western modernity and pre-Columbian tradition: "There is no contradiction between a magical conception and a rationalist conception, but rather that each character sees the

---

8 "Se habla así de novela indigenista; y se ha dicho que mis novelas Agua y Yawar fiesta que son indigenistas o indias. Y no es cierto. Se trata de novelas en las cuales el Perú andino aparece con todos sus elementos, en su inquietante y confusa realidad humana, de la cual el indio es tan sólo uno de los muchos y distintos personajes."

9 Arguedas's entire anthropological oeuvre, far more voluminous than his literary work, has been recently compiled in Seven Volumes in *José María Arguedas. Obra antropológica*, edited by Sybila Arredondo Arguedas, Horizonte, 2013. A cursory glance at the contents of this collections reveals the extent to which Arguedas's appraisal of the particularities of the Peruvian sierra and their relation to the coast and urban centers was coeval with a patient study of the manifold and different folkloric traditions, social formations, cultural values and history of the regions of Peru, complicating the binary antagonism between the rural and the urban worlds.

world according to their human formation"[10] (Arguedas 2000: 29, my translation here and below).

These lines reveal the essential point of contention between Arguedas and *indigenista* writers, but also his reservations with regard to Mariátegui's account of the rural Indian. The emphasis on apprehending the nature of divergent "human formations" clearly contrasts Mariátegui's dismissal of "cultural" issues as part of a sentimentalist idealization that conflicted with the pursuit of realism. For Arguedas, economic structures and relations remain inextricably bound to a system of cultural practices that define the cooperative ethos of the Andean world, without which the efficiency of their productive modalities could not be understood, let alone potentiated or appropriated.[11] The principle of reconciliation was thus not only a corrective to the extremes of occidentalism or ancestralism, but also implicitly a rejoinder against a lingering *economism* in Mariátegui's dialectical genealogy of Peruvian history, achieved through a rigorous *anthropological* approximation:

> Mariátegui did not possess information about Indigenous or Indian culture; he had not studied it, and he had no opportunity or time to do it; an account of Incan culture—about which a very voluminous bibliography exists—and the mode of being of contemporary Indigenous life was

---

10 Arguedas, José María, *La Mesa Redonda sobre Todas las Sangres del 23 de junio 1965*, edited by Guillermo Rochabrún, Pontificia Universidad Católica del Perú, 2000.

"No hay una contradicción entre una concepción mágica y una concepción racionalista, sino que cada personaje ve al mundo de acuerdo con su formación humana."

11 As several commentators have noted, Arguedas's descent to Indigenous culture by way of his scientific, anthropological research—for instance, as evinced his studies of the cultural preservation of the precolonial value-systems in the communities of the "southern sierra" of Huancayo and the Mantaro Valley—directly informs the unique appraisal of the potentials of the Indigenous world. For the analyses of these regions in particular, see Arguedas, José María. *Evolución de las comunidades indígenas*. Museo, 1957, pp. 78–151; *Folklore del Valle de Mantaro (provincias de Jauja y Concepción) Cuentos mágico-realistas y canciones de fiesta tradicionales*, in *Folklore Americano*, pp. 101–298. As Ángel Rama notes, these texts reveal a crucial complication of the simplification of the mentality and reality of the rural Indian in the northern and southern sierra endorsed by those who project a Manichean polarity between the rural and urban worlds, identifying this nuanced approach as setting his work apart not only from early *indigenismo* but from the novelistic work of Ciro Alegría, as well.

and probably remains still unknown.¹² (Arguedas 1970, my translation here and below)

This insufficiency in Mariátegui's work clarifies Arguedas's disavowal of the term "indigenismo" as a suitable characterization of his own project. For although *indigenismo* implied a decisive advance in thematizing, on scientific grounds, the reality and strife of the rural Indian—prefigured, according to Arguedas in the work of the generation of 900, and particularly in the work of archeologist Julio C. Tello, which stood against José de la Riva Aguero's and Victor A. Belaunde's *hispanismo*—it misrepresented the world of the "living Indian," its psychology, social practices and cultural values. Recounting the origins of his own literary and anthropological project after his encounter with the narratives of Lopez Albújar and García Calderon, Arguedas writes:

> [I] felt so appalled, so estranged, so disappointed, that I considered it indispensable to make an effort to describe the Indigenous man such as he was and such as I had come to know him through a very direct coexistence. [...] The two describe the Indian as a being of petrous expression, mysterious, inexcusable, ferocious, lice eating. (Arguedas 1971: 40, my translation.)¹³

It was not sufficient, however, to reject a deterministic conception of history and revolution, as Mariátegui had done, or to amplify the binary schema of class contradictions to account for the reality of a peasant proletariat and the semifeudal landlord oligarchic class. The idea of a "primary contradiction" that reduced social fragmentation to *class* divisions already involved an oversimplification that missed the inextricability between cultural and economic factors. This leads Arguedas to say that the category of contradiction is itself inadequate and not just in need of revision, complicating the central motor of the dialectical process endorsed by historical materialism:

---

12 Arguedas, José María. "Razón de ser del indigenismo en el Perú," in *Formación de una cultura nacional indoamericana*, edited by Ángel Rama, México, 1975, p. 192. The essay was first published in *Visión*, Lima, 1970, pp. 43–45.
13 "Me sentí tan indignado, tan extrañado, tan defraudado, que consideré que era indispensable hacer un esfuerzo por describir al hombre andino tal como era y tal como yo lo había conocido a través de una convivencia directa. [...] Los dos describen al indio como un ser de expresión petrea, misteriosa, inescrutable, feroz, comedor de piojos."

> Arguedas, José María, and Alejandro Romualdo. "Poesía y prosa en el Perú contemporáneo," in *Panorama actual de la literatura latinoamericana*, Fundamentos, 1971.

There are no contradictions, that is, contradictions are those which naturally exist between the different peoples in our country, between different ways of seeing the world. The great ambition of the book [*Todas las sangres*] was precisely to show this multiplicity of conceptions, in accordance with the degrees of approximation to a populous world.[14] (Arguedas 2000: 30)

Neither occidentalist nor ancestralist, Arguedas's principle of reconciliation aspired to a more nuanced process of integration for Peruvian society, where the ideal of an economic *appropriation* of Indian collectivist productive modalities had to be supplemented with a subjective cooperativist *ethics* and a politics of *transculturation*. It is to this aspect of Arguedas's project that we now turn.

Transculturation and Heterogeneity: Synthesis and Difference

In his classic 1982 study *Writing Across Cultures: Narrative Transculturation in Latin America* (*Transculturación narrativa en América Latina*), Ángel Rama describes the subjective transformation of the characters depicted in Arguedas's literary works in terms of what the Cuban anthropologist–musicologist Fernando Ortiz calls *transculturation*, grasped in turn according to what the Italian semiologist Vittorio Lanternari calls "cultural plasticity."[15] According to Rama, the thematic of transculturation becomes characteristic of the narrative impetus behind the so-called third phase of regionalist Latin American thought,

---

14 "No hay una contradicción entre una concepción mágica y una concepción racionalista, sino que cada personaje ve al mundo de acuerdo con su formación humana. [...] No hay contradicciones; es decir, las contradicciones son las que naturalmente existen entre las diferentes gentes que hay en nuestro r país, entre diferentes modos de ver el mundo. La gran ambición del libro fue precisamente mostrar esa multiplicidad de concepciones, según los grados de aproximación de un mundo populoso."

15 Rama first uses the term in his 1971 article *Los procesos de transculturación en la narrativa latinoamericana*. In its more mature formulation, however, he extends Ortiz's hermeneutic frame in discerning four distinctive kinds of relations and corresponding literary relational forms which involved characters caught within a process of transculturation, formative of what he calls a "general reconstruction of the cultural system": losses, selections, rediscoveries and incorporations. Across these four operations, the effects of transculturation result in what Rama calls a structural "Latin American perspectivism," in which the differences and tensional spaces of transit between cultural productive sites become thematized and explored in their relations, rejecting at once the "regionalist" closure of a culture into itself and the process of assimilation in acculturation (Rama 1982: chapters I and II).

to which the works of Ciro Alegría and José María Arguedas belong[16] (Rama 2012: 67). In Rama's appropriation of the term for literary criticism, narratives of "transculturation" describe the possibility of productive encounters between divergent cultural traditions, involving first and essentially a bidirectional mediation that encompasses but also complicates a twofold process: the *acculturation* through which one culture acquires the traits and becomes part of another culture, and the *deculturation* through which a former cultural identity loses parts of itself. And yet this simultaneous process of gain and loss also generates novel syntheses between different cultural forms and expressions, as part of a "creative movement" of *neoculturation*[17] (Ibid.). The following diagram illustrates the transcultural process outlined by Rama in its different facets, and as it becomes expressed by Arguedas in order to think the relation between the Andean World and Western culture.

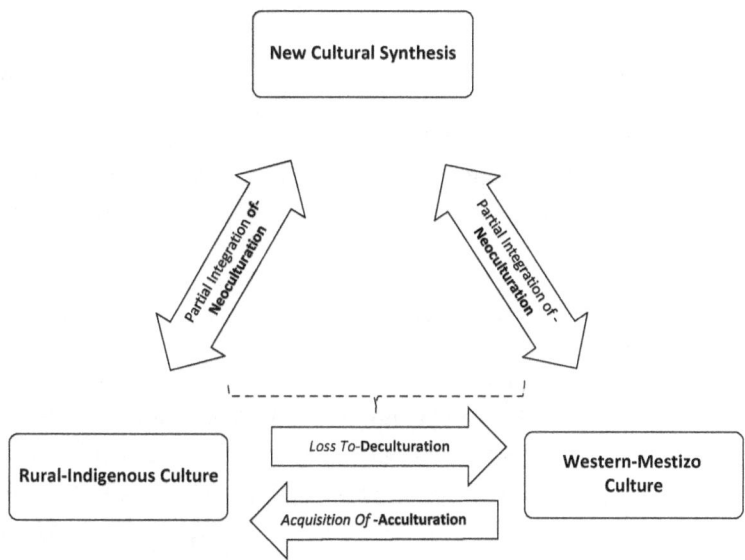

Diagram 3.1 Acculturation, Deculturation, Transculturation.

As Rama argues, every literary expression of a process of transculturation can therefore be identified as enacting a "double proof": (1) to produce

---

16 Rama, Ángel, *Writing Across Cultures: Narrative Transculturation in Latin America*, edited and translated by David Frye, Duke University Press, 2012.
17 As Silvia Spitta (1995) puts it, "the transculturated subject is someone who, like Arguedas, is consciously or unconsciously situated between at least two worlds, two cultures, two languages, and two definitions of subjectivity, and who constantly mediates between them all" (Spitta 1995: 24).

a mapping of the elements and qualities that define the culture(s) in relation with each other; (2) to depict the production of new forms that attest to the unprecedented emergence of a new transcultural subject in relation to existing cultural identities:

> On the one hand it notes that the current culture of the Latin American community (which itself is a product of long-term transculturation and in constant evolution) is composed of idiosyncratic values that can be identified as having been active since the remote past; on the other hand, it corroborates the creative energy that propels it forward, making it quite distinct from a simple aggregate of norms, behaviors, beliefs and cultural objects, for it is a force that acts with facility on situations arising from its own development as well as on contributions coming from elsewhere. (Rama, 2012: 19, my translation)

Abiding to the demands of this "double proof," Arguedas's transcultural literature, for Rama, retrieves the particularity of the Andean world in its tensional but holistic articulation within Western culture, while also anticipating a transformative process that gives rise to a new culture.[18] This process is also one of *universalization*, creating unforeseen mediations between local and foreign forms:[19]

> The link [to the Andean world] could universalize itself, extend; it showed itself as a concrete, acting example. The barrier could and had to be destroyed; the flow of the two nations could and had to unite. And the road did not have to be, nor was it possible that it was the only way, that under the empire of the exploiting victors, namely: that the defeated nation surrender its soul, even if not in appearance, formally,

---

18 According to Rama, if Latin American writers are to meet the pretensions to universality through literary creation, this can only be attained by recollecting and composing from the particularities of heterogeneous cultures, thus "recomposing from [previous cultural] material a superior discourse that could match or confront the most hierarchic products of a universal literature." Rama, Ángel. "Los Procesos de transculturación en la narrativa latinoamericana," in *Revista de Literatura Hispanoamericana*, issue 5, 1974, p. 37, my translation.

19 When, in his 1968 speech *No Soy un Aculturado*, Arguedas disavows the label of "acculturation" as an adequate description of his own relation to rural Indian reality, he overtly rejects that the sole destiny which escapes a futile resistance through nostalgic ancestralism must be the "occidentalist" assimilation of the autochthonous in the name of international integration and modernization. A third way is possible.

and that it take that of the victors, that is to say, that is become acculturated. (Arguedas 1968)[20]

The affirmation of new mediations that bind Indigenous culture in a "path to universalization" constitutes a rejection of the idea—endorsed above all by Antonio Cornejo Polar—that the only alternative to acculturation is a peaceful coexistence between already existing heterogeneous cultures or identities, and so that a literature written from within a unique historical and cultural context ought to remain, at best, a mutual and respectful distance from an inaccessible Other.[21]

By the same token, the productive potentials inherent in transculturation, for Arguedas, did not entail that heterogeneous identities had to unravel in the anticipation of an "ideal culture," like that conceived in Vasconcelos's mythos of a "cosmic race." Rather, transcultural hybridity functions as an *integrative* potential, preserving difference without compromising unity, and promoting

---

20 "El vínculo podía universalizarse, extenderse; se mostraba un ejemplo concreto, actuante. El cerco podía y debía ser destruido; el caudal de las dos naciones se podía y debía unir. Y el camino no tenia por qué ser, ni era posible que fuera únicamente el que se exigía con imperio de vencedores expoliadores, o sea: que la nación vencida renuncie a su alma, aunque no sea sino en la apariencia, formalmente, y tome la de los vencedores, es decir que se aculture."

> Arguedas, José María, *No soy un Aculturado*, speech given in 1968. Full text available at: https://www.servindi.org/actualidad/3252

21 While Ángel Rama's concept of transculturation emphasizes the synthetic and integrative potentials which obtain from the mediations between different terms, Antonio Cornejo Polar's (1978) reading sees the irreducibility and priority of difference and multiplicity, and the autonomy of divergent "contexts of realization-actualization-consumption." Following Cornejo Polar, Klára Schirová (2004), for instance, has argued that Arguedas in fact disavows transculturation in favor of "inculturation," in which heterogeneous cultures coexist in their differences within a new social space:

> José María Arguedas did not promote the idea of transculturation. He did not attempt to create a complimentary and ideal culture that was a combination of the best aspects of the two originary cultures. Arguedas formulated the Peru of everyone's blood, maintaining the primary cultural richness and expressing his faith in the process of "inculturation." [...] Arguedas' inculturation was a harmonic encounter (not a fusion) and constructive between cultures. [...] The purpose of the linguistic model is not, according to Cornejo Polar, integration and unification, but the justification of different cultural manifestations that live in contact with each other. (Schirová 2004: 99, my translation)

[a] revitalized examination of local traditions, which had become sclerotic, in order to find formulations that would allow for the absorption of external influences. External influences would thus be diluted into larger artistic structures that can still translate the problematics and the peculiar flavors they had continued to preserve. (Rama 1974: 37)[22]

This is as much a social as it is a linguistic and cultural process; indeed, to the extent that it involves the projective task of thinking new syntheses, literary transculturation functioned as a precursor to and imaginary for the prospects of a new cultural bond. Arguedas describes how the immediate task for literary imaginaries was to find a new language, apposite to describe the complex exchanges that exist between Quechua and Spanish, and to describe new forms of subjectivation that could arise on the basis of cultural exchange. In the next section, I attend to this productive task as it unfolds since Arguedas's early works, exemplifying how literary transculturation becomes a methodological condition to express the sociocultural process of integration between Western and Indigenous culture.

Form and Content: Literary Transculturation and the Search for a New Language

In retrospectively clarifying the potentials of a transculturation between the Western and pre-Hispanic worlds in Andean Latin America, Arguedas identifies a formal, constructive task that he would seek to realize in his literary works: the invention of a new expressive medium, through which the voice of a new *transcultural subject* could first be given voice. Such a transcultural subject would not only announce the subversion of the rural Indian as part of the global crusade against capitalism, but would compose a new language and thought to serve as a model for the transcultural process. In his essay *The Novel and the Problem of Literary Expression in Perú* (*La novela y el problema de la expresión literaria en el Perú*) Arguedas describes how, since his earliest works, he aimed to enrich the resources of the Spanish syntax and grammar to adapt its expressive resources and evince its historical mediations with Quechua. The absence of such a language within the Peruvian literary imaginary, he argues, remained the central boon that destined *indigenista* narratives to an inauthentic account of the Andean world, and by extension a distorting picture of its sociocultural reality: "Under a false language a world appeared as

---

22 Translated and cited by Moreiras, Alberto. *The Exhaustion of Difference: The Politics of Latin American Cultural Studies*, Duke University Press, 2001, p. 185.

invented, without marrow and bloodless; a typical 'literary' world, in which the word had consumed the work" (Arguedas 1976: 401, my translation here and below).[23]

In the same essay, Arguedas makes clear that the search for a language was continuous with the development of a new characterological framework, corresponding to two narrative arcs in his prose fiction: the narratives of the "big towns" ("*pueblos grandes*") that describes the major rural provinces and their capitals, from *Yawar Fiesta* (1941) to *Todas las sangres* (1964), and the narratives of the "village" ("*aldea*"), exemplified in the stories compiled in his collection *Agua* (1933) (Ibid.). But while the narrative of the village depicted a binary opposition between the landlords and the Indian villagers, the narratives of the big towns discerned five subjective types: the *rural Indian*; the fanatical-dogmatic *traditional landlord*; the institutionally servile *new landlord*; the town's wandering *mestizo* who lacks a mind and a future; and finally *the returning provincial student*, who returns to his place of origins after being educated in the city to imbue the community with an emancipatory horizon. In this framework, the role of the provincial student functions to reiterate a common trope of "third-wave regionalist" *indigenista* narratives, since at least the 1940s—evinced, for instance, in Ciro Alegría's *Broad and Alien Was the World* (*El mundo es ancho y ajeno*) in the figure of Benito Castro. In its generic traits, the provincial student turned revolutionary is defined by his amphibian quality, selectively appropriating aspects of Western and Indigenous thought; he is educated in the city, awakening a political consciousness and weaponizing his knowledge of the urban setting and world history as a practical lever to defy the hegemonic powers that besiege his culture:

> The fifth character is the provincial student that has two residencies; Lima and "his town"; a generally messianic type, whose soul blazes between love and hate; this human element, so noble, so tenacious, so abnegated, which is then swallowed by the implacable forces that sustain the social order against which he lacerated and spent his breath.[24] (Ibid.)

---

23 Arguedas, José María. "La novela y el problema de la expresión literaria en el Perú," in *Varios*, Casa de las Américas, La Habana, 1976.

"Bajo un falso lenguaje se mostraba un mundo como inventado, sin médula y sin sangre; un típico mundo 'literario,' en que la palabra ha consumido a la obra."

24 "El quinto personaje es el estudiante provinciano que tiene dos residencias, Lima y 'su pueblo'; tipo generalmente mesiánico cuya alma arde entre el amor y el odio; este elemento humano tan noble, tan tenaz, tan abnegado, que luego es engullido por las implacables fuerzas que sostienen el orden social contra el cual se laceró y gastó su aliento."

The linguistic and cultural mediations the educated rural student embodies, Arguedas argues, give "literary expression to the problem of universality," and stand against the threat of a parochial "regionalism." In this regard, Arguedas's vision of acculturation resists assimilation under the heading of "regionalism," positioning itself rather as an emblem of a vision that sublates the distinction between regionalism and universalism.

Following Vallejo's imagined "universal language" in which different nationalities would coalesce, tracking the "subtle displacements" between Spanish and Quechua became for Arguedas a way to traverse the choice between regional fidelity and universalist ambition. This continuity, Arguedas insists, is not only that between divergent subjective positions in the cultural or socio-economic spectrum, but also positions mankind within a natural lifeworld:

> There was and there is before the solution of these very special trances of literary expression to the problem of universality, the danger of regionalism that contaminates the work and parcels it. [...] To become realized, translated, to convert the diaphanous and legitimate torrent of the language that appears foreign; to communicate to the almost foreign tongue the matter of our spirit. That is the arduous, difficult question. The universality of this rare equilibrium of content and form, equilibrium achieved after intense nights of incredible work, is something to arrive in function of the human perfection achieved in the course of such a strange effort. [...] Only one could be the end: Spanish as a legitimate medium of expression of the Andean Peruvian world, the noble whirlwind in which different spirits, forged in different stars, struggle, attract, repel and mix, between the highest mountains, the deepest rivers, between snows and silent lakes, the freeze and fire.[25] (Ibid.: 402–3)

---

25 "Existía y existe frente a la solución de estos especialísimos trances de la expresión literaria, el problema de la universalidad, el peligro del regionalismo que contamina la obra y la cerca. [...] Realizarse, traducirse, convertir en torrente diáfano y legítimo el idioma que parece ajeno; comunicar a la lengua casi extranjera la materia de nuestro espíritu. Ésa es la dura, la difícil cuestión. La universalidad de este raro equilibrio de contenido y forma, equilibrio alcanzado tras intensas noches de increíble trabajo, es cosa que vendrá en función de la perfección humana lograda en el transcurso de tan extraño esfuerzo. [...] Uno sólo podía ser un fin: el castellano como medio de expresión legítimo del mundo peruano de los Andes, noble torbellino en que espíritus diferentes, como forjados en estrellas diferentes, luchan, se atraen, se rechazan y se mezclan, entre las más altas montañas, los ríos más hondos, entre nieves y lagos silenciosos, la helada y el fuego."

In a kind of dialectical resolution to the disjunction between tradition and modernization, Arguedas argues that the search for universality is also a question concerning the *spirit* of mankind, where human formations generate "narrow zones of confluence" for cultural expressions:

> Was and is this a search for universality carried through the struggle for form, and only form? Form, insofar as this signifies conclusion, or equilibrium, attained by the necessary mixture of elements that try to constitute themselves in a new structure. [...] To have sought to expression with a sense of universality through the steps that take us to the dominion of a foreign idiom, to have sought in the course of the leap; that was the reason behind the incessant struggle. The sought for universality, searched for without disfiguration, without the decline of earthly, human nature that one attempted to show; without giving in an apex to the external and apparent beauty of words. [...] It was not a matter then of a search for form in its superficial and commonplace sense, but a problem of the spirit, of culture, in these countries in which strange currents meet and throughout centuries do not conclude in fusing their directions, but rather form narrow zones of confluence, while in the deep and broad of the main veins they flow without rest, incredibly.[26] (Ibid.)

More strongly still, such a process of universalization through cultural hybridity attests to 'the possibility, indeed to the *necessity*, of more absolute act of creation, making mankind "one and unique," while resisting "the dangers of regionalism,"' as a definitive literary responsibility:[27]

---

26 "¿Fue y es ésta una búsqueda de la universalidad a través de la lucha por la forma, sólo por la forma? Por la forma en cuanto ella significa conclusión, equilibrio alcanzado por la necesaria mezcla de elementos que tratan de constituirse en una nueva estructura. [...] Haber pretendido expresarse con sentido de universalidad a través de los pasos que nos conducen al dominio de un idioma distinto, haberlo pretendido en el transcurso del salto; ésa fue la razón de la incesante lucha. La universalidad pretendida y buscada sin la desfiguración, sin mengua de la naturaleza humana y terrena que se pretendía mostrar; sin ceder un ápice a la externa y aparente belleza de las palabras. [...] No se trata, pues, de una búsqueda de la forma en su acepción superficial y corriente, sino como problema del espíritu, de la cultura, en estos países en que corrientes extrañas se encuentran y durante siglos no concluyen por fusionar sus direcciones, sino que forman estrechas zonas de confluencia, mientras en lo hondo y lo extenso las venas principales fluyen sin ceder, increíblemente."

27 "[L]a posibilidad, la necesidad de un acto de creación más absoluta."

But if language, thus charged with strange essences, allows one to see into the profound heart of humanity, if it transmits the history of its journey over the earth, universality may take perhaps long; but it shall arrive, since we know well that man owes its preeminence and reign to the fact of being one and unique.[28] (Ibid.: 33)

In the following sections, I briefly trace Arguedas's "narrative of the villages," focusing on the development of the militant Indian revolutionary subject in his short story *Agua*, before attending to the figurations of the subject in the narratives of the "big towns" since *Yawar Fiesta*, which reach its apex in *Todas las sangres*. Across this trajectory, the construction of a new language becomes progressively realized in a process of literary transculturation, where the projective ideal of a future subject that carries universality in mediating between the Western and Andean world emerges.

The Revolutionary Indian Subject in the Narratives of the Village: *Agua*

In the words of Jana Hermuthová, already in his 1935 short story *Agua*, Arguedas carries out with remarkable dexterity "changes in the lexicon, the morphology, and overall the syntax [of Spanish]" (Schirová 2004: 51, my translation, here and below).[29] In particular, she draws attention to Arguedas's displacement of the priority accorded to the sentence in Western languages, so as to capture the privileging of the verb that occurs at the end of the phrase in Quechua, which functions as indicative of pragmatic force or "the bearer of emotional nuance" (Ibid.).[30] Two asymmetrical worlds become suspended in this linguistic tension, "one that stabs, and one that bleeds" (Arguedas 1968: 402). A narrative woven from "pure hatred," as he describes it, *Agua*

---

28 "Pero si el lenguaje así cargado de extrañas esencias deja ver el profundo corazón humano, si nos transmite la historia de su paso sobre la tierra, la universalidad podrá tardar quizá mucho; sin embargo vendrá, pues bien sabemos que el hombre debe su preeminencia y su reinado al hecho de ser uno y único."

29 Jana Hermuthová, "El discurso experimental arguediano, in José María en el Corazón de Europa," in *José María Arguedas en el corazón de Europa*, edited by Klára Schirová, Universidad Carolina de Prada, 2004, p. 51.

30 Hermuthová also signals in this syntactical displacement between the two languages the accumulation of adjectives, and the repetition of entire phrases, both of which integrate mannerisms and modalities proper to the mediated form between Quechua and Spanish (Ibid.).

portrays a destructive furor which, however, nevertheless springs from what Arguedas calls "universal loves":

> *Agua* was written, yes, with hate, with the rapture of a pure hatred; that which springs from universal loves, there, in the regions of the world where two contradictory bands exist in confrontation with implacable cruelty, one which is harvested and the other which bleeds.[31] (Ibid.)

At the most abstract level, the story unfolds around a central antagonism, through which the rural Indian is positioned as a helpless agent against the mestizo oligarchic rule. Beyond this central antagonism, the Andean world appears as a multifaceted natural and cultural system: in the region of San Juan, where the story transpires, the landscape and fauna are invoked as parts of a holistic network of semantic valences: Ventanilla, once a great silver mine, is now forlorn and abandoned, reduced to a site for lovers to secretively meet, a shelter from the scorching sun for the cows during the day and a place of rest for mountain hogs to find solace throughout the quiet night. The analogical junction of nature and culture weaves a tensional but nevertheless singular ambience, split from within by the mark of economic subjugation and state abandonment. Arguedas does not indulge, however, in a redemptive, homeostatic vision of this scenery: before a hostile nature, harboring the memory of the mine's former prosperity and the stain of its current precariousness, the narrative voice scans its "hollow, black doors," revealing a voided space deprived of its past glory, and bereft of all promise for the future. In what appears as but a frustrated, inverted vitalism, we are told that "San Juan is dying"; its infrastructure collapsing, its population withering under the criminal rule of the gamonales and the neglect of the state (Arguedas 1933: 1).[32] The natural and cultural domains in *Agua* become then not only multifaceted in themselves, but porous and asymmetrical, distributing a social hierarchy: Don Braulio, predatorily scavenging his surroundings, "as the fox or hound" (as Ernesto describes him), usurps San Juan's water supplies not only from the Indians but from competing landlords.

If there is nostalgia in the narrative, it is vindicative rather than commemorative: Arguedas projects the indissociable bond between traditional Indigenous

---

[31] "*Agua* sí fue escrito con odio, con el arrebato de un odio puro; aquel que brota de los amores universales, allí, en las regiones del mundo donde existen dos bandos enfrentados con implacable crueldad, uno que esquilma y otro que sangra."
[32] Arguedas, José María, *Agua*, 1933, my translation here and below. Available at: http://home.snafu.de/angelam/rp/ES/Agua_JMA.pdf

folklore and the economic, productive activity of the commoners. At the outset of the story, the senior Indian leader, Vilkas, reproaches his fellow commoner for playing a celebratory song in times of drought, calling for him to instead "sing for rains" (Ibid., 1–3). The aging Vilkas, respectful of tradition is, however, also a figure of passivity and surrender, unwilling to defy don Braulio's rule, addressing the divinities with servitude in an innocuous plea for mercy. His respectful stance reveals, in the guise of melancholic despair, the danger of reactive inertia and of submissive pathos, where tradition becomes defanged of its emancipatory potentials and becomes a form of mournful evasiveness.

Marking a profound skeptical distrust about the future under the rule of the landlord oligarchy, but also staging an act of resistance against the imposition of Western culture and its religious idols, Arguedas displaces the impotence of Vilkas's musical prayer through revolutionary furor: standing in exception to the fearful and submissive Indians of the community, the young militant "*Mak'ta*" Pantacha questions the natural order depicted in the Indian song and curses the crimes perpetrated by don Braulio. Pantacha has returned from the coast with radical political ideas, reinforcing the idea that emancipatory consciousness originates and trickles down from the city. His song conveys the hostility and coldness of the Andean setting, sentencing its inhabitants to a perennial struggle. In contrast to Vilkas's submissive plea, the "student turned revolutionary" faces the sun with a defiant address: while the young Ernesto plays a chilling "tune from the *puna*," Pantacha indicts the colonial heritage for imposing the religious mythos of an indifferent messiah: "The rage of don Braulio is the cause. *Taytacha* [Jesus] does nothing" (Ibid.). Pantacha's demand then expands into a protest against the sun God (*Inti*), subverting the fate prescribed by the Andean myth as much as that imposed by the mestizo rulers:

> Pantacha stood in the chant of the corridor, gazing the *Inti tayta* eye to eye; and he blew the *wanakupampas'* horn with strength [...] the *Inti tayta* scorched the world. The stones of the mine Ventanilla shined like little mirrors; the hills, the mountains, the ravines, sizzled in the heat. It seemed as if the sun was burning the heart of the mountains; that it was drying the eyes of the earth forever. [...] The *Inti tayta* wanted, surely, the death of the earth, gazed forth, with all its might. His rage set the world aflame, and made men weep.[33] (Ibid.)

---

[33] "Pantacha se paró en el canto del corredor, mirando ojo a ojo al Inti tayta; y sopló bien fuerte la corneta de los wanakupampas. [...] El tayta Inti quemaba al mundo. Las piedras de la mina Ventanilla brillaban como espejitos; las lomas, los falderíos,

In a gesture reminiscent of Vallejo's metaphysical "cry of protest" in *Los heraldos negros* (cf. Chapter II), the elegiac arrest of the Indian song becomes transvalued from divine supplication into an act of political subversion. As he congregates with others amid inner conflict and unending exploitation, Pantacha promises to bind the divided commoners from the neighboring villages:

> The *tinkis* gathered around don Wallpa; the *sanjuanes*, silent, without calling to each other, convened on the other side.
>
> —There is no trust; commoners will not end well—Pantacha said, gazing toward the peoples separating in two bands.[34] (Ibid.)

Pantacha's pessimistic verdict in the face of internal separation carries, at its core, an implicit lesson: without organized action, the competitive spirit that animates the community risks fragmentation and ultimately dissolution; without political collectivization, cultural values become exhausted markers of a bygone past. As Juan Carlos Ubilluz argues, the insistence on organized action thus places Pantacha within the scope of "the classical solution" to "the problem of the Indian," thematized since Mariátegui's 1929 *Ideological Theses*, in which the urban avant-garde politically awakens the Indians to orient their revolutionary path (Ubilluz 2017: 117).

> This is, without doubt, the political solution that the indigenista narrative develops through the rural leaders like Benito Castro in *Broad and Alien is the World* (Ciro Alegría), Servando Huanca in *El Tungsteno* (César Vallejo), and even Demetrio Rendón Willka in *Todas las Sangres* (Arguedas). In all of these novels, they have educated themselves with leftist politicians on the coast, and have returned to their communities to organize them in view of rebellious action. (Ubilluz 2017: 117–18, my translation here and below)

The syntactical designator for the quantitative "many" ("*tantos*") becomes, through Pantacha's voice, folded into the singular qualitative form "much"

---

las quebradas se achicharraban con el calor. Parecía que el Sol estaba quemando el corazón de los cerros; que estaba secando para siempre los ojos de la tierra. [...] El tayta Inti quería, seguro, la muerte de la tierra, miraba de frente, con todas sus fuerzas. Su rabia hacía arder al mundo y hacía llorar a los hombres."

34 "Los tinkis se juntaron alrededor de don Wallpa; los sanjuanes, callados, sin llamarse, se entroparon en otro lado.—No hay confianza; comuneros no van a parar bien—dijo Pantacha, mirando a la gente separarse en dos bandos."

("*tanto*"), next to which the competing landlords appear but a disarticulated, feeble multiplicity: "But *comunkuna* much we are; principals, two, or three, at most there are" (Arguedas 1933).[35] As the story reaches its dramatic apex, the sun's fiery natural presence ("*Inti*"), divine symbol of the arid highlands, is cursed as the ruthless bringer of destruction; not the benevolent sun of the time of harvest, praised by Vallejo's elegiac poetic voice, but the sun of dereliction, whose natural indolence mirrors don Braulio's indifference. In response to this internal strife, in which nature is turned against Man just as Man turns against himself, Pantacha's voice reverberates: rather than a peaceful reconciliation, his outcry leaves neither myth nor reality intact, initiating a movement through which the collective rises against all normative orders, natural and human, mortal and divine, splitting the laws of the world in the name of justice.

This originary template for the collective revolutionary subject in Arguedas's works will become uniquely dispossessed of all semblance of egoism and individualization in *Yawar Fiesta*, the first of his great three narratives of the "big towns," to which we now turn.

The Collective Indigenous Subject in the Narratives of the "Big Towns": *Yawar Fiesta*

In *Yawar Fiesta*, often touted as Arguedas's most "technically" accomplished novel, the act of transcultural and linguistic hybridization achieves a further stage of maturity.[36] Alongside an increasingly nuanced description of mediations between Spanish and Quechua carried through manifold idiomatic representations, displacements and resonances, the novel enacts a transvaluation of the traditional antagonism between civilization and barbarism—typical of the Latin American social realist and telluric novel, ever since Sarmiento's *Facundo*—to describe the social rift in the Pucquio region of the Peruvian southern highlands. Arguedas disassociates the (eurocentric) ideological alignment of Western modernization with civilization, and of barbarism with

---

35 "Pero *comunkuna* somos tanto, tanto; principales dos, tres nomás hay."
36 The novel is preceded and anticipated by two short stories published in 1937, in which the divergent bullfighting traditions separating the Indigenous from Western subjects appears as central: the first of these, titled *The Dispossession*, was published in the April 4th edition of the magazine *Palabra* (Lima) and appears in rewritten form as the second chapter of *Yawar Fiesta*. The second, which works as an embryonic "draft" of the 1941 novel, titled simply *Yawar*, was published in the 156th edition of the magazine *Revista Americana* (Buenos Aires).

native pre-Hispanic traditions, while at the same time avoiding the temptation of a facile inversion through which modernity would be identified as the agent of barbarism in contrast to an idyllic Indigenous tradition. Instead, barbarism appears as a *structural* rather than intrinsic condition, binding both the creole, mestizo and the rural Indian within a degenerate socioeconomic order.

The entirety of *Yawar Fiesta* revolves around a single question: who will claim conquest of the untamable, quasi-mythical Andean mountain bull, Misitu, whose resilient presence stands both for the power of nature in general and for the hostility of the Andean world. More precisely, the presence of the bull within competing cultural rituals becomes the tensional point as the Indigenous tradition, deemed "barbaric" by the Westernized creoles, is threatened by the state's attempt to prohibit the *Yawar*, supplanting it with the "civilized" Western violence of Spanish bullfighting. Under the pretext of protecting the life of the Indigenous community from the brutality of their own rituals, the distant yet oppressive authority of the state thereby claims to save the region of Pucquio from what they deem "a savagery": "I ask that the Council sends a telegram to send a telegram to the director of Government, thanking him for this commandment that protects the life of the Indian. And that frees Pucquio from a savagery" (Arguedas 1968: 196, my translation here and below).[37]

The formality of the authorities' address is ironically undermined by the implicit hypocrisy of their message: the gamonales do not recognize their own rites nor their violence against the rural Indian as barbaric, as long as it conforms to the normative strictures of Western culture. It is thus not violence as such that is deemed barbaric, but only the violence that threatens the hegemony of one's own position, that is, one's own right to violence. The rhetoric of a civilizing movement against savagery encodes the persisting colonial impulse to enforce acculturation in the name of Western values.

The novel's punctual symbol for the division between the Indian and the mestizo, the bull Misitu, ultimately represents divergent mythologies and cultural spaces standing in tension, corresponding to two contrasting worldviews and belief systems. For the Indian commoners, the formidable bull reproduces

---

37 Arguedas, José María. *Yawar Fiesta*, epublibre. Available at: http://files.comunicatodos.webnode.es/200011834-6ab036ba9f/Yawar%20fiesta%20-%20José%20Maria%20Arguedas%20(1.)pdf

"Yo pido que el Concejo envíe un telegrama de agradecimiento al señor director de Gobierno por ese mandamiento que protege la vida del indígena. Y que libra a Puquio de un salvajismo."

the native myth of creation: the emergence of the God *Wirak'ocha* from Lake Titicaca, life rising from the waters "turned whirlwind at the center of the lake next to the large island, and from within this whirlwind thus emerged the Misitu, longing and shaking its head" (Ibid.: 307).[38] And yet, while Misitu ultimately stands for the power of nature in tension with the combative and collective prowess of man, the relation between the two is also inscribed in a cyclical temporality from which a new sequence of struggle springs forth: the surviving bulls from each year return, having learned how to fight back, so that even the appointed Spanish toreador falls into skepticism before the learned beast that now "knows how to kill"[39] (Ibid.: 377). Anticipating the futility of proscribing the *Yawar* and submitting the bull and the community to European cultural rituals, the Indian community leader, don Pancho, rhetorically undermines not only all human arrogance before nature, but the acculturation implied in the demand to supplant the *Yawar*:

> And the Government also: why will it intrude in the life of the towns? Who messes with the Government, then? [...] As fish in the broth, the Misitu shall waggle in that corral. Swiftly it shall seize the bullfighters.[40] (Ibid.: 404)

The frustrated imposition of acculturation in the novel signals the triumphant permanence of Indigenous culture: unable to command his subordinates, don Julian fails to bring the bull by force from the mountain, while the *K'ayau* Indians succeed in their cooperative attempt, finally allowing the *Yawar* to proceed. The commoners victoriously drag the broken bull, dispelled from his timeless omnipotence, as the sovereign authority of an infuriated don Julian likewise unravels, refusing to accept that the savages succeeded where he failed:

> In a little corner, the Misitu trembled. The *k'ayaus* gazed at him, saddened. It was an animal of the highlands, nothing more. There it was! Well strapped, well tempered by the Raura against the *k'eñwal*.[41]

---

38 "[...] se hizo remolino en el centro del lago junto a la isla grande, y que de en medio del remolino apareció el Misitu, bramando y sacudiendo su cabeza."

39 "Esos toros buscaban el cuerpo tras del poncho o de la capa, que embestían sobre seguro. Eran de experiencia, y sabían matar."

40 "Y el Gobierno también, ¿para qué se meterá en la vida de los pueblos? ¿Quién friega de aquí al Gobierno? [...] Como pescado en sopera, el Misitu coleteará en ese corral. Rápido agarrará a los capeadores."

41 A species of tree from the Andean regions.

There was no more rage; everyone stood silent. [...] They dragged him through the middle. In vain he resisted, in vain he sought to pull or turn. They pointed to the grassland with their helmets, dragging him on.[42] (Ibid.: 434)

Rather than the triumph of the "barbaric" rite, Arguedas takes the reaffirmation of the Indian collective as a symbolic act of subversion against centuries of oppression. Dragged down from the mountains by the commoners, Misitu is brought to die under the rule of the Indians in celebration of the *Yawar*, usurping the martyrdom of the Christian procession into a vindication of the ayllu.

The victory over Misitu thus speaks to the capacity of collective resistance against what Arguedas calls "mythic terror," through which institutional powers exert their hegemony by constructing narratives designed to disarm the possibility of insurgency:

They precipitate the Indian toward darkness, toward fear, toward that which we call in the university "mythic terror." [...] And the landlords, the very priests, all the people that exploit us, that make money at the expense of their ignorance, aim to confirm that this fear in the Indian toward the great forces of the earth is good and sacred. But if we were Government, brother! What would happen? We would shatter the borders that have made primitivism and servitude survive for so many centuries.[43] (Ibid.: 472)

The revolutionary Indian subject in *Yawar Fiesta* is not, however, concentrated in a singular individual who rises from the otherwise helpless masses to assume a heroic role, as is the case with *Tungsten*'s Huanca, or who returns

---

42 "En un rinconcito, el Misitu temblaba. Los *k'ayaus* lo miraban, tristes. Era un animal de puna no más. ¡Ahí estaba! Bien amarrado, bien templado por el *Raura*, contra el *k'eñwal*. Ya no había rabia; estaban todos en silencio. [...] En medio lo arrastraban. En vano se encabritaba, en vano quería jalar o voltearse. Señalaban el pajonal con sus cascos, arrastrándolo."

43 "Ellos precipitan al indio hacia lo oscuro, al temor, a eso que en la universidad llamamos 'el temor mítico'—[...] Y los terratenientes, los mismos curas, toda la gente que los explota, que hace dinero a costa de su ignorancia, procuran confirmar que este miedo del indio por las grandes fuerzas de la tierra es bueno y es sagrado. ¡Pero si nosotros fuéramos Gobierno, hermanos! ¿Qué pasaría? Romperíamos las causas que han hecho sobrevivir por tantos siglos el primitivismo y la servidumbre."

from the city as the privileged agent for emancipation, as is the case with *Agua*'s Pantacha. There are no clear protagonists in the novel; indeed, if there is a protagonist to be discerned, it is the Indigenous communities themselves, spearheaded by the *varayok* or local leaders from the four towns in Pucquio. The Indian commoners function as a collective subject that composes itself from the neighboring villages: they are mostly nameless, designated by their functional role within their communities and by the fortitude of their determination, forced to suspend the productive spirit of competition between themselves in a common struggle before the authorities. Describing this collective subject in *Yawar Fiesta*, in the Preface to the novel, Arguedas writes:

> There are almost no Indian names in *Yawar Fiesta*. It narrates the feats of the four towns in Pucquio; it tries to exhibit the soul of the community, what is lucid and dark in its being, the form in which the tide of its actual destiny disconcerts them[44] incessantly; how such a tide, beneath an apparent definition of limits, beneath the scab, obliges them to a constant effort of accommodation, of re-adjustment, to permanent drama. How long shall the tragic duality of the Indian and the Western in these countries, descendant from the Tahuantinsuyo and Spain, last? What profundity does the tide that separates them have in the present?[45] (Arguedas 2009: 154)

The integration of the neighboring villages that give rise to a subversive act acquires peculiar significance in the chapter titled *Los serranos*, where the ethereal, soaring echo of the mountains and the reach of the Indian voice are carried beyond the highlands and onto the coast through the products of communal labor. The *k'ayaus* take upon themselves to open the road to the Nazca province, building a bridge to the capital in a seemingly impossible endeavor:

---

44 In the novel, "the community" is disconcerted *in the plural* ("disconcerts them"/"*los desconcierta*"). This is another subtle indication of how Arguedas always thinks unity in multiplicity, and the generic identity of the collective to be woven from difference.

45 "Casi no hay nombres de indios en *Yawar fiesta*. Se relata la historia de varias hazañas de los cuatro barrios de Puquio; se intenta exhibir el alma de la comunidad, lo lúcido y lo oscuro de su ser; la forma cómo la marea de su actual destino los desconcierta incesantemente; cómo tal marea, bajo una aparente definición de límites, bajo la costra, los obliga a un constante esfuerzo de acomodación, de reajuste, a permanente drama. ¿Hasta cuándo durará la dualidad trágica de lo indio y lo occidental en estos países descendientes del Tahuantinsuyo y de España? ¿Qué profundidad tiene ahora la corriente que los separa?"

The ten thousand commoners extended the entire road to Nazca. The vicar established the path of the road, calculating the ravines, surrounding the gorges of stone that crossed the bridle path. The *varayok*'s straightened the path, according to their own judgment that the priest's was no good; they gathered, and consulting with each other, improved the way.[46] (Arguedas 1968: 262)

The local victory over Misitu, and the subsequent organization of the communities in the building of the road that connects the rural and urban worlds, initiates a projected, wider-scale process of collective subjectivation, through which the rural Indigenous communities not only defy corrupt local authorities, but also construct the emancipatory path toward a new future to overthrow the center of hegemonic power in the capital.

The novel closes by anticipating the moment of revolutionary upsurge against the center and source of state power, and not only against the landlord oligarchy:

Do you know, brothers, what it means that the *k'ayaus* dared to enter Negromayo? That they submitted the Misitu and dragged him across the entire *puna* all the way to the Pichk'achuri plaza? They have done it for pride, so that the entire world sees the strength that they have, the force of the *Ayllu*, when it wants. Thus, they opened the road to Nazca; because of that, 150 kilometers in 28 days! As in the times of the Empire. […]

By popular initiative, without support from Government. And so ever since, every town began. In the north, in the center, in the south, all the way to the jungle, they gathered in the town plazas, in large congregations; they sent telegrams to the Government, and began the work by themselves.[47] (Ibid.: 277)

---

46 "Los diez mil comuneros se extendieron en todo el camino a Nazca. El vicario hizo el trazo de la carretera, calculando las quebradas, rodeando los barrancos de piedra que cruzaban el camino de herradura. Los varayok's enderezaban el trazo, según su parecer, cuando el del cura no era bueno; se juntaban, y consultándose, mejoraban la ruta."

47 "¿Saben, hermanos, lo que significa que los *k'ayaus* se hayan atrevido a entrar a Negromayo? ¿Que hayan laceado al Misitu y que lo arrastren por toda la puna hasta la plaza de *Pichk'achuri*? Ellos lo han hecho por orgullo, para que todo el mundo vea la fuerza que tienen, la fuerza del ayllu, cuando quiere. Así abrieron la carretera a Nazca; por eso, ¡150 kilómetros en 28 días! Como en tiempos del Imperio. […] Por iniciativa popular, sin apoyo del Gobierno. Y desde entonces empezaron todos los

Abjuring the implicit teleology latent in the sacrificial conception of labor under capitalist production, the Indigenous communities embody the cultural avowal of *work for itself*.[48] And yet, the consummating moment of revolutionary upsurge remains obscure in its direct implications, as does the relation between the mestizo and the Indian collective. The image of the society to come, after the expansive movement into the city has taken place, is left as an uncertain horizon, relapsing to the familiar restorative dream (castigated by Mariátegui) of a collective effort that would match Indigenous ancestral glory, "as in the times of the Empire." One notices then that the threat of ancestralism returns, once the idealized Indigenous collective becomes the agent of a pure expansive movement, modeling the revolutionary process as the overtaking of the urban milieu by the Indian, rather than through the achievement of a productive mediation between the two.

Perhaps for this reason, Arguedas's subsequent elaboration of the narratives of "the big towns" would sketch a different image of the revolutionary agency to come, thinking a transcultural subject who would be situated beyond both the fiery defiance of the Indian turned revolutionary, as well as beyond the collective, migratory expansion of the integrated Indian community. Accordingly, in *Todas las sangres*, Arguedas not only anticipates the *emancipation* of the rural Indian from the mestizo through their integration, but imagines the production of a *post-Indian transcultural subject*, traversing the disjunction between the Western and Indigenous worlds, weaving itself from both traditions' cultures and beliefs. As we shall see in the next section, in constructing this new subjective figure, Arguedas conceives of a more complex

---

pueblos. En el norte, en el centro, en el sur, hasta en la selva se reunían en las plazas de los pueblos, en cabildo grande; pasaban telegramas al Gobierno, y comenzaban el trabajo por su cuenta."

48 Arguedas, José María. "Razón de ser del Indigenismo en el Perú," in *Formación de una cultura nacional indoamericana*, Siglo XXI, 1975, p. 193. Arguedas traces the historical roots of this conception to the Incan social organization of labor:

> [The Incas] [...] organized a society of a high level in what concerns technics, which rendered possible the abundance of goods, and a federal system with regard to religious beliefs, the arts, and modes of recreation; all of this systematic conjunction within a strict political order of such efficiency that the ancient Peruvian man worked without considered labor as a chore, much more that in any time, and as much as the most in the world. In this way it dominated an aggressive nature, threatening, apparently invincible, majestic, and tender. It converted abysses into gardens [...] irrigated desserts and constructed thousands of kilometers of excellent roads. (Arguedas 1975: 193, my translation)

characterological typology, concomitant with a different path toward social and cultural reconciliation through transcultural synthesis.

The Post-Indian Transcultural Subject: *Todas las sangres*

In her article "Todas las sangres: La utopía Peruana," Klára Schirová characterizes Arguedas's novel as an unprecedented attempt to "blur the line between literature and dialectics, creating ideological-poetic reflections which crucially depict the social background of the epoch" (Schirová 2004: 97, my translation, here and below).[49] Implicitly disputing Mariátegui's belief, she argues, Arguedas rejects the existence of an incommensurable gulf of intelligibility between the rural Indian and the mestizo, attesting to their integration in the antagonism against "a common enemy":

> Arguedas ascribes to the Indians the conduct of revolution, but never excluded the possibility that other races would sustain their struggle. On the contrary, José María Arguedas believed that a common enemy would destroy the barriers of cultural differences and establish the bonds of the community.[50] (Ibid.: 133)

This "common enemy" appears in the novel as the looming threat of imperial, international capital, in relation to which the interests of both landlords and the state become subordinated.[51] The consolidation of a united front, binding all social and ethnic groups, would not only resist the usurpation of national sovereignty but also consolidate a new collective bond for Peruvian society. In this way, Arguedas's work reiterates Mariátegui's hope

---

49 Schirová, Klára. "Todas las Sangres—La utopía Peruana" in *José María Arguedas in el corazón de Europa*, 2004, p. 97.
50 "Arguedas atribuye a los indios la conducta de la revolución, pero nunca excluyó la posibilidad de que otras razas sostuvieran su lucha. Al contrario, José María Arguedas creyó que un enemigo común destruiría las barreras de las diferencias culturales y entablaría los lazos de la comunidad."
51 Following Antonio Cornejo Polar, Irina Feldman argues that *Todas las sangres* constitutes above all the attempt to think the foundations for a collective, national liberation from and struggle against the international capital: "Arguedas creates a common front against imperialism and overrides the internal contradictions between bosses and workers, Indian s and the lords [...] the narrative underlines similarities between the formations of the hacienda and ayllu and explores them as theoretical ground on which the projection of the sovereignty of the Peruvian state can be built" (Feldman 2014: 30–32).

that liberal market capitalism needn't be a transitional period before the socialist future.[52]

In the novel, the opposition between the mestizo and the Indian becomes part of a more complex social typology. The story narrates the strife of the Aragón de Peralta family, who exert hegemonic control over the lands of San Pedro, in the region of Lahuaymarca. The pathetic agony of the patriarch Andrés at the outset of the novel, drunkenly ascending the church's tower to address the town's Indians, opens the narrative with an elegiac gesture: the looming death of the old oligarchy and the waning Christian hegemony from the colonial past. Falling to senile delirium and drunken stupor, don Andrés curses his fate as he addresses the congregated Indians in the town plaza, while a "castle of fires" blazes during the hour of Ascension: the church bells are covered with the blood of the patriarch, standing against the resilient sublimity of the town's protector, the mountain deity, Pukasira (Arguedas: 2001:7). Unmovable symbol of the ayllu, the mountain looms behind and above the church tower in the red hour of dusk; its plains covered in beds of *k'antu* ("*Cantuta*"), divine flower of the Incas, recalls the history of colonial bloodshed, insinuating historic retribution.[53] The death of the patriarch signals not only the agonic closure of the landlord oligarchy, of the Christian savagery since colonial times and of the rural economy under the latifundio; it recalls a fissure between the old feudal powers and the emerging power of capitalist, Western modernity. On the one hand, representing the "new landlord," don Bruno aspires to hegemonic control over the lands and Indian labor in *La Providencia*, routinely abusing the commoners, but eventually sinking into repentance before his Indigenous subordinates. Bruno's dogmatic verbosity becomes hyperbolized as he spirals into Christian fanaticism, revealing a delirious search for forgiveness addressed to divine transcendence, contrasting the communitarian values of the subjugated commoners. Appalled by the secular threat rising from the soulless pragmatism exemplified by his brother Fermín, Bruno's atonement unleashes a clownish, quixotic path toward martyrdom, prophesying the fatal and pathetic cessation of the latifundio by the end of the novel.

---

52 Commenting on this aspect of Arguedas's novel, Irina Feldman cites Tracy Strong's verdict, according to which "the liberal tradition no longer offers the intellectual resources to meet the challenges [...] of the modern world" (cited in Feldman 2014: 2).

53 The *Cantuta* is a bush which predominates in the Andes. The peculiarity of *k'antu* bush was precisely that it engenders only "flowers of the same name," a clear symbol for the presumed communitarian disposition of the rural Indian.

At the opposite end of the family feud, don Fermín incarnates the instrumentalist heart of the emerging capitalist class, with close ties to the state. Under his rule, the lives of the exploited Indians become reduced to a dehumanized labor force, slavishly provided by Bruno to work in the mine *Apar'cora* at the beginning of the novel. But Fermín is also an advocate of the "liberal solution," promoting the proletarization of Indian workers so as to secure an exploitable labor force after the end of the latifundio, coinciding with the industrialization of the nation in a process that would "transform barbarism into civilization" (306). Fermín's instrumental rationality and eurocentrism thus present the secular obverse of Bruno's religious pathos, anticipating the assimilation of the rural economy into urban industrial capitalism, while naturalizing inequality and socioeconomic privilege as the only path to civilization. The liberal dream of urbanization and "professionalization," continuous with a "rationalist" and "pragmatic" conception, becomes revealed in its true motivation: to perpetuate the servitude of the rural Indian under the rule of the new capitalist class.

> We have to make of them lucid factory workers, and very regularly, open a tailor-made door so that they ascend to technicians. The future world is not and will not be one of love, of "fraternity," but of the power of a few, most serene and free from passions, over inferior ones that must work. "Fraternity" is the path of regression to barbarism. God made man unequal in his faculties. [...] The fraternity of the miserable is the worst enemy of human greatness, its deceitful negation.[54] (Ibid.: 306)

The contrast between the brothers is clear: Bruno's waning appeal to divine authority and moralistic indignation before modernization recalls the time where "every landlord was a Spanish king," while Fermín's thirst represents the secular power of a growing capitalist class (40).[55] Each of the two indicts the other as the source of degradation of the family's prosperity. For Bruno, it is Fermín's secularism and individualism that corrupts the divine law supporting the feudal oligarchic structure, eroding the moral tenets of Christian

---

54 "Hay que hacer de ellos lúcidos obreros de las fábricas y, muy regularmente, abrir una puerta medida para que asciendan a técnicos. El mundo futuro no es ni será del amor, de la 'fraternidad,' sino del poder de unos, de los más serenos y limpios de pasiones, sobre los inferiores que deben trabajar. La 'fraternidad' es el camino de retroceso a la barbarie [...] la fraternidad de los miserables es el peor enemigo de la grandeza humana, su negación mentirosa."
55 "Desde la República, cada hacendado era un rey español."

faith: "You drove us all to evil. Me! Me too!" (22).[56] In turn, Fermín chastises the hypocrisy behind Bruno's pathetic, moralizing stance, sustained in the reactionary dogma that "God and civilization are irreconcilable" (67). Recalling his brother's brutal sexual abuses against the Indians, Fermín exposes the hypocrisy behind Bruno's sophistic beatitude as a deferral of responsibility when appealing to divine justice: "Which beast, what pig raped that miserable creature that my mother protected? Who was found with the beasts, and poor creatures without the age for judgment?" (22).[57] Beyond the ideological divergence between the brothers, however, the novel suggests a deeper complicity at work between the competing modern and feudal worldviews, operating in sinuous synergy for exploitative control over the Indians and their future. Thus, while Bruno keeps the commoners in poverty and ignorance so as to avoid their uprising against the feudal rule, Fermín draws on them as a labor force in the mine *Apar'cora*, manipulating his brother's anachronistic zeal, and forging a temporary truce to gain advantage over competing city capitalists.[58]

This structural bind through which capitalists and landlords subordinate the Indian becomes definitively threatened by the looming intrusion of international capitalism into the nation, incarnated by the ominous presence of the mining consortium, Wisther and Bozart. The latter stands as a symbol for the danger of global capital to overtake not only the interests of the emerging national capitalist class, but moreover all forms of cultural identity and local sovereignty, subordinating Indians, creoles, and mestizos alike. In the novel, the young landlord Aquiles extends this diagnosis to its nihilist conclusion, identifying foreign interference not as an imperial venture driven by a foreign nation-state, but rather as a soulless financial tropism eroding the integrity of all national fidelities: "[t]he consortiums have no fatherland; they have overcome such a concept" (265).[59] Next to the global reach of the private consortiums, the national capitalists remain impotently bound to the

---

56 "Tú empujaste a todos al mal! ¡A mí! ¡A mí también!"
57 Here "poor creature" translates the colloquial Spanish expression "pobre criatura," which is used to refer to helpless youths or children. The indictment of barbarism is thus doubled, as Bruno's systematic violence treats the victimized, cognitively undeveloped Indigenous children like animals to be used and abused.
58 As Irina Feldman (2014) notes—following Benjamin, Milstein and Agamben—the distinctive placement of Fermín and Bruno coins two modes of sovereign violence: the "divine," dogmatic or "kingly" violence exerted by Bruno over *La Providencia* (literally, The Providence), eventually surrendered in messianic repentance, contrasting the objective violence of the proletarization of the Indian under the structural logic of competition and the telos of capitalist production.
59 "Los consorcios no tienen patria; han superado ese concepto."

domestic sphere: "Aragón is limited by the 'nation,' which it seeks to exploit and develop to his own benefit. The consortium guarantees the calculated misery of all the men of the world to rule; however, the growth of this empire needs also to a certain extent, development" (Ibid.: 380).[60] The implied diagnosis is ruthlessly objectivizing: capitalists cannot be merely identified as a "unified" group or social class, in contradiction to the workforce they exploit. Driven by the logic of competition, capitalism sacrifices *loyalty* in the name of competitive growth, requiring one to turn against "one's own" so that allegiance is always only a provisory, strategic compromise. Even the family bond is no exception to this rule. Having "overcome the concept of nation," global capital appears unbound from human ends, individual or collective, national or international. Whatever development it brings remains instrumental; social utility serves it, not the other way around.

In view of the impending collapse of the degenerate bind between Bruno's archaic violence, don Fermín's capitalist venture and the exploited Indigenous community, Arguedas presents a new kind of transcultural subjectivity that weaves itself from all existing positions, through the anomalous figure of the educated "Indian mestizo," Rendón Willka. Like Benito Castro in Ciro Alegría's *Broad and Alien Was the World*, and *Agua*'s Pantacha, Wilka represents the prodigal son, returning to his hometown from the city as an educated man, potentiating the Indigenous labor force outsourced to Fermín's mines, as well as earning Bruno's trust to eventually become his successor as the leader of *La Providencia*. Recalling young Wilka's departure to the city, Arguedas narrates how the townswomen intoned a fateful *harawi*—a traditional Andean folk song, addressing the daily hardships of rural life—prophesizing the homecoming which would bring back to the community the necessary knowledge from the city. This ideal is reiterated through the book's primary symbol: the search for *the blood of the Other*, the retrieval of which enables a return to and for one's own blood:

> You shall not forget, my son
> Never shall you forget
> You go in search of the blood
> You shall return for the blood

---

60 "Aragón tiene la 'limitación' de la patria, a la que desea explotar y hacer desarrollarse en su beneficio. El consorcio procura la miseria calculada de todos los hombres del mundo para imperar; sin embargo, el crecimiento de ese imperio necesita también en cierto modo el desarrollo."

Fortified
Like the hawk that observes it all
And whose flight nobody reaches.[61] (78)

Unlike Pantacha's overt, vocal antagonism against the local authorities, or the anonymous collectivity of *Yawar Fiesta*'s Indigenous community, Rendón Willka's conduct unfolds as that of a diligent strategist, selectively appropriating elements from Indian collectivism, the feudal landlord oligarchy and the secular capitalist class, becoming thus a point of convergence for the commoners, Bruno and Fermín. Accordingly, he identifies with the cooperativist ethics of the Indian commoners, but also with Bruno's fervent Christological martyrdom, as well as with Fermín's rational pragmatism. His singularity lies in his methodical capacity to negotiate with all positions across the cultural spectrum, forging a rational organizational acumen above blunt insurrectionary affect. If the tragic end common to Pantacha and Willka is nonetheless the same, as figures of martyrdom, what they leave behind and make possible differs both in scope and consequence. For as Arguedas himself states, Willka is not a figure of the rural Indian, but rather of a different, *post-Indigenous transcultural subjectivity*, a new kind of mestizo no longer defined by the preponderance of Western culture, but diagonally integrating different identities: at once a mestizo and an Indian, a free-thinking secular rationalist and a spirited communitarian.

Answering to the charges of provincialism raised by the historian Henri Favre in the infamous roundtable on *Todas las sangres*, Arguedas unambiguously states:

> There is no contradiction between a magical conception and a rationalist conception, rather, each character sees the world according to their human formation. [...] Rendón Willka is not an Indian [...] [he] does not believe in the mountain-Gods; he makes use of that belief to achieve a political end. He is totally rational or rationalist; [...] He is an atheist! He does not believe in the catholic God nor in the local Gods; and he considers that the machine, the technical, is indispensable for the development of the country [I]n Rendón Willka there is an [...] an [...] an integration [...] of this world rationally comprehended, and that of which is still capable of having, in itself, this Indigenous conception of the world. (Arguedas 2000: 47)

---

[61] "Vas en busca de la sangre / has de volver para la sangre, / fortalezido; / como el gavilán que todo lo / mira / y cuyo vuelo nadie alcanza."

Rendón Willka is therefore not the emblem of an idyllic fusion between tradition and modernity: just as he rejects the individualistic spirit of capitalist competition and the reactionary theism of Christian teleology, he likewise rejects the vitalist cosmology of the ayllu. He promotes instead a *secular teleology* that merges rational calculation, sacrificial fervor and a cooperativist labor ethics. In this regard, Arguedas insists that the novel does not favor tradition over modernization; rather, it subtracts rationalism from capitalist individualism and cooperativism from mythological–religious archaism: "The ancient community may serve as the base for a [...] for a modern community. [...] Peruvian society must be transformed, but in the sense of converting it into a society in which fraternity and human solidarity become the element that drives the march of Man, and not competition" (47).[62]

The mediation between modernity and tradition becomes inscribed across all levels of determination, from the syntactic to the political. Confronting the sarcastic praise of the treacherous engineer Cabrejos, who rhetorically asks Rendón Willka about his correct pronunciation of the word *"cabildo"* after having returned from the city—"You don't say *'cahuildo'* anymore?"—the latter retorts with ironic, passive aggression, accepting that he indeed has learned from the city, while in the same stroke rejecting its unqualified embrace.[63] He answers in a grammatically deviant, yet precise and laconic subjunctive, proper to the Indian Spanish, mediated by Queuchua, in prophetic tenor: "In Lima, Indian learns" (*"En Lima, Indio aprende"*) (Arguedas 2001: 202).[64] Willka's syntactic blunder is also a semantic displacement, in which impropriety with regard to the norms of the Spanish language becomes transvalued into an act of cultural and political resistance: his defiant "error" thus undermines Cabrejos's false compliment, subverting the implied prescription of acculturation in the rhetoric of education as a civilizing process.[65]

---

62 "La comunidad antigua puede servir de base para una, una comunidad moderna. [...] Rendón Willka ha tomado estos elementos de la ciudad [...] la sociedad peruana debe ser transformada, pero en este sentido de convertirla en una sociedad en que lo fraternal y la solidaridad humana sea el elemento que impulse la marcha del hombre, y no la competencia."
63 "(Ya no dices 'cahuildo'?)"
64 "En Lima, indio aprende [...]"
65 In this regard, Fredric Jameson has described such a process as the dual condition for all discursive acts proper to a revolutionary practice: to resist at once "the transparency of common sense and everyday speech" (Feldman 2014: 18).

The power of this new language is recognized toward the climax of the novel, as don Bruno hands over the future of *La Providencia* and of the Indian commoners to Willka's care. He prophetically captures the revolutionary potential in Willka's speech, describing it as a Spanish that is "barbaric" and yet permeated by a "rational clarity," a "divine language":

> La Providencia and its people depend on your intelligence, on your cleverness for the good. Come into my library. Read at night, calmly. Your Spanish is like that of [...] no, not like that of the *cholos*; it is of another class; you speak as if our infant God (*niño Dios*) rejoiced through your mouth. Barbaric Spanish, but clear. Demetrio.

Such a new language, however, is not put to the service of any "restoration." On the contrary, Willka states that while "tradition" is also a source of enlightenment, it risks a cultural protectionism that inhibits growth: "tradition is a double edged sword: it illuminates, but contains" (102). Responding to Anto's fatalism concerning the community in sight of don Fermín's mining venture, Willka speaks with disarming realism yet also with laconic tenderness. For the Indians will meet a certain end, he claims, in a return to the Earth ("*pachamama*"), at the same time as the Earth is reduced to its banal materiality, in the diminutive form ("*tierrita nomas*"): "To the Earth only, brother Anto—little dirt only" (102).[66] Implicitly disavowing both Indigenous vitalism and Christian theism, Willka identifies with the secular pragmatism of the capitalist class, but from the collectivist perspective of the ayllu: "don Fermín is like me, but from the other side" (38).[67]

By the same token, for Willka, Bruno's fanatical spirituality amounts to nothing but expiring messianic grandiloquence. He coldly denounces the falsity of the "God he carries within," who does not "lend him an eye," indirectly condemning the landlord's spiritual invocations and rhetorical pomp.[68] As Fermín and Matilde judge with dispassionate cynicism, Bruno's penitential martyrdom toward the Indians is not so much a productive novelty, but compounds the excesses of religion and authoritarianism, in a "feudal barbarism dangerously contaminated by the Indian one" (346).[69]

---

66 "La tradición es un arma de dos filos: ilumina, pero contiene."
67 "Don Fermín, como yo es, aunque del otro lado."
68 "el Dios que tiene en su adentro no la da ojo"
69 "Un barbarismo feudal, peligrosamente contaminado por el del indio."

Belonging neither to the mythological vision of the world of the ayllu, nor the created Earth of Christian religious myth, nor the Godless earth of capitalist instrumentalism, Willka's "divine language" becomes the instrument through which Indigenous cooperativism is reconciled with the sacrificial pathos of Christianity, as well as the secular, materialist bases of Western culture. In an act of symbolic passage, don Bruno's handing over of *La Providencia* emblemizes the self-effacement of the legacy of the latifundio and the emergence of a new truce between the mestizo and the Indian: as the departing soul of Bruno's deceased mother is handed to the verdict of the Indian mayor Maywa, she is described as venturing barefoot to the mountain *K'oropuna*, not to rest, but to joyously work with the departed commoners, as their equal: "We shall take you where our dead go to work" (280).[70] In the end, it is the source of a new cultural pact that redeems the colonial past of the family lineage, as cooperation becomes the key to reconciliation. Irrupting in the dialogue between Maywa and Bruno, Willka accepts control over *La Providencia*, not as the successor landlord, but as the bringer of the definitive interruption of such succession. The figure of the *gamonal* then disappears in the advent of a new subject and collective destiny.[71] As Bruno's mother is embarks onto *K'oropuna*, that sacred fortress which "is never finished," Willka accepts the protection of Bruno's child as his own:

Will you defend my son if I die?
With my arms, my thought, with the Lahuaymarcas.[72] (Ibid.: 296)

The anticipation of labor in the mountains in the afterlife becomes simultaneously a site of struggle in the present: the mine *Apar'cora* prefigures the emergence of a new social bond, in which workers from different provenances and ideologies meet and work. The forecasted synthesis allows Arguedas to extend Mariátegui's proposed appropriation of Indigenous modes of production-labor and collective property to the cultural sphere. More precisely, Arguedas describes how the *collectivist productive* modality celebrated

---

70 "Te llevaremos adonde nuestros muertos trabajan."
71 This conflicts with Feldman's identification of Bruno as a "revolutionary" figure, recognizing that "the time of the haciendas is over" (Feldman 2014: 33). As Feldman correctly shows, however, Bruno's penitence is of a piece with the dissolution of the quasi-divine authority of the landlord, unraveling the "kingly sovereignty" of the colonial past.
72 "Vas a defender a mi hijo, si yo me muero? /—Con mis brazos, con mi pensamiento, con los lahuaymarcas."

by Mariátegui remains indissociable from a cultural matrix that embodies a *cooperativist ethics* of "labor for itself." Cooperativism defies the individualistic logic of competition and the instrumental conception of labor promoted by the capitalist mode of production and the liberal conception of modernization in a valorization of labor as an end, and not only as a means. For Arguedas, the synthesis of this cooperativism with rationalism gives way thus to a *secular spirituality*:

> The old community may serve as the base for [...] a modern society. [...] Rendón Willka has taken these elements from the city. [...] Peruvian society must be transformed, but in the sense of converting it in a society in which fraternity and human solidarity becomes the element that drives the march of man, rather than competition. (Ibid.)

Developing a theme emphasized since his novel *The Sixth* (*El sexto*), Arguedas depicts partisan attachments as much as ethnic or social polarizations as obstacles to collectivization, recognizing all identities as being equally subject to the threat of international capitalism. Meditating over K'oyowasi's prayer, Willka affirms man's creative powers with lyric heroism: the search in the mines promises to unearth not gold, but the radiance of light itself, coming into being as the essence of man's labor: "The light within the world can be done! We shall make it! Great is man!" (Ibid.: 137).[73] Describing the resounding echo of the *pututus* before the productive glory of the collective *faena*, which makes of work a collective project, Fermín stands in awe, reckoning the power of the Indian commoners:

> The Indians do not take this task in the mine as ordinary work, but as a communal project (*faena*). That is, they work in competition. To see who yields more! [...] They are called *pututus*. They are played when work is to be done in a competitive, sporty way, and in sight of common benefit.[74] (Ibid.: 132)

Foreseeing the appropriation of such an ethos in a future social bond for Peruvian society as a whole, the engineer Palacios imagines that sociocultural

---

73 "La luz dentro del mundo puede hacerse! La haremos. El hombre es grande."
74 "Que los indios no toman esta tarea de la mina como trabajo ordinario, sino como una faena comunal. Es decir, que trabajarán, en competencia. ¡A ver quién rinde más! [...] Se llaman pututos. Los tocan cuando el trabajo ha de hacerse a manera de competencia deportiva y en beneficio común."

reconciliation must be supported in overcoming the alienation of man from labor, where the latter is not seen as the instrument (of wealth-property) but again as an end itself, subverting subordination to both the landlords and capitalists:

> Understand, my fellow. If we could all work like this. [...] Work would not be a curse. Understand that one day we shall be like them, when we no longer work to strengthen those who exploit us. [...] For nothing! Understand that! Only for work itself, for competing in work itself, when it is for themselves.[75] (135)

As the narrator of Arguedas's "Second Diary" (*Segundo diario*) declares, Willka's ultimate act of martyrdom at the end of the novel announces the victory of the Andean *yawar mayu*: the restless river of blood of the traditional Indigenous song, through which the community celebrates the "fertility, initiation, renovation"[76] of its cultural rites. This torrential movement is not purely destructive, however, but one that reconstitutes itself from whatever is contained within the limits it shatters. The traditional rite becomes thereby apposite to a transcultural shift within the prospect of a revolutionary upsurge. In the words of William Rowe, the *Yawar Mayu* emerges thus as "a tidal wave of passion that breaks all boundaries," where the limits that separate bodies and cultures are destroyed in a "raging torrent" which is thus a movement of universalization (Rowe 1996: 78):[77] "A river of blood in [his] eyes; the *yawar mayu* of which the Indians spoke. The river was about to break its banks over him with more power than any sudden upsurge of the raging torrent that ran through a gorge, five hundred meters beyond his own hacienda's canefields" (437).

Nevertheless, the hopes for such a conciliatory transformation, for Arguedas, would soon unravel in the face of changing historical circumstances, making the prospects of transculturation appear ever less plausible. During the years between *Todas las sangres* and the publication of his last novel, *El zorro de arriba y el zorro de abajo* (henceforth *The Foxes*), Arguedas faced the eventual frustration of the transcultural dream to reconcile "the magical and rational"

---

75 "¡Entiende, compañero! Si pudiéramos trabajar así todos. [...] El trabajo no sería una maldición. ¡Entiende que algún día seremos como ellos, cuando no trabajemos para fortalecer a los que nos explotan."
76 Poole, Deborah. *Rituals of Movement, Rites of Transformation: Pilgrimage and Dance in the Highlands of Cusco, Perú*, 1983, pp. 23–24.
77 Rowe, William, *Ensayos Arguedianos*, Casa de estudios SUR, 1996.

conceptions of the world. In the last and final section, I trace how in this work the figure of the transcultural subject vanishes, giving way to the obscure figuration of a *post-cultural revolutionary subject* in the narrative of the emerging cities.

The Limits of Transculturation and the Post-Cultural Subject: *The Foxes*

During the infamous 1965 roundtable about *Todas las sangres*, Sebastián Salazar Bondy and Henri Favre, among others, indicted Arguedas's novel for allegedly reiterating a Manichean polarity between a maligned mestizo and a fetishized rural Indian.[78] As Guillermo Rochabrún (2000) recounts in his assessment of the discussion, these criticisms ultimately concerned factual questions about the novel's depiction of the rural south, castigating its evident ideological inflections: the portrayal of a system of castes ("*castas*") that was no longer operative being among the most pressing. Moreover, the novel, it was argued, presented two incompatible accounts of change, where the prospects for social transformation and the preservation of an idealized Indigenous culture were artificially superposed. According to Rochabrún, however, these criticisms stemmed from a sociological bias, according to which Westernizing modernization was to be taken as a definitive destiny, reducing the prospects for transcultural appropriation to a reactive ancestralism:[79]

> In the social sciences of the time, "modernization" provided the most widely accepted answer [to questions about social change]: according to it, a society such as Peru's was in a process of modernization, that is, in transit from a traditional to a modern society [...] in a movement whose direction cannot go but in the direction of the modern which, though

---

[78] The title assigned by the publication of the roundtable in 1983, *Have I lived in Vain?* ("*He vivido en vano?*"), indexes Arguedas's profound deliberation that, as his critics argued, he might have indeed failed to produce an account of the rural Indian which would be conducive to the emancipatory process of the rural Indian and the constitution of a future societal frame for the Peruvian nation.

[79] Rochabrún correctly notes that the novel in fact depicts a more complicated terrain of social positions and subjectivities than the bipolar interpretation of its sociological and literary critics suggested. Which is to say that, as we have seen in the last section, the structural complexity in which the characters in *Todas las sangres* are situated so as to resist such a simplistic, Manichean placement. For Arguedas anticipates a prospective space for mediations proper to a schema of "intermediary" subjectivities in transition, whose fate opens a different future other than the "*cholification*" of the Indian into the urban space, through acculturating modernization (Quijano).

they wouldn't hope was that of capitalist modernity, could nevertheless only be defined as that of a productivist occidental rationalism. (Rochabrún 2000: 94-97, my translation)[80]

Rochabrún is certainly correct in that the criticisms against Arguedas missed how the transcultural dream was designed to resist the singular destiny of modernization as assimilation to Western culture. It is misleading, however, to suggest that Arguedas's primary task was to formulate an alternative *to* modernization. It would be more correct to say that Arguedas imagined a path toward an alternative modernity, in accordance with the ideal of a socialism adapted to the Peruvian context that begins with Mariátegui's heterodox socialist project, and in which aspects of non-Western cultural traditions become activated potentials for a new social bond.

With this in mind, it is difficult to underestimate the effects on Arguedas of persistent polemics and charges of having unwittingly relapsed to a fetishistic idealization of the Indian. Reduced to "an impotent and passive spectator of the formidable struggle that Humanity is carrying on in Peru and everywhere," the forecasted cooperative truce and transcultural phase would not arrive, and the hegemony of international capital instead exacerbated atomization through industrial expansion and urbanization.[81] Already in his 1952 essay *El complejo cultural en el Perú*, Arguedas observed the tectonic shift implied in the migratory process from the highlands to the coastal cities. By the middle of the 1960s, the system of "roads and airplanes" which had taken the place of the feudal communication system appeared in inevitable tension with the preservation of cultural tradition. Moreover, Velasco's 1968 agrarian

---

80 Rochabrún, Guillermo. "Las trampas del pensamiento: Una lectura de la mesa redonda sobre *Todas las sangres*," in *La Mesa Redonda sobre Todas las Sangres del 23 de Junio de 1965*, ed. Guillermo Rochabrún, Pontificia Universidad Católica del Perú, 2000.

"En las ciencias sociales de la época la 'modernización' proporcionaba la más difundida respuesta a tales interrogantes: según ella una sociedad como la peruana estaba en proceso de modernización, es decir, en tránsito de una sociedad tradicional a una sociedad moderna [...] un movimiento cuya dirección no puede ir sino hacia el polo de lo moderno, el cual si bien ellos no desearían que fuese la modernidad capitalista, no alcanzan a definirlo sino como un racionalismo occidental productivista."

81 "Como estoy seguro que mis facultades y armas de creador, profesor, estudioso e imitador, se han debilitado hasta quedar casi nulas y sólo me quedan las que me relegarían a la condición de espectador pasivo e impotente de la formidable lucha que la humanidad está librando en el Perú y en todas partes, no me sería posible tolerar ese destino."

reform did not bring about the desired restitution of the Indian, but only led to a contraction of the rural economy and a movement of mass migration. In the wake of such shifting historical circumstances, Arguedas could no longer afford anticipating the dream of an integral nation, host of an alternative modernity in which "the magic" survives. His last literary works thus express a crippling helplessness, where the formerly solemn aspiration toward utopia fades away.

This dispersion becomes particularly acute in his last, truncated novel, *El zorro de arriba, zorro de abajo* (henceforth, *The Foxes*). In this work, Arguedas inscribes the Indigenous cosmological separation between *Hanan* and *Hurin*, the "land from up above and from down below,"[82] to trace the cultural disintegration that follows from the thwarted descent of the Indian into the urban space. The novel narrates the migratory arrival of Indigenous communities to the coastal city of Chimbote, where they will suffer irreversible spiritual and bodily corruption. As Ángel Rama (1984) argues, the novel attests to the triumph of individualistic "bourgeois culture," pitting technological and urban growth against the cultural foundations of collective life, and bringing about

> material improvements with abysmal disequilibriums, but above all the loss of roots, the destruction of a cultural equilibrium that is not replaced by an equivalent one, the desecration of a communitarian

---

82 Already in his poem *Ode to the Jet* Arguedas assaults the warped and oppressive utopianism of the occidentalist view, ironically addressing "the [earthly] world from above," projected through the aerial, panoptical gaze of a modern subject whose omniscience and omnipotence trump the wonders of the Earth. He semantically transforms the verticality of the traditional Indian cosmology, to designate the patronizing utopianism of occidentalism: the "world from above" (*Hanan*) no longer designates the regional divide between the *Chinchansuyo* (comprising the northern and central coasts of Peru) and the *Antisuyo* (the south and central Andes), but is amplified as a topological model which identifies the all-encompassing, quasi-divine gaze of the modern subject, whose secularizing impetus extends even to its own religious emblems in a kind of anthropocentric frenzy. By the same token, the "earthly world" (*Hurin*) no longer merely comprises the *Collasuyu* and *Cuntisuyo*, but concentrates the entirety of the urban and rural landscape, as well as the totality of natural and cultural beings comprising the material world. In this way, we obtain a delirious modern gaze which disenchants the world at the same time as it elevates itself to the rank of divinity, as the inversion of "Man turned God," coupled to a forlorn and trivialized "Earth" whose richness and multiplicity appear relatively flattened, trivialized and ordinary.

worldview replaced by the "skeptical individualism" of contemporary bourgeois culture. (Rama 1984: 193, my translation)

A vertical logic organizes the novel's progression, tracking not only the movement of migratory descent but the erosion of the cultural bond which ties individual bodies into a collective history. At heart, one finds a structural complicity between the objective appropriation of labor to industrial capitalist modernity and the subjective appropriation of libido in the city space. The ideal of integrative mediation dissolves in an inconsistent multiplicity of nameless, aberrant individualities populating the urban milieu, once again exploited by private interest and forlorn by the state.

The British philosopher Nick Land has described the general logic of this process: as societies enter the vortex of urban capitalist life, alienation becomes exacerbated as opposed to remedied, spewing wandering bodies, extirpated not only from their present, but from their own history and past, so that all forms of individual and collective determination shatter:

> Once the commodity system is established there is no longer a need for an autonomous cultural impetus into the order of the abstract object. Capital attains its own "angular momentum," perpetuating a run-away whirlwind of dissolution, whose hub is the virtual-zero of impersonal metropolitan accumulation. At the peak of the productive prowess the human animal is hurled into a new nakedness, as everything stable is progressively liquidated in the storm.[83] (Land 1992: 80)

Arguedas's novel posits an unambiguous pessimism about the degenerative process of urbanization under capitalism: at the outset, Arguedas annuls the "choral" and dialogic style that organized *Todas las sangres*, stripping the human voice from all eloquence, and reducing it, much like Vallejo, to a meaningless "babble." As Alberto Moreiras writes, the novel speaks thus of a failed teleology, a "narrative of the end of narratives," in the task to rethink utopia from *the rabble of culture*:

> El *zorro* is a narrative of the end of narrative, it would be reductive to call that writing of writing's collapse an "appropriation and defiance" of modernity. What else can it then be? [...] For Arguedas, at this point,

---

[83] Land, Nick. *The Thirst for Annihilation: Georges Bataille and Virulent Nihilism*, Routledge 1992.

a drastically urgent if perhaps already desperate task lay at hand: to re-appropriate, to re-symbolize, life in Chimbote into a possible utopia, the only hope for the future. The magical-real machine was then emblematically in place—or apparently so. But in that limit-situation transculturation could only happen as a failure of transculturation—through the failure itself. (Moreiras 2001: 197)[84]

Throughout the story, references to the Indian cultural world no longer carry the brilliance of a synergetic rapport with the natural world under cooperativist labor, but instead express the tragic dissolution of the social bond. The novel thus dismantles the triumphant, insurrectionary passion of the *yawar mayu*, whose obliteration of all boundaries prevailed at the end of *Todas las sangres* as a restorative and integrative force, instead giving way to the image of the flood (*"huayco"*), in a disintegrative temporality of alluvial derailment, debasement, and waste. The Indian creative mythos becomes perverted by the corrupting intrusion of Western modernity: the disciplined pilgrimage of the deity Tutaykire—literally, the "Warrior from the above," avatar for the difficult path of the wandering Indian without a destiny—is separated at once from the mountain qua site of labor by a throat (symbol of drunkenness and debauchery) and from the fertile sea by a gaping abyss (symbol of carnal surrender).[85] Derailed from his journey, and sentenced to fall asleep besides the road, the God's stoic resilience is "dispersed" by the seductress "fox" (*"zorra"*; also derogatory slang in Peruvian Spanish for prostitute). He becomes seized by her panoptical gaze, "trapped by a 'sweet and contrarian fox,' among the *yungas*. From the *El Dorado* mountain she sees from up above and down below" (Arguedas 2013: 45).[86] The image of collective *mobility*, the forging of the roads to the coast, which since *Agua* and *Yawar Fiesta* served to celebrate Indigenous productivity, now leads to perdition and ruin.

In the novel, the lowly "fox" is etched within the city space across a series of figures, signaling libidinal arrest and degeneracy. The quasi-divine sovereign authority of oligarchic rule that claimed rights over the body becomes disseminated into the social body writ large, reproducing the verticality of the master–slave logic across all human relations once the subject has become

---

84 Moreiras, Alberto. *The Exhaustion of Difference: The Politics of Latin American Cultural Studies*, Durham and London, 2001.

85 This mythological figure first appears in Arguedas's work in his 1968 translation of "the Huarochiri transcript," titled *Dioses y hombres de Huarochiri*.

86 "[...] quedo atrapado por una 'zorra' dulce y contraria, entre los yungas. Desde el cerro el Dorado ve arriba y abajo."

commodified. The sexual violence imparted by Bruno on the Indian commoners at the outset of *Todas las sangres* becomes the basis of a general social economy in *The Foxes*: the wretched figure of the prostitute Fidelia, presaging the commodification of the body as it enters into the intensifying circuit of market exchange; the torn voice of the homosexual and incestuous Chueca (literally, *deviant* or *bent*), bastard son of prostitution; the identification of the "the Argentine" prostitute with a "*vizcacha*" (a rodent); Tinoco's procuring of both his sister Felicia and his wife Gerania; the abandoned Orfa, whose child is orphan to a nameless father; the "double jawed" Aymara Apasa, who procures three women as he purchases lands in the Santa valley, and so on.

At the novel's dramatic apex, the citizens of Chimbote relocate the crosses of the dead to a new and deserted burial site, while leaving the corpses in their place. The names and spirits of the dead are brutally amputated from the bodies that correspond to them, just as the migrating bodies of the citizens compose the "living dead," all dislocated from their individual and collective identities:

> With the crosses over their shoulders, everyone approached the wooden row that carried the legends of their names toward the arc, raising them by the head, placing them over their other shoulder. And all of the indebted marched, dune below, with crosses over both shoulders. They formed thus a very large collective that descended raising dust, a mass of people moved forward without speaking.[87] (Ibid.: 96)

Under exploitative wage labor in the factory, and the equally imprisoning hedonistic vortex of city life, labor in *The Foxes* becomes reduced to a reiterative cycle of outsourced energy. Don Braschi's triumph in the anchovy fishing market against his competitors maps the sanguine logic of capital accumulation onto the libidinal deviations of misogynous virility, endowing him the title of "*culemacho*," contrasting the impotence of "*cochos*" (literally, aging men lacking virility) (42). Hegemonic control over the coastal natural and socioeconomic environs erupts with a metaphor from the patron, morphing lyricism into plundering vulgarity: "I make the sea give birth," outperforming competing capitalists by "making the small anchovies give

---

87 "Con las cruces al hombro se acercaron todos a la fila de maderos que tenían las leyendas de sus nombres hacia el arco, las alzaron por la cabeza y se las pusieron al otro hombro. Y cada deudo desfilaba, medano abajo, con cruces sobre los dos hombros. Formaban así una comitiva muy grande que bajaba levantando polvo, una masa de gente avanzaba sin hablar."

birth to bills" (45).[88] This sinuous agency, however, is not the abstract, faceless figure of international capitalism; in his direct physical presence and limitless capacity for individualized violence, Braschi reiterates the "divine sovereignty" of feudal rule within the secular urban space and through capitalist wage labor.

The following diagram traces the binary system of subordinating oppositions that the novel articulates across divergent series and scales of determination.

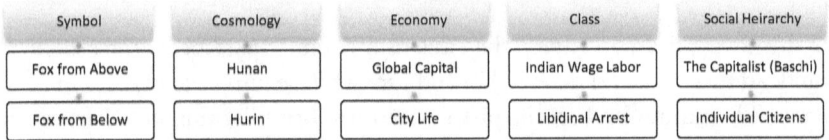

Diagram 3.2 Strata in The Foxes.

Just as Arguedas can no longer wrest a "rational" kernel from the competitive logic of capitalism, so the colonial legacy can no longer sustain the preservation of its sacrificial ethos, and Western religious spirituality becomes as a result unredeemable: don Diego, the "inca hippy" works as a petty subordinate for the major patron, don Braschi, lacking any semblance of repentance or bond to a culture or religion (Ibid.: 147).[89] The mythical subversion of Willka's "divine language" becomes disfigured and unrecognizable in the ramblings of "crazy Moncada," whose errant sermons oscillate between patent lunacy and messianism, woven from morsels of Indian and Christian religiosity. At the same time, Arguedas anticipates in this context an obscure subversive agency, beyond transculturation; Moncada vulgarly accurses the "drunken-stars" of foreign-imperial intrusion, as they "amass the incandescence of the sun, the fortune power" (174):

> There are drunkards that screw it over, drunkard stars, luminaries, foreigners that imbibe liqueur from their town-nation and screw over the people-nation in which the incandescence of the sun is amassed, the

---

88 "Estos amos de fábrica hacen parir billetes a cada anchovetita. [...] Yo hago parir a la mar."
89 "¡Extraño pendejo éste que me han mandado de Lima; extraño hippi 'incaico'! ¡Y gracioso, carajo, y simpático, carajo! Muy extraño. Este Braschi se consigue auxiliares de toda laya," pensaba don Ángel.

fortune power that I may volatize or spite, aromatize with my voice which the constellations hear.[90] (174)

The disfiguration of identity exemplified by Moncada timidly insinuates the embryonic potentials for a new *post-cultural subject*, woven from the inconsistent plurality of exploited bodies that populate the urban space. In this regard, William Rowe (2011) notes how the novel harbors the promise of an unprecedented admixture of discursive modes and subjective types: no longer the idyllic mediation between Quechua and Spanish that informed the transcultural dream from *Agua* to *Todas las sangres*, but anomalous forms woven from different sociolects and idiolects, articulated from what we have called *the rabble of culture*, the ashes of a failed transculturation:

> The rupture of isolating walls encourages the intermingling of sociolects and idiolects, producing "alluvial discourses." The extraordinary mutual enrichment between discourses tends to relate with sexuality ("the Stutterer") or with death and birth (Moncada and Esteban de la Cruz). At the grammatical level we find parataxis, not only as the result of Quechua influence but also as the aesthetic product of the new ferment between social forces. [...] The rupture of barriers, now grammatical, produces new multivalent discourses. (Rowe 2011: 298)[91]

This unprecedented subjective figure can no longer be indexed to the mediation between previously existing social positions and cultural traditions; rather, pulverized identities come to reconstitute the social bond in unprecedented ways. As Horacio Legrás (2008) argues, assessing the bigamous figure of Bazalar, who assumes a leading role in the procession of the crosses toward the abrupt closure of the novel, Chimbote's displaced subjectivities attest to a radical *anti-foundationalism* that extirpates cultural belonging from the emancipatory process. In its radical hybridity and anomalous quality, *The Foxes'* embryonic post-cultural subject approximates, if anything, Vallejo's universal human subject, who lies beyond any circumscription to nation, ethnicity and

---

[90] "Hay borrachos pa'que se zurren en él, hay borrachos estrellas, astros, extranjeros que toman licor de su pueblo-nación y se zurran en el pueblo-nación donde amasan la incandescencia del sol, la fortuna poder que yo puedo volatilizar, vitriolizar, aromatizar con mi voz que oyen las constelaciones."
[91] Rowe, William. "Reading Arguedas' Foxes," in *The Fox From Up Above, The Fox From Down Below*, translated by Frances Horning Barraclough, Pittsburgh University Press, 2011, p. 298.

culture. In the *Last Diary*, Arguedas directly attests to this change of emphasis in his thought, overtly recognizing Vallejo as the returning precursor of this new subjective figure of the future:

> Perhaps with me one historical cycle draws to a close and another begins in Peru, with all that this represents. It means the closing of the cycle of the consoling calender lark, of the whip, of being driven like beasts of burden, of impotent hatred, of mournful funeral "uprisings," of the fear of God and the predominance of that God and his protégées, his fabricators. It signifies the opening of a cycle of light and of the indomitable, liberating strength of the Vietnamese man, of the fiery calender lark, of the Liberator God. That God who is coming back into action. Vallejo was the beginning and the end.[92] (292)

But while the purity of Vallejo's "militiaman" produced a clamor for the world of justice to come in "the time of harvest," Arguedas hijacks the individualist logic of capitalism *from within*, as the new subject composes itself from impure subjectivities, drawing a diagonal across all orders of representation. The possibility of finding universality within the ruins of a failed modernization is thus actualized in speeches at the interface between reality and delirium, eloquence and nonsense. The unintelligibility of this anomalous language, emblematized by the voices of Moncada, Bazalar and the indiscernibility of their place of enunciation, suggests that the exponential fragmentation of identities under capitalism may still give way to a new collective hope.

In the end, *The Foxes* provides no definitive resolution, as those carriers of Mariátegui's revolutionary dream congregate in somber defeat at the priest's office in *La Esperanza* (literally, *The Hope*), pondering the uncertain path toward emancipation. The group discuss the future for revolutionaries on the brink of defeat, divined under the vigilant gazes of *Ché Guevara* and the Christ. As the American priest Cardozo reiterates the possibility for a secular spirituality, he identifies the prophetic return of the Messiah, and the anticipation of a heroic leftist spirit of revolution, symbolizing the inextricability of individual sacrifice and collective struggle: "The revolution will not be deeds

---

[92] "Quizá conmigo empieza a cerrarse un ciclo y a abrirse otro en el Perú y lo que él representa: se cierra el de la calandria consoladora, del azote, del arrieraje, del odio impotente, de los fúnebres 'alzamientos,' del temor a Dios y del predominio de ese Dios y sus protegidos, sus fabricantes; se abre el de la luz y de la fuerza liberadora invencible del hombre de Vietnam, el de la calandria de fuego, el del dios liberador. Aquel que se reintegra. Vallejo era el principio y el fin."

but instead will be the work of these two examples, one divine and the other human, who was born of that divine one: Jesus and Ché" (Ibid.: 281).[93]

Herein lies perhaps Arguedas's final offering to the revolutionary spirit of *indigenismo*: the tender reduction of the solemn transcultural dream into the affirmation of the priority of collective interest against a savage individualism. His verdict is clear: the figure of the rural proletarian, even in its post-Indigenous transcultural form, can no longer play the role of a privileged agent for collective emancipation.

The following diagram summarizes the different figurations of the revolutionary subject in Arguedas's works that we examined before:

FIGURES OF THE REVOLUTIONARY SUBJECT IN ARGUEDAS' WORKS

Militant Indian Subject	Collective Indian Subject	The Transcultural Post-Indian Subject	The Post-Cultural Generic Subject
• Agua - Pantacha	• Yawar Fiesta - The K'ayau indians	• Todas Las Sangres - Rendon Wilka	• The Foxes - Bazalar Moncada

| Narrative of the Small Towns | Narrative of the 'Big Towns' | Narrative of the New Cities |

Diagram 3.3 Figures of the Subject in Arguedas' Works.

The fragmentary effects witnessed in *The Foxes* would only intensify in the decades following Arguedas's late works, making the prospects of a revolutionary process organized under the persistence of Indigenous cooperativist values implausible, however reconciled with the Western "rational worldview." And yet, in the midst of ruin, an elegiac heroism before absolute despair lingers, refusing to surrender once and for all the possibility of wresting hope back from the rabble of culture. Even at the threshold, engulfed by wallowing despair, Arguedas never abandons the heroism of agonic struggle, as Flores Galindo wrote in his characterization of Mariátegui's spirit.

In the next chapter, we shall assess the consequences of this ongoing historical process for *indigenista* narratives and socialist thought in the decades following Arguedas's work, as well as its implications for the contemporary Peruvian sociopolitical and literary context.

---

93 "—La revolución—se oyó la voz irme de Cardozo—no será obra sino de estos dos ejemplos, uno divino, el otro humano, que nació de ese divino: Jesús y el 'Che.'"

Chapter 4

THE CONTEMPORARY SCENE: THE FUTURE OF *INDIGENISMO* AND THE COLLAPSE OF THE INTEGRATIVE DREAM AFTER ARGUEDAS

Introduction: A Brief Retrospective—*Indigenismo* after Arguedas

In the last instance, Arguedas's work implies a decisive extension of the project of appropriation which grounded the socialist *indigenista* spirit, overcoming what he perceived as a lingering economism in Mariátegui's vision. In understanding the Peruvian nation as a complicated nexus organizing not only relations of class, legal status and ethnicity, but profoundly divergent cultural traditions, he correlates the collectivist Indigenous mode of production to a worldview grounded fundamentally in an affirmation of work-for-itself. But despite his attempt to think of sociocultural difference across a complex set of relations and subjective positions, Arguedas's articulation of the "magical and rational conceptions of the world" still reproduced a Manichean contradiction between Western and Indigenous cultures. In this way, he ultimately conceived of an idealized process of transculturation that would render modernity and tradition compatible, a destiny other than the savagery of modern capitalism, to be seized after the collapse of the latifundio.

The agrarian reform initiated in 1968 by Velasco's military rule proved ultimately unsuccessful in succeeding the rent-based labor economy imposed historically by the landlord oligarchy, instead exacerbating the disenfranchisement of the rural Indian by the state. As described in Arguedas's *The Foxes*, mass migration into the cities implied a tectonic transformation of Peruvian society, through which Indigenous populations became subject to new forms of alienation and exploitation. Government institutions would prove just as inefficient and corruptible when protecting the Indian workers in the cities from the new capitalist oligarchies as they had been when standing in complicity with the rural landlord oligarchy of the latifundio.

In response to this historical sequence, we saw how Arguedas's late work delivered an obscure forecast, in which the promise of a transcultural collective life unravels before an ever more obscure and uncertain future. Accordingly, the image of the "post-Indigenous subject" that mediated strategically between "rational and magical" conceptions of the world no longer promised national integration: the martyrdom of the hero who achieves collective emancipation through transcultural production, expressed in the figure of Rendón Willka, ceased to be a plausible model for a new subject and for emancipatory action. In *The Foxes*, as we saw, the rural Indian becomes subject to the libidinal capture of urban decadence under wage labor, run by a capitalist class that takes the place of the old landlord oligarchy, perpetuating the historical complicity of the creole and mestizo with state institutions. In this process, it is not only individual agency that becomes reduced to its "material bases," as in Vallejo's *Trilce*, but the collective cultural heritage of the Indian which becomes dissolved into inconsistent identities.

In the end, Arguedas's truncated narrative describes the horrors of an ever more fractured society as the colonial shackles of semifeudal rule are supplanted by the degeneration of life and work in the industrially developing city. Whatever productive potentials may once have existed in Indigenous modes of production and belief systems, these dissolve as the urban setting devours individuals and communities alike. And if, already since its liberal expression, *indigenismo* was but the promise to restore the social fracture that afflicted the Peruvian nation, then Arguedas's fatal prognosis is that capitalist modernization, rather than bringing about a felicitous process of integration for Peruvian society, results in an ever more pronounced process of individual and collective disarticulation. Rather than the acculturation imagined by the liberal modernizers since the nineteenth century under the dream of pedagogical transmission and professionalization, what transpired was a process in which individuals were divided from their native traditions and alienated from their labor.

What are we to say, then, of the development of *indigenista* literature in the decades following Arguedas's death, in light of his somber verdict, once the economic and cultural foundations of the appropriative ideal appeared equally implausible as mediating vehicles toward collective emancipation? In what follows, I examine some of the major tendencies and problems that emerge in *indigenista* literature after Arguedas, facing the progressive collapse of the revolutionary socialist ideal. At heart, I focus on how a new sequence of *indigenista* narratives appears in this context, conceiving of a *postrevolutionary subjectivity* that resists subversive violence and reimagines the possibilities of a productive mediation between the Western mestizo and the rural Indian.

In the first section, I focus on Edgardo Rivera Martínez's seminal 1993 novel, *País de Jauja*, which aligns the ideal of transculturation to a new version of the "educated mestizo," which is also a pacifist and self-proclaimed "apolitical" response to the traumatic experience of subversive violence following the insurgency of the Shining Path and its brutal repression by the Fujimori regime in the early 1990s. Through this narrative shift, *indigenismo* departs from its utopian mode and political role and becomes delivered once more to an *ethical* imperative to guard against all forms of human violence. As we shall see, this position coincides with the humanist postrevolutionary orientation that recent philosophy and political theory names "the ethical turn." Accordingly, the postrevolutionary subject ceases to be a figure of collective mobilization and becomes the emblem of the modest promise that future generations may awaken a multicultural consciousness.

In the second section, I situate Rivera Martínez's attempt to separate the tasks of literature and politics within the spectrum of the democratic and humanitarian critique of the "ethical turn," which argued the utopian aspirations of the twentieth-century revolutionary projects. This allows us to situate the Peruvian *indigenista* socialist tradition in the context of a wider retrospective assessment of the revolutionary ideal, as well as engaging in an evaluation of its past and its prospects. In particular, I focus on the critique of the concept of violence as correlated with the utopian aspirations of the socialist project, and consider how the *indigenista* socialist tradition sought, however provisionally, to escape this predicament through a predominantly constructive vision of revolutionary practice.

Considering these criticisms and historical limitations, in the third section I address the contemporary crisis of the productivist ideal that grounded the image of the postcapitalist future for socialist narratives since Mariátegui. This crisis, I argue, is not only a problem for socialist political practice, but an essential problem when attempting to move beyond the Marxian and transcultural paradigms offered by socialist *indigenista* authors in the twentieth century. The collapse of productivism and the ayllu after the end of the latifundio was thus not only correlated with failures of the concrete socialist political experiences of the last century, but also with the failure of the figure of the proletariat subject as the motor of historical change. The search for a new productivism becomes in this light indissociable from the search for a novel kind of revolutionary subjectivity and an unprecedented vision of the future, beyond the hegemonic mantle of global capital.

To complete our assessment, in the fifth section I briefly recount the development of the postrevolutionary, reformist turn of Peruvian socialism after the

1960s, attending to emerging leftist proposals concerning the future for the Peruvian economy and society in general, and concerning the rural Indian in particular. I conclude with a promissory, provisional attempt to clarify how the integrative ideal guiding *indigenista* narratives can be assessed in the contemporary context, considering the changing circumstances of Peruvian society and the place of the rural Indian within it.

The Collapse of the Revolutionary Ideal in Literary *Indigenismo* after Arguedas

As Ismael Marquez has persuasively argued, *indigenista* literary production since the 1940s—particularly, after the publication of Ciro Alegría's *Broad and Alien is the World* and Arguedas's *Yawar Fiesta* in 1941—responds to progressive changes in the Peruvian social and economic landscape, describing the "urban milieu as a pervasive, negative influence" and offering a new cultural hero: "the individual with Andean roots who, transformed by his experience in the city, returns to his place of origin as an agent of an alternative modernity" (Marquez 2005: 146).[1] And although in many cases such narratives continue to express an optimistic vision of the future—well into the 1960s—the *indigenista* novel since the 1950s also begins to confront the uncertain fate of Peruvian society, where a rekindling of the communitarian aspects of the rural world becomes threatened by capitalist modernization.[2] In the decades following Arguedas's diagnosis of the failures of transculturation in the urban space, *indigenista* authors would accordingly seek to delineate the contours of new forms of subjugation, as well as indicate a possible emancipatory figure beyond that of the socialist revolutionary subject.

At the same time, the consistency of *indigenismo* as a genre in which literature assumes the task of thinking the prospects for national integration becomes, if not impossible, exceedingly obscure. From the 1960s onward, following Arguedas's fatal diagnosis in *The Foxes*, many writers show a growing skepticism with respect to the idea that modernization could in the end offer a solution to Peru's social fragmentation—Julio Ramón Ribeyro's *Los geniecillos*

---

1 Marquez, Ismael. "The Andean novel," in *The Cambridge Companion to the Latin American Novel*, edited by Efraín Kristal, Cambridge University Press, 2005, p. 146.

2 Marquez follows Cornejo Polar in identifying the *indigenista* production since the 1940s under "neo-indigenismo," in which the ambiguities concerning the future and the privileged role of the returning student from the city to bring about the desired alternative modernity.

dominicales (1965) and Oswaldo Reynoso's *En Octubre no hay milagros* (1965), being two paradigmatic exemplars of this development.³ These works not only recoil from the socialist revolutionary imaginary and its political aspirations, but express a frustration before a thwarted modernization that perpetrated social inequalities or else imposed new ones.⁴ In fact, these works retroactively assess the limitations of the utopian visions that animated socialist *indigenista* writers, which eventually lead down the path to an ideologically misguided vindication of insurrectionary violence, and which did not reflect the sentiment of the rural Indian farmers. As Manuel Scorza declares apropos his last novel, *La danza inmóvil*, published in 1983, with regard to the failures of the armed insurrection of Indigenous guerrillas in the rural south:

> I know that many will find my novel irritable, since I pose themes such as my disenchantment after experiencing great defeats. The Peruvian guerrilla was exterminated because of an erroneous conception of reality; the guerrillas did not know their country well, their ideological instruments did not coincide with the mentality of the farmers.⁵ (Scorza 1991: 141, my translation)

---

3 The ensuing decades after general Velasco's 1968 agrarian reform would not shatter but ratify the disintegration of both the Indigenous community and of the urban efforts to integrate the Indian's struggle to an integral political and literary vision of Peruvian society. In 1978, Francisco Morales Bermudez called for the creation of the Constitutional Assembly, and in 1979 an electoral process, ceding power to Fernando Belaunde Terry's presidency and signaling the interruption of military dictatorship. In the decades following the 1970s, the progressive consolidation of a liberal market economy and the continued disenfranchisement of the Indian would devolve in an unprecedented fragmentation and diversification of leftist groups. Among these, we saw the consolidation of new radical factions inspired by Maoist ideals (the party *Bandera roja*) derived from the PCP, which would eventually devolve in violent, subversive struggle throughout the 1980s, under the idea that armed confrontation and civil war provided the only solution for the Indian—particularly under Abimael Guzmán's group *Sendero Luminoso* (*The Shining Path*), concentrated in Ayacucho—culminating in the genocidal and brutal counterinsurgency campaign waged largely in rural Peru in the early 1990s, under the Fujimori regime.
4 Indeed, in the decades that follow some authors go as far as diagnosing the potential danger in a process of thwarted modernization, leading to the radicalization of Indigenous rebellious groups, for instance, culminating in the violent measures of *The Shining Path* as seen in Vargas Llosa's *Lituma en los Andes*. Ismael Marquez (2005) recapitulates some of these developments.
5 Scorza, Manuel. *La danza inmóvil*, Siglo XXI, 1991.

   "Yo sé que a muchos mi novela les va a irritar porque planteo temas como el del desencanto que tengo después de haber asistido a grandes derrotas. La guerrilla peruana fue exterminada por una concepción errónea de la realidad, los querrilleros no

The critical distance from the revolutionary imaginary opened the way, however, for new figures for emancipation to succeed those imagined by socialist writers. Like Arguedas's post-cultural subject, and echoing Vallejo's solemn invocation of generic fraternity, Scorza anticipates an unborn subject who, though no longer defined by cultural belonging or local mediations, becomes the abstract avatar binding "all the dreams of History" to a future beyond past tragedies:

> All of the dreams in History! The New Man shall understand that love and happiness are the truly subversive facts. But this man is as yet unborn. We live not in the present but in the past. And between past and future there is a pit. Perhaps this pit may only be filled with our corpses. It is necessary that it be so, because it is necessary that above our own corpses Humanity comes to pass.[6] (Scorza 1991: 181, my translation)

For Scorza, this oblique insinuation of humanist solidarity demands an implicit critical retrospective, correcting the socialist *indigenista* representational matrix: a recognition of the lingering distance that separated socialist utopian aspirations from the empirical reality of the rural Indian, despite its own pretenses, and the necessity of escaping the fate of violence into which the revolutionary dream degenerated. This dual demand would intensify in the tragic aftermath of armed insurgency since the 1980s, leading to a disenchantment with the revolutionary ideal, and even to its disavowal. As Carlos Vilas and Richard Stroller argue, the war against the Shining Path revealed the terminal degeneration of both the revolutionary ideal and hegemonic state rule:

> The war between *Sendero Luminoso* and the Peruvian State throughout the 1980s can be seen as a struggle between two poles of power for political-military control of disputed territory, with both sides' strategies based upon unusual levels of violence. Insurgency and counter-insurgency alike destroyed communities and forced inhabitants to take part in atrocities or to keep silent. (Vilas and Stroller 2008: 103–8)

---

conocían bien su país, sus instrumentos ideológicos no coincidían con la mentalidad de los campesinos."

6 "¡Todos los sueños de la Historia! El Hombre Nuevo comprenderá que el amor y la felicidad son los hechos realmente subversivos. Pero ese hombre no ha nacido. No vivimos en el presente sino en el pasado. Y entre el pasado y el futuro hay una fosa. Quizás esa fosa sólo podrá llenarse con nuestros cadáveres. Es necésario que así sea, porque es necésario que por encima de nuestros cadáveres pase la Humanidad."

In any case, already since the agrarian reform that led to the abolition of the latifundio, one finds *indigenista* writers adapting the transcultural ideal to a pacifist alternative. Engaging the undoing of the rural Indian in the city, their narratives bear witness to the return of the figure of the enlightened mestizo that characterized the "cosmopolitan" progressive liberal tradition at the end of the nineteenth century, and which Mariátegui took as the direct precursor of socialist *indigenismo*.

Two brief examples should suffice for our purposes: in Alfredo Bryce Echenique's 1970 autobiographical novel *A World for Julius* (*Un mundo para Julius*), the *Bildungsroman* form is adapted to tell the life of young Julius, an aristocrat mestizo living in Lima during the years before Velasco's 1968 agrarian reform. In the novel, Julius becomes increasingly sensitive to the poor Indian servants who work for his family: the nursing housemaid, Vilma, whose eventual fate is to become a prostitute, simultaneously operates as a symbol for his embryonic erotic drives, but also for his ethical awakening to a social reality within which he is at once an actor and yet without clear place. The fractured family unit remains woven by the ominous, absent figure of the stepfather, Juan Lucas, representative of the new bourgeois aristocracy whose ties to the global market promise to save the nation's waning old oligarchy, contrasting but also perpetuating the ruthlessness of the landowning ascendancy of Julius's family. The ethereal rapport between Julius and Vilma, contemplative and fetishistic, traces the fragmentary shards of a twofold corruption, where the alienated mestizo child who remains dislocated within his own family identifies in his solitude with the plight of the subjugated Indian worker. No redemptive destiny is prefigured at the end of this process, however, as the novel's conclusion signals impotence in the face of inequality, commensurate with the hollow, degenerative triumph of urban modernity.

In a similar way, Edgardo Rivera Martínez's 1993 novel *País de Jauja* imagines a process of reconciliation by way of generational renovation: the story presents another Bildungsroman in which the shattered innocence of the mestizo child follows not only a developmental process of sexual and psychological maturation, but signals the advent of a multicultural subject, situated beyond the division between the mestizo and rural Indian. Set in the idyllic region of Jauja, at the end of the 1940s, the novel affirms cultural enrichment by direct immersion and humanistic education. The young protagonist, Claudio, incarnates the purified, infantile gaze of a new mestizo generation, whose sensitivity and openness to different forms of cultural production places Indigenous traditions alongside Western ones. For example, he transcribes Quechua music for the piano, transforming the lyrical content of the Andean oral tradition into a voiceless expression, encoding a peaceful, silent correspondence. Conversing with his friend Georgiou Radulesco at the Jauja hospital toward the end of the novel, Claudio draws a parallel between the European academic musical appropriation of folkloric traditions and pre-Hispanic musical forms, suggesting a reconciliation between modernity and tradition: he finds an unlikely resonance between the Indian *huayno* and the academic music of the Hungarian Bartók, who enhanced the Western musical idiom by appropriating native folkloric form.

As Claudio notices a series of invariances between Western and Indigenous cultures, he also realizes that Western forms can develop and become enriched and informed by local, native traditions:

> And what do you think of Andean music?—At first, I did not like it, but then I started growing fond of it, and even more so when I discovered that it resembled somewhat the works of Béla Bartók. […] A Hungarian composer who has been greatly inspired by the popular music of his country, and who has recreated songs and danceable music of more or less pentatonic form, somewhat similar thus to the Indian *huaynos*.[7] (Rivera Martínez 1993: 353, my translation here and below)

No longer appointed as the facilitator of the rural Indian's acculturation, the postrevolutionary enlightened mestizo adapts the liberal-humanist ideal of transculturation through pedagogical transmission, one which includes not only Western canonical forms, but also Indian native ones. This multicultural consciousness becomes adequate to a "reformed modernity" that simultaneously overcomes liberal occidentalism and separates the ethics of cultural mediation from the revolutionary imperative, fostering what Rivera Martínez calls a "universal culture":

> Our contribution to universal culture may only be valuable to the extent that it is original and positive, and among us it is only our pre-Hispanic past that is original, although this legacy has been enriched, developed,

---

7 Rivera Martínez, Edgardo. *País de Jauja*. La Voz, 1993.

"Y qué piensa usted de la música andina?" "Al comienzo no me agradaba, pero luego fui tomándole un cierto gusto, y aún más cuando descubrí que se asemeja en algo a la de Béla Bartók." "¿Bartók?" Un compositor húngaro que se ha inspirado mucho en la música popular de su patria, y que ha recreado canciones y música de baile de estructura más o menos pentatónica, un tanto parecida por eso a la de los huaynos serranos" (Ibid.: 353).

or re-elaborated, later through miscegenation, and through an increasing assimilation of the conquests of Western culture.[8] (Rivera Martínez 1999: 28, my translation)

The unbinding of modernity from the ideological excesses of occidentalist liberalism, as much as revolutionary socialism, is achieved by non-conflictive communication and generational renovation. The young Claudio incarnates this spirit in his wondrous openness to Western and Indigenous traditions and emerges not as a figure of political upheaval or collective struggle, but of affective and cultural reconciliation. He fulfills the promise of a synthesis between the urban and Indigenous world, between cosmopolitanism and localism, without the necessity of insurrectionary violence or nationalist-utopian

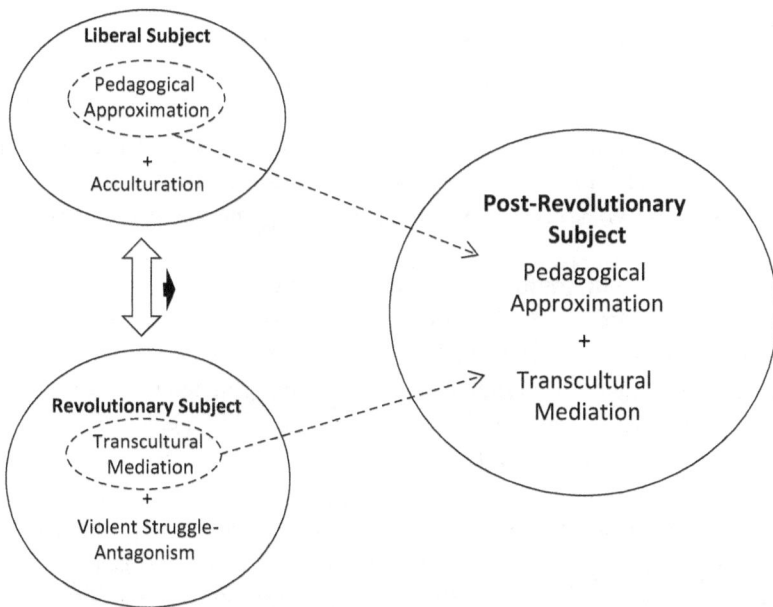

Diagram 4.1 The Post-Revolutionary Subject.

---

8 Ferreira César, and Ismael P. Márquez. *De lo andino a lo universal: la obra de Edgardo Rivera Martínez*, Fondo Editorial PUCP, 1999.

"Pues nuestro aporte a la cultura universal sólo puede ser valioso en la medida en que es original y positivo, y, entre nosotros sólo es original—por lo menos hasta hoy—lo que proviene de nuestro pasado pre-hispánico, aunque ese legado haya sido enriquecido desarrollado o reelaborado por el mestizaje, y por una creciente asimilación de las conquistas de la cultura universal."

proclamations. The diagram 4.1 captures the construction of the post-revolutionary subject in *indigenista* narratives after Arguedas.

This anti-utopianism does not only reflect the collapse of the revolutionary project, but proscribes the latter as complicit with an intolerable violence that frustrates authentic reconciliation. Recalling his reaction to the tragic outcome of the 1992 Tarata bombing during the insurgency of the Shining Path, Rivera Martínez (2003) describes the pragmatic difficulty of "dreaming of a different world" in the context of the ensuing armed conflict: "What could I, a writer, do in this terrain of confrontation with subversion? Not much, I believe, right? Merely to dream with a different world, as the one proposed in my novel"[9] (Rivera Martinez 2003: 41, my translation).

The transcultural process envisaged in *País de Jauja* appears thus to separate literary imagination from the pretense of a prescriptive political program. As a "pure object of literary hope," unbound from the demands of political agitation, Rivera Martinez claims to give not a manual for general conduct nor, even less, a prediction for how emancipation will ultimately be attained. He remains content to "dream" within the bounds of local possibility, where emancipation realizes itself, however slowly, across generations. As Mirko Lauer summarizes, four principles guide this vision:

> (1) Harmony, not conflict, lies at the center of the Andean narrative, although this does not cease to be problematic for the author. (2) An Andean social group emerges exerting its limitless capacities, in this case the powers of the cultural fantasy of the enlightened middle classes. (3) The Western is presented as a complement of Quechua—again, the theme of non-conflict—in this case, Ancient Greek above all, but also the cosmopolitanism that filters to Jauja through the sanatorium and socialist ideas. (4) There is a direct confession of the provincial that runs the risk [...] of seeking to seduce a reader construed as a kind of "national stranger." (Lauer 1998: 171, my translation[10])

Claims for political neutrality and oneiric purity, however, cannot conceal the idealized process of cultural exchange that takes place in the novel. For its

---

9 Rivera Martínez, Edgardo. "Jauja: Ciudad de Fuego. Conversación con Edgardo Rivera Martínez," in Lienzo no. 24, 2003. Full interview available at: https://revistas.ulima.edu.pe/index.php/lienzo/article/viewFile/1135/1088

10 Lauer, Mirko. "Rivera Martínez, Edgardo. *País de Jauja*," in *Inti: Revista de literatura hispánica*, no. 48, Peisa, 1998, pp. 169–172.

reformed modernity is also a reformed representative vindication, through which the fate of the rural Indian is merely instrumental in the upbringing of a new multicultural consciousness. Rivera Martínez's "universal culture" operates through humanistic and humanist integrative ambition, yet also expresses a circumscribed localism at the level of practice, describing transculturation as a strictly apolitical process. In the last instance, his figure of the purified mestizo, and of alternative modernity, imagines an angelic subject, the anonymous mestizo Child freed from the vengeful desire of revolt against institutional and economic hegemonic powers, voided of any political ambition. Its idyllic transmission sharply contrasts with the nineteenth- and twentieth-century *indigenistas* demand for social realism in concert with an emancipatory politics: to face the fragmentation of the nation by articulating intellectual, artistic and political action in the image of a future, integral nation.

The Ethical Turn and Democratic Materialism

As we have seen, the deflation of the universalist ideals of modernity and socialism in *indigenista* narratives, in the name of a recognition of invariances across cultural and aesthetic productive forms, appears as the complementary obverse of abjuring of a collectivist global political horizon in favor of a localized ethics of peaceful exchange. This shift in the literary and ideological imaginary of *indigenista* narratives responds to the carnage unleashed by the revolutionary experiences of the twentieth century across the globe. Castigating subversive violence as much as the authoritarian excess of socialist regimes and insurgencies in Latin America, such a *postrevolutionary consciousness* promotes an unconditional respect for the life of the Other, a defense of human rights above all ideological motivations, and finally a vindication of democratic politics against totalitarian temptation. In this process, Bruno Bosteels argues, one notes not only the proscription of all violent insurgency, but also a disavowal of "political subjectivation as such," so that "the irrefutable radicalism of one's openness to the Other" is sustained precisely "in order preemptively to strike at the dogmatic nature of all processes of political subjectivation" (Bosteels 2012: 305).

Along the same lines, Juan Carlos Ubilluz has recently argued that the movement away from emancipatory politics in Peruvian political history coincides with a historical process that has been named—following Jacques Rancière, Slavoj Žižek and Alain Badiou—"the ethical turn," defining "an ideological posture which consecrates a 'democratic' humanitarian ethic to the point of inhibiting the politics of emancipation" (Ubilluz 2017: 232). Contextually relating the Peruvian situation to the global context, he claims:

This position exists in parallel to the revolutionary sequence, but situates itself in the world from the failure of the Soviet experiment. From then on, the cultural horizon follows the certainty that all revolutions would end in a totalitarian State and in the concentration camp. In fact, in Peru the ethical turn becomes entrenched with even greater strength given the apparition of The Shining Path, with its terrorist attempts, its "retreats" to the mountains and its genocidal incursions against the Indigenous communities.[11] (Ubilluz 2017: 232 my translation here and below)

This general disposition implies also a definitive cessation of the dream of universality that animated Mariátegui's conception of an "active philosophy," binding autonomous processes in the arts, sciences and politics.

Moreover, this diagnosis itself corresponds to a global phenomenon: at the outset of *Logics of Worlds*, Alain Badiou names "democratic materialism" the contemporary ideological zeitgeist proper to the ethical turn, prescribing prudence against the temptations of both utopian politics and philosophical universalism. In its ontological basis, democratic materialism upholds the idea that there is only a multiplicity of "bodies and languages," but no universal truths, including those of the political domain, that is, it denies that there is grand transhistorical horizon beyond individual and cultural–linguistic differences to fix the horizon of collective thought and action. The derogation of universalism is then premised on the legal and humanistic protection of the singularity of what Badiou calls "the rights of the living":

> [T]he contemporary consensus, in recognizing the plurality of languages, presupposes their juridical equality. Hence, the assimilation of humanity to animality culminates in the identification of the human animal with the diversity of its sub-species and the democratic rights that inhere in this diversity [...] democratic materialism does stipulate a global halting point for its multiform tolerance. A language that does not recognize the universal juridical and normative equality of languages does not deserve to benefit from this equality. A language that

---

[11] "Esta postura existe paralelamente a la secuencia revolucionaria, pero se afianza en el mundo a partir del fracaso del experimento soviético. Desde entonces se instala en el horizonte cultural la certea de que todas las revoluciones terminan en el Estado totalitario y el campo de concentración. De hecho, en el Perú el giro ético se afianza con aun mayor fuerza debido a la aparición de Sendero Luminoso, con sus atentados terroristas, sus 'retiradas' al monte y sus incursiones genocidas a las comunidades indígenas."

aims to regulate all other languages and to govern all bodies will be called dictatorial and totalitarian.[12] (Badiou 2008: 2)

Such a democratic materialism has been leveraged to propose a critique of socialist *indigenista* narratives, among others by Mario Vargas Llosa who, in *La utopia arcaica*, argues that the collectivist ideal guiding all revolutionary utopias is grounded in a nefarious desire for "forced collectivization" and "absolute homogeneity," against individual freedoms and differences between individuals. This general disposition, however, also forms part of recent attempts to retrospectively vindicate the indigenista tradition, separating the latter from its integrative–universalist ambitions. For example, Antonio Cornejo Polar's insistence that Arguedas's work is ultimately not oriented toward transcultural synthesis, but rather aims toward a preservation of "heterogeneity" between incommensurable "contexts of production-actualization-consumption." In both cases, the authors emphasize the recognition of difference and tolerance before the Other against what they perceive as the authoritarian excess of utopian, socialist pursuits for integration and homogeneity.

With this said, one might ask: Why should a democratic politics oriented toward humanitarian protection necessarily entail the inhibition of emancipatory politics? Put differently: why is an articulation of revolutionary political and artistic production incompatible in principle with democracy or with the protection of "human rights," if after all the latter cannot but presume a given standard for universality that ethically binds all individuals and cultures? Is not the circumscription of politics to a respect for human *rights* and a democratic *state*, at best, a reformist agenda that ratifies the sovereignty of Western juridical norms and values? The very essence of the "generic communism" imagined by Marx in the 1844 philosophical manuscripts and the antistatist modality of Leninist politics, Badiou argues, clearly establish the incompatibility between a democracy subordinate to state politics and the politics of emancipation:

> [Marx] [...] insists that democracy should in truth always be understood as a form of State. "Form" means a particular configuration of the separate character of the State and of the formal exercise of sovereignty. In declaring democracy to be a form of State, Lenin enters into the filiation of classical political thought, including that of Greek philosophy,

---

12 Badiou, Alain. *Logics of Worlds: Being and Event II*, translated by Alberto Toscano, Continuum, 2008, p. 2.

which declares that "democracy" must ultimately be thought as a figure of sovereignty or power: the power of the demos or the people; the capacity of the demos to exert coercion for itself. [...]

If democracy is a form of State, what strictly philosophical use is this category destined to have? For Lenin, the aim or idea of politics is the withering away of the State, the classless society, and therefore the disappearance of every form of State, including, quite obviously, the democratic form. This is what one might call generic communism, whose principle is provided by Marx in the 1844 Manuscripts.[13] (Badiou 2005: 79)

If the institutional frame of democratic politics remains inextricably bound to state sovereignty, however, it remains unclear why the revolutionary path requires a violent confrontation with this power, a confrontation ultimately destined to betray its own aims, perpetuating brutally authoritarian forms of governance. The implicit premise is that any attempt to pursue the derogation of institutional power can only do so by unwittingly reiterating what it seeks to overthrow. It would be no different for *indigenista* socialists: Was not the imagined "national consciousness" woven from "everyone's blood" but a justification for forced collectivization and insurgency by imposing "absolute homogeneity" in the social order?

Along these lines, Vargas Llosa argues that the utopianism of socialist *indigenista* narratives reveals the lingering idealist kernel underlying the "materialist" rhetoric of integration as collectivization. For it is impossible, he claims, to form a cohesive set from the differences that divide individuals and groups, and even more so to formulate a criterion from which common destinies could be anticipated or prescribed:

Other than in an administrative and symbolic sense—that is to say, the most precarious there is—"The Peruvian" does not exist. There are only Peruvians, a panoply of races, cultures, languages, degrees of life, uses and customs, more different than similar to the other, whose common denominator reduces, in most cases, to living in the same territory, submitted to the same authority.[14] (Vargas Llosa 1993: 210–11, my translation here and below)

---

13 Badiou, Alain. *Metapolitics*, translated by Jason Barker, Verso, 2005.
14 "Salvo en un sentido administrativo y simbólico—es decir, el más precario que cabe—,'lo peruano' no existe. Sólo existen los peruanos, abanico de razas, culturas, lenguas, niveles de vida, usos y costumbres, más distintos que parecidos entre sí, cuyo

In the last instance, having reduced the fictional integrity of the coming nation to an irreducible difference, the telos of socialism is diagnosed as inherently pathological. The impetus against representation and mimicry would then be realized not in the fantasy of an authentically self-representing and self-emancipating transcultural subject, but rather in relinquishing the very desire for authentic representation and the ideal of a collective destiny under a cohesive "national consciousness." Far from freeing themselves of idealization in the name of a "materialist" science of history and social realist aesthetic mode in literary matters, socialist *indigenista* narratives would have remained just as idealized as any other utopian vision that takes as a historical necessity what is in truth an ideologically mediated fiction.

Seen in this light, Rivera Martínez's postrevolutionary prospects aim to correct the utopian idealism of the socialist imaginary through ethical and humanistic attunement: a new subject, embryonic but pure, situated beyond the hostilities of racism and classism, capable of bridging comprehension between different cultures and traversing social fragmentation by transcultural exchange. Moreover, *País de Jauja* realizes what, according to Vargas Llosa, would amount to nothing less than a corrected Arguedas: a return to the oneiric tenderness, ethical innocence and sentimental pathos from *Los ríos profundos*, decanted from all subversive furor. The tender and unwritten innocence of Ernesto's empathic gaze becomes then reinscribed and cleansed in Claudio's patient labor of human exchange and growth. Rivera Martinez would have succeeded in giving shape to an *indigenismo* under a reformed *critical realism*, freed from utopianism, at once representing the oppression of the Indian without confusing itself for a model for future society.

Beyond the Ethical Turn: The Critique of Violence and the Politics of Creation

The apparent choice between the authoritarian tendencies of utopian idealism and critical realism enjoins us to raise the question we suggested above once more: Why are aspirations toward universality and utopia rendered *necessarily* incompatible with a democratic politics or pathologically destined to a vindication of insurrectionary violence? More precisely, why is the integrative ideal of socioeconomic equality deemed inherently incompatible with the preservation of heterogeneity? Such a conclusion certainly follows if one

---

denominador común se reduce, en la mayoría de los casos, a vivir en un mismo territorio y sometidos a una misma autoridad."

collapses, as Vargas Llosa does, the general idea of collective organization and the desire for "forced collectivization," where the pursuit of equality or integration is equivalent to a desire to abolish diversity. But to essentialize the link between emancipatory politics and violent insurrection is not so much to castigate utopian excess as to proscribe opposition to state power when it consolidates itself under the aegis of democracy.[15] The sovereignty of state democracy, it would follow, simply cannot be challenged outside of its own selective procedures and institutions. However susceptible to repression and corruption these institutions might be, their continuity and integrity is to be protected, for they eventually will be the bringers of prosperity and peace. Accordingly, whatever deficiencies such democracies might suffer, these cannot be equated with the horrors of totalitarian violence; if nothing else, democratic governance appears as "the lesser evil" in relation to revolutionary-totalitarian politics.

This historical constellation corresponds to what Slavoj Žižek names "the liberal utopia," which encapsulates the idea of liberal democracy as the "best possible world," rendering itself immune to challenge as an instance of sovereign power.

> The claim to want nothing but the lesser of evils, once asserted as the principle of the new global order, gradually takes over the very feature of its enemy it wanted to fight. The global liberal order clearly asserts itself as the best of all possible worlds; the modest rejection of utopias ends with imposing its own market-liberal utopia which will become reality when we will properly apply market and legal Human Rights mechanisms. Behind all this lurks the ultimate totalitarian nightmare, the vision of a New Man who left behind the old ideological baggage. (Žižek 2007)

The irony is thus that the anti-utopian fervor of proponents of the ethical turn is premised on a utopian idealization of democratic politics and its institutionalized forms of legal-representative power as the only admissible vehicles

---

15 It is not sufficient to claim that the revolutionary imaginary projects "ideal fictions" which it confuses for social reality; for one of Marx's essential points is that capitalism itself functions as a system woven from "real abstractions," historically realized in its specific social and economic productive modes of organization, for example, the concepts of value, commodity, labor. See Brassier, Ray. "Concrete-in-Thought, Concrete-in-Act: Marx, Materialism and the Exchange of Abstraction," *Crisis and Critique*, Vol. 5, no. 1, 2018, pp. 111–119.

toward social emancipation. To the extent that such institutions and such power, however, can be seen as no less susceptible to corruption and violence than what they seek to oppose, the "liberal utopia" is itself in need of criticism and retrospective assessment, and with it the prospects for a emancipatory politics.

These observations, however, immediately suggest the following question: If the ideal of collective emancipation were to be successfully dissociated from a violent utopianism of the sort denounced by proponents of the ethical turn, while also challenging the limits of the democratic sovereign state, then what form could it take? Not without modesty, Juan Carlos Ubilluz (2017) proposes that the ensuing legacy of the socialist *indigenista* tradition goes beyond a reactive-critical gesture against hegemonic powers, but also carries the promise of following the emerging social movements of its time, as it "enables the thought of a literature that not only denounces the crimes of the state or of the progressive party (as that of armed conflict) but follows closely current processes"[16] (Ubilluz 2017: 245). In turn, Bruno Bosteels (2012) insists that, before any reactivation of positive emancipatory goals can be achieved, a retrospective *critical* task is in order, avoiding facile moralism or blind exculpation. To accomplish this retrospective critical task, Alain Badiou (1975) gives a general imperative or "axiom": to avoid at all costs the reduction of political issues to the terms of what he names "post-political discourse," directed against the perils of extremism, fanaticism, totalitarianism, and so on. For the moralist abhorrence and legalist-humanitarian circumscription guiding the rhetoric of democratic materialism results in complacency before hegemonic state power in the name of a fetishized "democratic" ideal. At heart, for Badiou, revolutionary consciousness must interrogate and displace the role of insurrectionary violence within the materialist dialectic of history and its understanding of emancipatory action.

Already in his 1975 book *Theory of the Subject*, Badiou denounces the moralist castigation of "totalitarian terror" for its political impotence, arguing that "the denunciation of the repressive and bloody character of a mode of politics does not amount to the real criticism of this politics, nor does it ever enable one to be done with it" (Badiou 2009: 294). To initiate the necessary historical critique, Badiou traces the issue back to Hegel's account of the "Reign of Terror" in *The Phenomenology of Spirit*, which appears as a necessary moment

---

[16] "A su vez, el estudio de la narrativa indigenista ayuda pensar la posibilidad de una literatura que no solo denuncie los crímenes de Estado o del partido vanguardista (como la del conflicto armado) sino que siga de cerca procesos políticos actuales."

where "absolute freedom" and "sacrificial death" are dialectically identified in a purely negative movement toward universality:

> Universal freedom, therefore, can produce neither a positive work nor a deed; there is left only *negative* action; it is merely the fury of *destruction*. [...] The sole work and deed of universal freedom is therefore death, a death too which has no inner significance or filling, for what is negated is the empty point of the absolutely free will. It is thus the coldest and meanest of all deaths, with no more significance than cutting off a head of cabbage or swallowing a mouthful of water.[17] (Hegel 2018: 235–36)

Badiou does not shy away from accepting the idea that such a destructive moment is essential to the process of subjectivation, but follows Marx in localizing revolutionary agency in a process that does not identify with but separates itself from state power. For revolutionary terror is not, as Hegel conceived, a despotic violence that functions as "the mechanical result of the modern State" or as the "faction of the victorious" taking the place of power. Rather, it concentrates collective action so as to become subtracted from state power, by dismantling the machinery of capitalist production.

In the classical Marxist narrative, the subtractive process outlined before occurs through the projected escalation of class struggle, which finally unravels the class system supporting the proletariat's identity as a wage laborer as it destroys the machinery of capitalist appropriation. For Badiou, as for Marx, the revolutionary subjective process, however, cannot be reduced to a *destruction* of Law, or to proletariat insurgency, since the revolutionary act would thus relapse into a purely negative gesture, driven by a nihilistic anxiety where "the real kills the symbolical, rather than splitting it [...] [and] subjectivation blocks the rule without annulling its space" (Badiou 2009: 291). In other words, Badiou argues that the revolutionary act is not only a "blocking" of the existing law but its "splitting," a "blurring of the places" under which the collective is structurally repositioned in a local situation (Ibid.). In short, the critical assessment of revolutionary violence, Badiou claims, begins not by analyzing the *objective* effects of the acts themselves on the basis of an antecedently agreed legal–moral register. Rather, it begins by recognizing the one-sidedness of a subjective disposition whose antagonistic furor becomes voided of positive content to the point of impotence, thus revealing "anxiety's

---

17 Hegel. G. W.F. *The Phenomenology of Spirit*, translated by Michael Inwood, Oxford University Press, 2018.

incapacity to effectuate the division" (Ibid.: 293). As Bosteels emphasizes, the revolutionary subject to come must thus effectuate the "internalization of the past" in which "shame, anxiety and uncertainty" prevent a relapse into the temptation of power. This is the imperative for an emancipatory political act whose subversive potential may be achieved without taking the place of state power:

> [I]f authoritarianism always lies in wait as a sinister constitutive outside of all democracy precisely due to the totalitarian desire to incarnate it, then the new radical politics to come will consist in keeping firm in the shame, the anxiety, and in the uncertainty, without giving in to the impudence of wanting to fill the empty place of power—that is, without giving in to the metaphysical temptation to give body to the ghost of effective justice. (Bosteels 2012: 187)

The message is therefore clear: the revolutionary process is irreducible to destruction or antagonism, but involves the constructive vision of what Vallejo named in *Salutación angélica* "the time of harvest," after the time of war and beyond insurrectionary furor (cf. Chapter II). Such reconstitution cannot be idealized as an unperturbed process *after* the revolutionary process, however, but must be seen as immanent to it, leading to the construction of a new mode of organization and production for society beyond state power and class difference.

In a more recent formulation, as we briefly surmised in the first chapter, Badiou goes on to explain this positive function inherent to the revolutionary act as a process of *subtraction* from, rather than mere *destruction* of, the Law, through which the bodies and languages which democratic materialism deem irreducible become incorporated into a new collective process. Accordingly, Badiou identifies two "deviations" in the revolutionary process: a toothless reformism that obviates the role of destruction ("subtraction without destruction"), and the nihilistic-anarchic reduction of revolution to violent sublimation, underwritten by anxiety ("destruction without subtraction"):

> [I]f destruction is separated from subtraction, we have as result the impossibility of politics, because young people are absorbed in a sort of nihilistic collective suicide, which is without thinking and destination. [...]
> We can now conclude: the political problems of the contemporary world cannot be solved, neither in the weak context of democratic opposition, which in fact abandons millions of people to a nihilistic destiny,

nor in the mystical context of destructive negation, which is another form of power, the power of death. Neither subtraction without destruction, nor destruction without subtraction. It is in fact the problem of violence today. Violence is not, as has been said during the last century, the creative and revolutionary part of negation. The way of freedom is a subtractive one; but to protect the subtraction itself, to defend the new kingdom of emancipatory politics, we cannot radically exclude all forms of violence. [...] We have to learn something of nihilistic subjectivity.[18] (Badiou 2007)

Badiou's argumentation entails the reformation of the revolutionary subject in its bases, thinking the indissociable link between antagonistic resistance and creative action as part of the singular process of "subtraction." In the same direction, as we have seen, Mariátegui's voluntarist emphasis on affirmation was premised precisely as overcoming both the nihilistic sublimation of a pure anarchic confrontation with the mestizo (as in the late work of González Prada) and the distorting idealizations of the Indian which obfuscate its structural subjugation under the latifundio in an idealized vision. The concrete negation of the latifundio could only be accomplished by satisfying the *demand* of the Indian's right to land, not in the legalist sense of assimilating it into the small-property ownership of a new capitalist class, but rather by constructing an integral social collective of workers and intellectuals, as well as Indigenous and Western forms of production. In Badiou's terms, we can thus say that creative antagonism, at heart, "subtracts" the rural Indian from its structural subordination to the mestizo rule, conceiving of an alternative that supersedes both the medieval vestiges of the latifundio and liberal capitalist modernity. Radicalizing this basic impetus, Arguedas established the indissociable bind between a new subjective disposition toward labor and a new productive model for society, avowing the particularity of Indigenous culture in conceiving of the potentials for integration. Without the latter, he argued, one simply could not understand the bond that organized the cooperativist economy of the ayllu. Rather than assaulting heterogeneity in the name of collectivization, Arguedas's revolutionary agency gave way to integrative figures of a post-Indigenous and even post-cultural subject which, like Vallejo's generic human subject, was built from the inexhaustible differences and identities

---

18 Badiou, Alain. "Destruction, Negation, Subtraction," presented at Art Center College of Design in Pasadena—February 6 2007. Full text available at: http://www.lacan.com/badpas.htm.

composing Peruvian society, however fractured in their individualities, even when torn from their place of origin and their cultural milieu.

In the last instance, the project of a Peruvian socialism imagined by *indigenista* writers was also one that expressed a unique reformulation of the universalist and utopian aspirations of revolutionary politics, attending to the priority of integrative production as primary in relation to the uniqueness of Peruvian social reality. If a universalism can never be an idealism that distorts and elides the intricacies of the particular, then a fetishistic "telluric" localism can neither be an authentic regionalism, insofar as one severs the particular from the larger contextual–historical placement. As Nick Srnicek and Alex Williams (2016) put it, following Ernesto Laclau's logic of "populist reason," universality cannot be conceived abstractly, divided from its structural place; the universal is always a particular that concentrates a site of collective "hegemonic struggle," woven from and productive of differences:

> Universals emerge when a particular comes to occupy this position through hegemonic struggle. [...] The universal, then, is an empty placeholder that hegemonic particulars (specific demands, ideals and collectives) come to occupy. It can operate as a subversive and emancipatory vector of change with respect to established universalisms, and it is heterogeneous and includes differences, rather than eliminating them. (Srnicek and Williams 2015: 77-78)[19]

This impetus toward the necessity of new constructive mediations is, more than any antiquated ancestralism, the promise and aspiration that guided the revolutionary sequence of *indigenista* thinking, and the perceived role that intellectuals, philosophy and literature should play in relation to emancipatory ends. It is this aspect of Mariátegui's conception of socialist philosophy, as a productive practice, that must be salvaged through the critical retrospective task, to bear on the assessment of the violent legacy of Peruvian socialism, beyond the indictments of a facile moralism. For Mariátegui recognized as the essence of the *indigenista* moment and promise, above all, the disciplined experimental labor which allowed a critical approximation of social reality through new theoretical principles, aesthetic paradigms and political ideals.

---

19 Srnicek, Nick, and Alex Williams. *Inventing the Future: Postcapitalism and a World Without Work*, Verso, 2015.

The Collapse of Socialist Productivism and the Proletariat Subject

Nevertheless, as we have seen, Arguedas attested to the failure of attempts to align revolutionary politics with a figure of the transcultural subject, through which Indigenous culture would not only survive but actively participate in the constitution of a new collective spirit. Facing the dissolution of cultural identity through urbanization as depicted in *The Foxes*, Arguedas timidly sought to find the conditions for a new subject in such a latent inconsistency and inarticulacy, to no avail. With no concrete expression in the syndicate, party or the cultural bond of the community, this subject existed only as a wandering abstraction within the urban capitalist space; it was not a figure of proletariat collective insurgency, but an indiscernible voice emerging from a growing surplus population. In Arguedas's waning, uncertain hope, this nameless universality becomes but an abstract insinuation of a different future, a faint murmur of Vallejo's radiant universality, woven from what we called "the rabble of culture"—that is, from the aberrant subjectivities born of a thwarted modernity.

More broadly, the crisis of the Peruvian socialist dream becomes symptomatic of and continuous with the problematic search for a new image of the political subjective process and its ultimate result, traversing the critique of violence and the affirmation of creation. For once the productivist ambition to supersede capitalism as a mode of production is shorn from programmatic specificity, revolutionary action becomes only measurable against the exorbitant capacity of global capitalism to assimilate crises, suppressing every form of collective struggle by internalization. Put differently, without the economicist hope to "free the forces of production from capitalist relations of production," the revolutionary dream becomes incapable of producing a concrete vision of the future, and the celebration of construction and invention rings hollow.

Explaining the global failures of the classical Marxist dialectic when anticipating capitalist momentum and the ultimate advent of a postcapitalist society, Nick Land diagnoses two principal factors: (1) its *theoretical* incapacity to anticipate how the prospects of an escalating contradiction between capital and labor would be modulated by ever more prescient bureaucratic-political intervention into the dynamics of market, thereby restricting the nihilist tendencies of competition; (2) the *practical* failure of socialist regimes and experiments to realize the promise of a superior mode of production to capitalism in practice, that is, the failure of the productivist dream (Land 1992: 38).

Despite its manifold adaptations and overt resistance to economist dogmatism, these general problems clearly become revealed in the Peruvian historical process, eroding the socialist dream of economic and cultural appropriation. The failure of potentiating the productive prowess of rural peasant communities toward the constitution of a "global proletariat" not only faced the insurmountable problem of their inarticulacy but, moreover, underestimated the assimilation of rural labor by capital in the cities after the collapse of the latifundio. It is hardly surprising, then, that Arguedas's late work becomes depleted of the strategic, positive clarity proper to the transcultural hero and national dream in *Todas las sangres*, returning instead to the amorphousness of Vallejo's stateless subject. As the attempt to amend Marxian economism relinquishes aspirations for an alternative mode of production, the revolutionary subject and the future of collectivism can only appear on condition of its unrecognizability, which is to say, its programmatic vacuity.

Perhaps because of the conceptual and practical difficulty of matching the productivity of capital by formulating a productivist alternative, such obscurity paradoxically becomes transvalued into the only gesture of uncompromising resistance. For instance, Slavoj Žižek defines the revolutionary subjective spirit as carrying simultaneously an absolute *resignation* in the face of an impossible future and the universal *enthusiasm* of traversing this impossibility: "Enthusiasm and resignation, then, are not two opposite moments: it is the 'resignation' itself, that is to say, the experience of a certain impossibility, that incites enthusiasm"[20] (Žižek 1990: 259). Finding solace in defeat, this gesture transforms impotence into the promise of victory, such that revolutionary action can only proceed from the absolute refusal of programmatic specificity.[21] Only a powerless, reactive subjectivity remains, no longer underwritten

---

20 Žižek, Slavoj. "Beyond Discourse-Analysis," in *Reflections of our time*, by Ernesto Laclau, Verso, 1990, pp. 249–260.
21 It is instructive to understand the essential underestimation of capitalism which inheres in traditional Marxist historicism, which remains centered in the thought of a process of a central escalating contradiction (labor and capital) which ultimately sublimates the difference between the terms. This is the generative dynamic leading to the conditions for revolutionary moment, by virtue of which urbanization disintegrates the autonomy of rural economies through the expropriation of land, and the absorption of workers into industrial wage labor, that is, the process by which the European peasantry underwent a process of capitalist "enclosure" at the end of the fifteenth and beginning of the sixteenth century, reiterated in the Peruvian situation

by the anxiety of terror, but rather by the lull of resignation. Shorn from all positive content, such a vision camouflages a general impotence in response to the voracious tendency of capitalism to reintegrate all qualitative forms into its ruthless expansion and self-transformation. As collective resignation and enthusiasm become pragmatically indiscernible, in the end it becomes evident that collective production and the dynamics of market competition cannot be pulled so easily apart. Unable to match the protean capacity of capitalist production, such a politics diagnoses the positive project to think a different future as inherently pathological.[22] Land names this position "transcendental miserabilism" and uses it to designate the pessimism of the predominant "Frankfurtian spirit" that overtakes the socialist imaginary once productivist ambitions collapse:

> The Frankfurtian spirit now rules: Admit that capitalism will outperform its competitors under almost any imaginable circumstances, while turning that very admission into a new kind of curse. [...] [N]o substantial residue of Marxian historicism remains in the "communist" version of this posture. In fact, with economics and history comprehensively abandoned, all that survives of Marx is a psychological bundle of resentments and disgruntlements, reducible to the word "capitalism" in its vague and negative employment: as the name for everything that hurts, taunts and disappoints. [...]
>
> The Marxist dream of dynamism without competition was merely a dream, an old monotheistic dream re-stated, the wolf lying down with the lamb. If such a dream counts as "imagination," then imagination is no more than a defect of the species: the packaging of tawdry contradictions as utopian fantasies, to be turned against reality in the service of sterile negativity. "Post-capitalism" has no real meaning except an end to the engine of change. (Land 2012: 623–26)

The obscure image of the future given in Arguedas's last novel emerges as the natural result of the ongoing unraveling of the revolutionary prospect, and

---

under the migratory economic transformation coeval with the liquidation of the latifundio after the agrarian reform.

22 See Critchley, Simon. "Declaration on the Notion of the Future," at *The International Necronautical Society* December 2010, http://www.believermag.com/issues/201011/?read=article_necronautical

as creation becomes assimilated into the vortex of capitalist modernization. After all, Mariátegui's hope for productive appropriation of the collectivist labor of the *ayllu*, and Arguedas's derailed transcultural dream to reconcile the "rational and magical conceptions of the world" in a postcapitalist world, were still guided by the prospect of a possible peace between the pursuit of productive success and a collective loyalty between social–cultural groups or classes to social ends. A peace, that is, capable of avoiding the atomization brought about under capitalist modernization, industrial wage labor and the cannibalistic tendencies of market competition.

The Crisis of Democracy and the Peruvian Situation Today

Given the obscurity that shrouds the idea of a "postcapitalist future" and the nefarious legacy of past insurgencies, it comes as no surprise that the predominant political orientation of socialist thinkers has been to progressively move away from the utopian aspirations of revolutionary politics. Postrevolutionary socialists and anti-utopian humanitarian democrats agree on one fundamental point: beyond implausible collectivist utopias, a powerful and efficient state is ultimately necessary for social emancipation to obtain. A far cry from the internationalist and post-state politics of revolutionary socialism, nationalism and state expansion are thus considered necessary instruments to guarantee social justice. Under the juridical protection of a democratic politics, grounded in a respect for human rights, one hopes that the expansion of state power may be leveraged efficiently within a market economy to emancipatory ends. Only then can the egalitarian ideal attain a tolerable degree of traction on social reality. As far as radical emancipatory projects go, these tend to wallow in the absence of productivist postcapitalist and post-statist ambition, absorbed within the scope of horizontal and local struggle, as universalism dissolves into divergent forms of regionalist politics. As Ray Brassier argues, this moderation emerges as perhaps the most salient feature of the collapse of the communist project and its association with totalitarian rule:

> This scaling down of political ambition by those who espouse the ideals of justice and emancipation is perhaps the most notable consequence of the collapse of communism as a Promethean project. The best we can hope for, apparently, is to create local enclaves of equality and justice. But the idea of remaking the world according to the ideals of equality

and justice is routinely denounced as a dangerous totalitarian fantasy.[23] (Brassier 2014: 469)

The question dividing the political spectrum will be then that of specifying the admissible balance between the private and public powers, and the reach of the state to intervene into the dynamics of market in the interest of social utility. Where the extension of the state does not relapse into the temptation of authoritarian repression, the socialist embrace of institutional governance within a democratic political frame also fulfills the public demand for historic repentance: it disavows the tragedies of the insurgent past, without thereby betraying the pursuit of equality. The Marxian, utopian aspirations for a "postcapitalist" and "post-state" society are in this way scaled down: the collective organization of civil society is expressed by and delimited to participation in local-horizontal struggle or state politics, while electoral representation through the party and the syndicate concentrates and redirects social demand to the state machinery, as well as to the private sector.

The consolidation of new democratic socialist groups within the last decades in Peruvian political history illustrates this process with clarity: following the radical subversive uprising of the Shining Path and the Tupac Amaru Revolutionary Movement, the country saw economic growth in tandem with the atomization of new leftist fronts, aiming at electoral representation. These would remain in close connection not only with various labor unions and syndicalist institutions but also with emerging organizations addressing issues of cultural, ethnic and gender rights. A new, social democratic left thus extended the integrative ideal to different forms of minoritarian struggle and public discontent, linking with the representation of Indigenous communities in the provinces. The task of collective political organization was in this way taken beyond the party and syndicate, to the oftentimes disjointed labor of NGOs and humanitarian groups, making the prospects of a general consensus toward a singular "leftist front" increasingly precarious.

A brief retrospective is in order: in 1978, the Revolutionary Vanguard (*Vanguardia Revolucionaria*) convened with 14 other syndical groups in the formation of the Popular Democratic Unity (*Unidad democratica y popular*) (UDP), participating in that year's election of the Constitutional Assembly. In 11 September 1980, the UDP, alongside several other leftist

---

23 Brassier, Ray, "Prometheanism and its Critics," in *#Accelerate: The Accelerationist Reader*, Urbanomic, 2014.

parties and groups, became part of the new coalition party, the United Left (*Izquierda unida*), achieving considerable electoral support in the 1980 and 1983 municipal elections.[24] In 1984, a group led by José Diez Canseco founded the Mariáteguist Union (*Unidad Mariáteguista*), leading to the formation of the Unified Mariáteguist Party (*Partido unificado mariáteguista*) (PUM), attaining second place in the 1984 presidential elections in coalition with the United Left, only to disintegrate by 1990. The PUM explicitly identified itself with a rekindling of Mariátegui's ideal to adapt socialism to Peruvian reality through the syndical-party organization of rural and urban workers, only this time under the institutional mantle of participative democracy. In doing so, they converged toward traditional forms of social democracy, issuing a demand for the nationalization of natural resources, rights for the Indigenous communities, and a stimulation of internal market toward economic decentralization. The PUM expanded its representative bases representative bases, organizing worker groups to include concerned with issues of ethnicity, gender, ecology and cultural rights, that is, under growing hegemony of so-called identity politics. It reconvened its bases under the name Peruvian Socialist Party (*Partido socialista del Perú*) in 2006. It would later unite with various other groups in 2012—predominantly, through the leadership and electoral inscription of Marco Arana's ecologist group *Tierra y Libertad*—in the formation of another leftist coalition: the Broad Front (*El frente amplio*), which quickly gained significant momentum.[25]

Through the candidacy of Veronika Mendoza, the 2016 electoral contest saw *El frente amplio* reintroduce the principles outlined by the PUM to the national agenda, adapting Mariátegui's ideals to a reformist-institutional agenda.[26] The historic "problem of the land" that determined the fate of the rural Indian was in this way aligned with a prospective shift in the nation's industrial priorities toward a stimulation of internal markets, a progressive movement toward the formalization of labor and the legal reinforcement of ecological and property rights in Indigenous communities. With regard to the

---

24 These comprised the following associations, comprising a wide range of leftist ideological orientations: *Partido Comunista Peruano, Partido Comunista Revolucionario, Frente Obrero Estudiantil y Popular, Unión de Izquierda Revolucionaria, Unidad Democrática Popular, Partido Comunista de Perú—Patria Roja*.
25 These comprised the following: *Ciudadanos por el Cambio, Movimiento de Afirmación Social, Tierra y Libertad, Fuerza Social, Patria Roja, Partido Socialista del Perú*.
26 The complete governmental plan of *El Frente Amplio* can be found in full at: http://aplicaciones013.jne.gob.pe/pecaoe/sipe/PlanGobiernoPDF.aspx?koznY8YcptP43Os e4J6sXEp7zp8dpHvRUaHy9cZM4BU

latter, the choice between a collective or small-property model for Indigenous communities that divided socialists and liberals persisted at the core of the political debate, however stripped from any larger prospect toward appropriation or integration in a post-market economy. In particular, the economic program proposed by *El frente amplio*—elaborated, among others, by the economists Pedro Francke and Oscar Dancourt—moved away from the predominant "trickle-down" economics (*"chorreo"*) of the "extractivist" primary export model of the last decades,[27] driven by the revenue accrued from the mining industrial sector. In turn, they proposed a diversification of economic productivity, oriented toward the growth of internal markets; emphasizing, for example, agriculture and tourism through the extension of credit for small entrepreneurs and farmers.

In the political domain, the new leftist front opposed social conflict, generated above all in the state violence against Indigenous communities protesting the incursion of mining companies into their territories. This was considered as much a matter of historic retribution as a question of economic reform. This required, it was argued, both a regulation of the private sector and a protection of the collective property rights of the Indigenous communities, against the atomizing tendencies of capitalism. As Zulema Burneo de la Rocha writes with regard to the effects of the growth of the mining enterprise since the 1990s for rural communities:

> The community's collective property is affected, since mining ventures are generally "open pit." The community cannot oppose itself legally to the giving of a mining concession; at most, it may demand a payment for the lands in which he won't be able to work during the mining operations, and an additional indemnity in case a building belonging to the community is damaged. (Burneo de la Rocha 2008: 6)

The protection of the integrity of the rural Indigenous collectivist practices was thus conceived in a protectionist form as the obverse of state regulation

---

27 It was argued that mining could not continue to be the primary motor of economic and social growth in the decades to come, for economic, ecological and social reasons: the international fall in the prices of minerals (particularly, for Peruvian production, those of copper and gold) in relation to the 2002–14 period, as the de-accelerating growth of the Chinese economy lowered the demand and prices considerably; the persistent environmental contamination and ecologically unsustainable extractive practices produced by the mining enterprise against the will of the communities, and in violation of their property and human rights.

of private companies, rather than as part of a larger social project of potentiation. It finds its proximate origins in the so-called *New Land Law* ("*Nueva ley de tierras*"), passed during the Fujimori regime in 1995, which promoted the integration of the rural economy into the market by allowing the transfer of land by individual families, seeking to create thus a small-property class of landowners within the communities.[28]

As Jorge Luis González Angulo argues, this led to the fragmentation of land ownership, unraveling the legal basis for the collective property model to survive:

> To give the community the faculties to decide [for a privatization of the land] and take from it the legal protection that it enjoyed in the 1979 Constitution signifies, in general terms, to leave aside that form of communal organization, to extract it from the system and abort it as an institution.[29] (González Angulo 2004: 99)

To address the internal fissure within the communities that resulted from the privatization of the land, *El frente amplio* proposed a fortification of a collective property rights schema for Indigenous communities, implying the derogation of the New Law, and even a return to the legislation of the 1979 Constitution, which proscribed individual-familial transfer of communal land. This alternative, however, arguably conflicts with a long-standing sentiment of those commoners who saw the "liberalization of the land" as a means to escape the protectionist authority of community leaders.

> Individual ownership would liberate them from the social control that the community still exerts over productive decisions, and they would be able to ask for credit to financial entities and banks. This does not imply, however, that commoners desire the dissolution of the community. [...] What is true is that the community leaders and guild representatives at the regional and national levels have a strong position against individual

---

28 See Eleodoro Romero Romaña's *Derechos Reales*, Volume II, Second edition 1993.
29 González Angulo, Jorge Luis, "La nueva ley de tierras y el derecho de propiedad de las comunidades campesinas," in *Themis*, 2004, pp. 95–100. Available at: http://revistas.pucp.edu.pe/index.php/themis/article/download/11484/12004

> "Sin embargo, otorgar a la Comunidad la facultad de adoptar tal decisión y restarle la protección legal de que gozaba con la derogada Constitución de 1979, significa, en términos latos, dejar de lado esta forma de organización comunal, extraerla del sistema y abortarla como instituto."

ownership of the lands. They demand even a return to the protectionism of communal property [guaranteed by the 1979 Constitution], which the community would not have freedom to dispose of their lands.[30] (Burneo de la Rocha 2008: 7)

This internal rift affecting the rural indian populations indicates that the contradiction between the collectivist principles of the community and the individual private thrust of the cities has become internalized and redoubled within the communities themselves, facing the historic stagnation of the rural economy, as well as the pressures and incentives of integration into the market economy. Reinforcing the regulation of private companies, and in response to the prescient divide between the state and rural Indian communities, *El frente amplio* promoted enhanced mechanisms of approximation to and incorporation of the rural communities into the political decision-making process of debate through the practice of "prior consultation" ("*consulta previa*"), guaranteeing the sovereignty of the communities over their territories.[31] If a productive dynamism without market mechanisms remains unthinkable, it was hoped, at least the state may tame the market toward social ends. And if the idea of a new revolutionary subject remains proscribed, at least the organization of dissent in mass protests into the reformist demands may function as the democratic watchdog for the state, protecting the human integrity and cultural autonomy of rural populations.

There are several problems with these programmatic prospects, but they are fundamentally related to the historical rift between civil society and its representative powers, given the state's institutional precariousness, and its

---

30 Burneo de la Rocha, Zulema, "La propiedad colectiva y las comunidades campesinas del Perú," CEPES. Text available at: http://www.cepes.org.pe/pdf/observatorio_tierras/propiedad_colectiva_tierra.pdf

> "Al decir de algunos comuneros, el título individual los liberaría del control social que aún ejerce la comunidad sobre las decisiones productivas, les permitiría solicitar créditos a entidades financieras y bancos. Todo lo anterior, no implica, sin embargo, que los comuneros deseen la disolución de la comunidad. [...] Lo cierto es que líderes comunales y representantes gremiales a niveles regionales y nacionales tienen una fuerte postura contraria a la titulación individual de las tierras. Ellos reclaman incluso la vuelta al proteccionismo de la propiedad comunal, con lo cual la comunidad campesina no tendría libre disponibilidad de sus tierras."

31 Cynthia A. Sanborn, Verónica Hurtado, Tania Ramírez, "La consulta previa en el Perú: avances y retos," in *Diario Uno*, August 10, 2016. Available at http://diariouno.pe/2016/08/10/fa-presenta-proyecto-de-ley-para-mejorar-consulta-previa/

concomitant incapacity to ensure representation and suppress corruption through democratic-legal means. As it turns out, the political class consolidated through electoral representation in the decades after the Fujimori dictatorship revealed itself to be no less prone to degeneracy or corruption, and neglect of rural Indigenous communities remained a constant.[32] Facing the greatest crisis of corruption since at least the Fujimori regime in the face of the scandal with the Brazilian construction companies (*"Lava Jato"*) and a growing cannibalistic relation between the major political powers, public distrust extended across all of the state institutions and against the entirety of the political class.[33] The temporary illusion of prosperity generated by the mining export model between the years 2002 and 2014, and the victorious sentiment of democratic recovery after the Fujimori dictatorship, comes to an end as productivity declines, economic growth decelerates and democratic institutions lose the population's trust. Rather than upholding a sanguine liberalism beholden to capitalist competition in a free market, it became apparent that the relation between public and private institutions operated with impunity in a mercantilist economy, in which competition was thwarted by endemic corruption. At a loss for any great national collective projects, civil mobilization remained delimited to acts of protest and manifestations of public dissatisfaction, rather than programmatic consensus centered on proposals. The December 2017 national civilian march, calling for a complete overhaul of the political class (*"Que se vayan todos"*), was perhaps the paradigmatic gesture of this generalized frustration, in which a desperate demand for purification in the absence of constructive ideals was directed against the entire political class, pointing to an institutional crisis.[34] Left at the hands of precarious institutions, mass action devolves into castigation of the memory of dictatorship and outrage against the ubiquity of corruption, expressing the frustration of a population betrayed by its political class, yet unable to consolidate a plausible counter-hegemony. This sequence implied the return to the destructive

---

32 Indeed, the major electoral presidential candidacies and groups that reached or approached power in the last decades have been unduly financed by the corrupt enterprise of the Brazilian companies: see https://elcomercio.pe/politica/contribuciones-intermediarios-jorge-barata-noticia-501801
33 As a point of reference, *Ipsos* reported the following poll figures, dating from December 2017: https://elcomercio.pe/politica/ipsos-57-favor-ppk-deje-cargo-presidente-noticia-482244
34 Secada, Pablo. "Que se vayan todos los corruptos," in *La República*, December 20, 2017, available at: http://larepublica.pe/politica/1160278-marcha-que-se-vayan-todos-los-corruptos-colectivos-salen-a-las-calles-este-miercoles-en-vivo

one-sidedness of collective anxiety, no longer nested in the carnage of revolutionary subversion, but rather in the lull of historical disappointment.

This is the end of the democratic utopia that emerged in the dusk of the Fujimori dictatorship and the concomitant derailment of the revolutionary socialist left. The destiny of *indigenismo* as not only a literary style but as part of a social integrative project becomes equally obscure, as the future remains unthinkable outside the scope of capitalist modernization and as the Andean cultural world continues to unravel. Indeed, the failure to formulate even imaginative potentials for collective emancipation and radical invention within the exigencies of the contemporary world, beyond the historic prescience of fragmentation and alienation, offers no future other than disintegration. For only in retrieving the productivist alternative may the prospects of collective action be situated beyond mere vituperation, and only on those grounds may a relation to the Andean world be conceived beyond the protection of cultural rights—that is, without merely resisting dissolution in the circuit of capitalist production. Such a future, however, cannot merely reiterate the figure of the proletarian revolutionary, or indeed even the post-Indian subjectivity envisaged by Arguedas, but would have to forge unprecedented means of emancipation and collective struggle. Which is not to say, of course, that these multiple figurations for a "Peruvian socialism" remain simply obsolete in the wake of shifting historical circumstances.

From Mariátegui's dream for a "national consciousness," we underscore the practice of an "active philosophy" oriented by the dream of a "national consciousness," integrating aesthetic production and philosophical-literary ideals to political experiments, in a process where theory becomes a matter of appropriative construction in relation to one's historical context. From Vallejo's generic human subject and his aesthetics of transmutation, we underscore the boundless scope of the universalist spirit that aims to traverse national, natural and cultural boundaries, forging an uncompromising concept of justice beyond contingent orders of difference, firmly situating thought beyond the horizon of identity politics under "democratic materialism" and the subjective disposition of the "ethical turn." Finally, from Arguedas's post-Indigenous subject and post-cultural subject, we underscore the inextricability between productivist ambition and cultural–normative determination, in which productive mediations and novel constructions weave themselves from various orders of difference, beyond Manichean contradictions.

Taken together, we can say that the ideal of an "alternative modernity" cannot obtain without a new conception of the emancipatory process, which entails both a new figure of collective subjectivation and a new image of the future. These faint indications, given over to us by the memory not only of failure, but of a persisting labor and hope for social justice, cannot by themselves support the dream of creative integration or be themselves sufficient to produce a new figure of the revolutionary subject. Nor do they prophesy its inevitable emergence, in what would amount to a relapse into teleological delirium. Yet the only possible destiny for the labor of transcultural synthesis, for universality and utopia, to the extent that such a destiny remains not *necessary* but *possible*, is to find the means to subtract the process of collective emancipation from its historical avatars, rekindling the productivist dream beyond the economicist and transcultural configurations offered by the twentieth-century *indigenista* socialist tradition and its postrevolutionary sequels. This project points toward that unmovable kernel which remains invariant in the revolutionary spirit informing the socialist *indigenista* tradition: to transform the present in sight of a possible future, however uncertain, by imagining new forms of collective existence, beyond a world ridden with fragmentation and oppression.

BIBLIOGRAPHY/CITED WORKS

Aragón, Luis. *El proletariado del espíritu*, in *Amauta*: no. 15, Lima, 1928.
Arguedas, José María, *Agua*, 1933. Available at: http://home.snafu.de/angelam/rp/ES/Agua_JMA.pdf
Arguedas, José María. "Evolución de las comunidades indígenas: El Valle de Mantaro y la ciudad de Huancayo," in Revista del Museo Nacional N°26, Lima, 1957, pp. 78–151.
Arguedas, José María. "Folklore del Valle de Mantaro (provincias de Jauja y Concepción): Cuentos mágico-realistas y canciones de fiesta tradicionales," in *Folklore Americano*, Lima, pp. 101–298.
Arguedas, José María, *José María Arguedas. Obra Antropológica*, edited by Sybila Arredondo Arguedas. Lima: Horizonte, 2013.
Arguedas, José María, *La Mesa Redonda sobre Todas las Sangres del 23 de junio 1965*, edited by Guillermo Rochabrún. Lima: Pontificia Universidad Católica del Perú, 2000.
Arguedas, José María. "La Novela y el Problema de la Expresión Literaria en el Perú," in *Qepa Wiñaq [...] Siempre Literatura y antropología*, edited by Dora Sales. Lima: Iberoamericana, 2009.
Arguedas, José María. *No soy un Aculturado*, 1968. Available at: https://www.servindi.org/actualidad/3252
Arguedas, José María. "Primer diario," in *Amaru*, no. 6, April–June, Lima, 1968.
Arguedas, José María. "Razón de ser del indigenismo en el Perú," in *Formación de una cultura nacional indoamericana*, edited by Ángel Rama, México, 1975, p. 192. Lima: The essay was first published in *Visión*, 1970, pp. 43–45.
Arguedas, José María. "Razón de ser del indigenismo en el Perú," in *Formación de una cultura nacional indoamericana*, edited by Ángel Rama, México: Siglo XXI, 1975, p. 192.
Arguedas, José María. *Todas las Sangres*. Lima: Peisa, 2001.
Arguedas, José María. *Yawar Fiesta*, epublibre. Available at: http://files.comunicatodos.webnode.es/200011834-6ab036ba9f/Yawar%20fiesta%20-%20Jose%20Maria%20Arguedas%20(1.)pdf
Arguedas, José María. *Yawar fiesta*. Lima: Editorial Universitaria, 1968.
Arguedas, José María, and Alejandro Romualdo. "Poesía y prosa en el Perú contemporáneo," in *Panorama actual de la literatura latinoamericana*. Madrid: Fundamentos, 1971.
Badiou, Alain. *Age of the Poets: And Other Writings on Twentieth-Century Poetry and Prose*, translated by Bruno Bosteels. New York: Verso, 2014.
Badiou, Alain. *Logics of Worlds: Being and Event II*, translated by Alberto Toscano. New York: Continuum, 2009.
Badiou, Alain. *Metapolitics*, translated by Jason Barker. New York: Verso, 2005.

Badiou, Alain. *Peut-on penser la politique?* Paris: Le Seuil, 2008.
Badiou, Alain. *Subtraction, Destruction, Negation*, presented at UCLA, 2007. Available at: http://www.lacan.com/badpas.htm
Badiou, Alain. *Theory of the Subject*, translated by Bruno Bosteels. Continuum, 2011.
Barbusse, Henri. "El presente y el porvenir," in *Amauta*: New York, no. 8; pp. 9–11.
Bosteels, Bruno. *Marx and Freud in Latin America: Psychoanalysis, and Religion in Times of Terror*. Verso, 2012.
Brassier, Ray. "Concrete-in-Thought, Concrete-in-Act: Marx, Materialism and the Exchange of Abstraction," *Crisis and Critique*, Vol. 5, no. 1, 2018, pp. 111–119. https://crisiscritique.org/2018h/brassier-v1.pdf
Brassier, Ray, "Prometheanism and its Critics," in *The #Accelerate: The Accelerationist Reader*. Falmouth: Urbanomic, 2014.
Burneo de la Rocha, Zulema, *La propiedad colectiva y las comunidades campesinas del Perú*. CEPES, 2005. Available at: http://www.cepes.org.pe/pdf/observatorio_tierras/propiedad_colectiva_tierra.pdf
Castro Arenas, Mario, *La novela peruana y la evolución social*, Lima: J. Godard, 1967.
Tord, Luis Enrique, *El indio en los ensayistas Peruanos 1848–1948*. Lima: Editoriales Unidas, 1978.
César, Ferreira and Ismael P. Márquez, eds., *De lo andino a lo universal: la obra de Edgardo Rivera Martínez*. Lima: Fondo Editorial PUCP, 1999.
Clayton, Michelle. *Poetry in Pieces: César Vallejo and Lyric Modernity*. Berkeley and Los Angeles: UC Press, 2011.
Cornejo Polar, Antonio. "Aves sin Nido como alegoría nacional," in Matto de Turner, Clorinda, *Aves Sin Nido*. Lima: Biblioteca Ayacucho, 1994.
Cornejo Polar, Antonio. "El indigenismo y las literaturas heterogéneas," in *Revista de Crítica Literaria Latinoamericana*. Lima: Latinoamericana Editores, 1978, pp. 6–21.
Cortázar, Julio. "Carta Abierta a Roberto Fernández Retamar," in *SIMO, Ana María. Cinco miradas sobre Cortázar*. Ana Maria: Tiempo Contemporáneo, 1968.
Cortázar, Julio. "Letter to Fernández Retamar," in *Casa de las Américas*, no. 45, 1967. Available at: http://www.mundolatino.org/cultura/juliocortázar/cortázar_3.htm
Coyné, André. *César Vallejo y su obra poética*. Lima: Letras Peruanas, 1957.
Critchley, Simon. "Declaration on the Notion of the Future," at *The International Necronautical Society*, December 2010. Available at: http://www.believermag.com/issues/201011/?read=article_necronautical
Deborah, Poole A. "Rituals of Movement, Rites of Transformation: Pilgrimage and Dance in the Highlands of Cusco, Peru,"in Pilgrimage in Latin America. N. Ross Crumrine and Alan Morinis, New York: Greenwood Press, 1991, pp. 307–338.
Degregori, Nieto. "Los narradores andinos herederos de Arguedas," in *Arguedas y el Perú de Hoy*, edited by Carmen María Pinilla, Gonzalo Portocarrero Maisch, Cecilia Rivera, and Carla Sagástegui. Lima: SUR Casa de Estudios del Socialismo, 2005.
Escajadillo, Tomás. *La narrativa indigenista peruana*. Lima: Amaru Editores, 1994.
Escobar, Alberto, *Cómo leer a Vallejo*. Lima: P.L. Villanueva, 1973.
Feldman, Irina, *Rethinking Community From Peru: The Political Philosophy of José María Arguedas*, University of Pittsburgh Press, 2014.
Flores, Galindo, *La Agonía de Mariátegui: la polémica con la Komintern*, DESCO, 1980.
González, Angulo, and Jorge Luis, "La nueva ley de tierras y el derecho de propiedad de las comunidades campesinas," in *Themis*, 2004, pp 95–100. Available at: http://revistas.pucp.edu.pe/index.php/themis/article/download/11484/12004

González Prada, Manuel. "Conferencia en el Ateneo de Lima" en Sobrevilla" in Manuel González Prada. ¡Los jóvenes a la obra! Textos esenciales, Lima: Fondo Editorial del Congreso del Perú, 2009, pp. 226–227.
González Prada, Manuel, "Discurso en el Politeama," in *Pájinas libres*, edited by Thomas Ward, 1998. Available at: http://evergreen.loyola.edu/tward/www/gp/libros/paginas/pajinas6.html)
González Prada, Manuel, "Nuestros Indios," in *Horas de lucha*, translated by Harold Eugene Davis, in "Our Indians, Latin American Social Thought," Washington: The University Press of Washington, 1961, pp. 339–340.
Gutierrez Girardot, Rafael, *César Vallejo y la Muerte de Dios*. Bogota: Panamericana, 2003.
Hegel, G. W.F. *The Phenomenology of Spirit*, translated by Michael Inwood. New York: Oxford University Press, 2018.
Hermuthová, Jana, "El discurso experimental arguediano, in Jose María en el Corazón de Europa," edited by Klára Schirová, in *José María Arguedas en el corazón de Europa*. Prague: Universidad Carolina de Prada, 2004.
Katscher, Leopold. "Taine – A Literary Portrait," in *The Nineteenth Century*, Vol. XX, Surbiton, UK, 1886, pp. 51–73.
Khan, Sholom J. *Science and Aesthetic Judgment: A Study in Taine's Critical Method*. New York: Columbia University Press, 1953.
Koselleck, Reinhart. *Futures Past – On the Semantics of Historical Time*, translated by Keith Trible. Baskerville: Columbia University Press, 2004.
Kristal, Efraín. *The Andes Viewed from the City: Literary and Political Discourse on the Indian in Peru, 1848–1930*. New York: P. Lang, 1987.
Land, Nick. *Fanged Noumena: Collected Writings 1987–2007*, edited by Robin McKay and Ray Brassier. New York: Urbanomic, 2012.
Land, Nick. *The Thirst for Annihilation: Georges Bataille and Virulent Nihilism*. New York: Routledge, 1992.
Lauer, Mirko. "Rivera Martínez, Edgardo. *País de Jauja*," in *Inti: Revista de literatura hispánica*, no. 48. Lima: Peisa, 1998, pp. 169–172.
Legrás, Horacio. *Literature and Subjection: The Economy of Writing and Marginality in Latin America*. University of Pittsburgh Press, 2008.
Mariátegui, José Carlos. "Aniversario y Balance," in *Amauta*, Vol. 17, 1928. Available at: https://www.marxists.org/espanol/mariateg/1928/sep/aniv.htm
Mariátegui, José Carlos, "Breve Epílogo," in *Variedades*, March 13, 1929. https://www.marxists.org/espanol/mariateg/oc/historia_de_la_crisis_mundial/paginas/breve%20epilogo.htm
Mariátegui, José Carlos, *Correspondencia, 1915–1930*, edited by Antonio Melis. Lima: Empresa Editora Amauta, 1984.
Mariátegui, José Carlos, "El 'Freudismo' en la literatura contemporánea," in *Variedades*, August 14, Lima, 1926. Available at, https://www.marxists.org/espanol/mariateg/oc/el_artista_y_la_epoca/paginas/el%20freudismo.htm
Mariátegui, José Carlos. "El problema de las razas en la América Latina," in *Tesis Ideológicas*, 1929. Available at https://www.marxists.org/espanol/mariateg/oc/ideologia_y_politica/paginas/tesis%20ideologicas.htm
Mariátegui, José Carlos. "El problema de las razas en America Latina," in *Tesis Ideológicas*, my translation. Available at https://www.marxists.org/espanol/mariateg/oc/ideologia_y_politica/paginas/tesis%20ideologicas.htm

Mariátegui, José Carlos, *Estatutos de la Confederación General de Trabajadores del Perú*, 1929. Available at: https://www.marxists.org/espanol/mariateg/oc/ideologia_y_politica/paginas/estatutos.htm

Mariátegui, José Carlos. "Existe una Inquietud Propia, En Nuestra Época," in *Mundial*, March 29, 1930, https://www.marxists.org/espanol/mariateg/oc/el_artista_y_la_epoca/paginas/existe%20una%20inquietud%20propia.htm#1a

Mariátegui, José Carlos. *José Carlos Mariátegui: An Anthology*, edited and translated by Harry E. Vanden and Marc Becker. NYU Press, 2011.

Mariátegui, José Carlos, "La Crisis doctrinal del socialismo," in *La Escena Contemporánea*, 1925. Available at: https://www.marxists.org/espanol/mariateg/oc/figuras_y_aspectos_de_la_vida_iii/paginas/la%20crisis%20doctrinal.htm

Mariátegui, José Carlos. "La economía liberal y la economía socialista," in *Defensa del Marxismo*. Available at: https://www.marxists.org/espanol/mariateg/oc/defensa_del_marxismo/paginas/ix.htm

Mariátegui, José Carlos. "La filosofía moderna y el Marxismo," in *Defensa del Marxismo*, Publisher unnamed, 1974. Available at: https://www.marxists.org/espanol/mariateg/oc/defensa_del_marxismo/paginas/iv.htm

Mariátegui, José Carlos. "La Misión de Israel," in *Mundial*, May 3, 1929, my translation. https://www.marxists.org/espanol/mariateg/oc/figuras_y_aspectos_de_la_vida_iii/paginas/la%20mision.htm#*a

Mariátegui, José Carlos. *Marxist determinism*, translated by Celina María Bragagnolo, 1928, https://www.marxists.org/archive/mariateg/works/1928/marxist-determinism.htm

Mariátegui, José Carlos. "Lo Nacional y lo Exótico," in *Mundial*, December 9, 1924. Available at: https://www.marxists.org/espanol/mariateg/oc/peruanicemos_al_peru/paginas/nacional.htm

Mariátegui, José Carlos. "Presentación de *Amauta*," in *Amauta*, year 1, no. 1, 1926. Available at: https://www.marxists.org/espanol/mariateg/1926/sep/amauta.htm

Mariátegui, José Carlos. "Presentación to El Movimiento Obrero in 1919," in *Amauta*, Lima, 1928.

Mariátegui, José Carlos. "Programa del Partido Socialista Peruano," in *La organización del proletariado*. Comisión Política del Comité Central del Partido Comunista Peruano, 1967. Available at: https://www.marxists.org/espanol/mariateg/1928/oct/07a.htm

Mariátegui, José Carlos. "Prologo" in *Tempestad en Los Andes by Luis*. E Valcarcel, 1927. Available at: https://www.marxists.org/espanol/mariateg/1927/oct/10.htm (my translation.)

Mariátegui, José Carlos, *Seven Interpretative Essays on Peruvian Reality*, translated by Jorge Basadre. Austin: University of Texas Press, 1971.

Mariátegui, José Carlos, *Seven Interpretative Essays on Peruvian Reality*, translated by Marjorie Urquidi. University of Texas Press, 1988. Available at: https://www.marxists.org/archive/mariateg/works/7-interpretive-essays.htm

Mariátegui, José Carlos, *The Heroic and Creative Sense of Socialism*. New Jersey: Humanity Books, 1996.

Martos, Marco and Elsa Villanueva, *Las palabras de Trilce*. Lima: Universidad de San Marcos, 1989.

Marquez, Ismael. "The Andean Novel," in *The Cambridge Companion to the Latin American Novel*, edited by Efraín Kristal. New York: Cambridge University Press, 2005.

Marx, Karl. *Pre-Capitalist Economic Formations*, translated by Cohen. New York: International Publishers, 1964.

Matto de Turner, Clorinda, *Aves sin Nido*. Lima: Biblioteca Ayacucho, 1994
Matto de Turner, Clorinda. *Herencia*. Lima: Impresa Masías-Baquijano, 1895.
Matto de Turner, El *Perú ilustrado: 23 de Noviembre de 1889*. London: Forgotten Books, 2017.
Meillassoux, Quentin, "The Divine Inexistence," in *Quentin Meillassoux: Philosophy in the Making*, edited by Graham Harman. Edinburgh: Edinburgh University Press, 2011.
Moran, Dominic. "The Author's Favorite, But is it Any Good? Some Thoughts on El Palco Estrecho," in *Politics, Poetics, Affects: Re-visioning César Vallejo*, edited by Stephen Hart. Newcastle: Cambridge, 2013, pp. 67–87.
Moreiras, Alberto. *The Exhaustion of Difference: The Politics of Latin American Cultural Studies*. Durham & London: Duke University Press, 2001.
Ortega, Julio. "Prologue" to critical edition of *Trilce*. Madrid: Cátedra, 1993.
Ortega, Julio. *Teoría poética de César Vallejo*. Providence: Del Sol, 1986.
Rama, Ángel. *La ciudad letrada*. Ediciones del Norte, 1984.
Rama, Ángel. "Los Procesos de transculturación en la narrativa latinoamericana," in *Revista de Literatura Hispanoamericana*, no. 5, Maracaibo, 1974.
Rama, Ángel. *Transculturación narrativa en América Latina*. Siglo XXI, Buenos Aires, 1982.
Rama, Ángel, *Writing Across Cultures: Narrative Transculturation in Latin America*, edited and translated by David Frye. Durham and London: Duke University Press, 2012.
Rivera Martínez, Edgardo. "Jauja: Ciudad de Fuego. Conversación con Edgardo Rivera Martínez," in Lienzo no. 24, 2003. Full interview Available at: https://revistas.ulima.edu.pe/index.php/lienzo/article/viewFile/1135/1088
Rivera Martínez, Edgardo. *País de Jauja*. Lima: La Voz, 1993.
Rochabrún, Guillermo. "Las trampas del pensamiento: Una lectura de la mesa redonda sobre *Todas las sangres*," in *La Mesa Redonda sobre Todas las Sangres del 23 de Junio de 1965*, edited by Guillermo Rochabrún. Lima: Pontificia Universidad Católica del Perú, 2000.
Romero Romaña, Eleodoro. *Derechos Reales*, Vol. II, Second edition, Lima: Editorial Pontificia Universidad Católica del Perú, 1993.
Rowe, William, *Ensayos Arguedianos*. Lima: Casa de estudios SUR, 1996.
Rowe, William. "Reading Arguedas' Foxes," in *The Fox From Up Above, The Fox From Down Below*, translated by Frances Horning Barraclough. Pittsburgh: Pittsburgh University Press, 2011.
Rowe, William. "The Political in *Trilce*," in *Politics, Poetics, Affects: Re-visioning César Vallejo*, edited by Stephen M. Hart. Cambridge: Cambridge Scholars Publishing, 2013, pp. 3–19.
Sanborn, Cynthia A., Verónica Hurtado, and Tania Ramírez, "La consulta previa en el Perú: avances y retos," in *Diario Uno*, August 10, 2016. Available at http://diariouno.pe/2016/08/10/fa-presenta-proyecto-de-ley-para-mejorar-consulta-previa/
Schirová, Klára. "Todas las Sangres – la utopía peruana," in *José María Arguedas en el corazón de Europa*. Pardubice: Universidad Carolina de Praga, 2004.
Scorza, Manuel. *La danza inmóvil*. Madrid: Siglo XXI de España Editores, 1991.
Secada, Pablo. "Que se vayan todos los corruptos," in *La República*, December 20, 2017. Available at: http://larepublica.pe/politica/1160278-marcha-que-se-vayan-todos-los-corruptos-colectivos-salen-a-las-calles-este-miercoles-en-vivo
Sherman, Adam. "Vallejo Fragments," in *Politics, Poetics, Affects: Re-visioning César Vallejo*. edited by Stephen Hart. Cambridge: Cambridge Scholars Publishing, 2013, pp. 89–100.
Schirová, Klára. *Todas las Sangres – La utopía Peruana*, in *José María Arguedas in el corazón de Europa*, Prague: Universidad Carolina de Praga, 2004.

Sicard, Alain. "La dialéctica de la carencia en la poesía de César Vallejo," in *Zama*, Francia: Universidad de Poitiers, 2016, pp. 109–115. http://revistascientificas.filo.uba.ar/index.php/zama/article/view/3091/2732

Sobrevilla, David, "La visión del mito en José Carlos Mariátegui, Mariano Iberico y Luis Alberto Sánchez," in *Escritos Mariáteguianos*. Lima: Universidad Inca Garcilaso de la Vega, 2012.

Spitta, Silvia. *Between Two Waters: Narratives of Transculturation in Latin America*. Texas: Rice University Press, 1995.

Srnicek, Nick, and Alex Williams. *Inventing the Future: Postcapitalism and a World Without Work*. London: Verso, 2015.

Tanaka, Martín, *Reflexiones a propósito de la nueva edición de Clases, Estado y nación en el Perú, de Julio Cotler*. Instituto de Estudios Peruanos, 2005. Available at: https://www.scribd.com/doc/9295942/Reflexiones-a-proposito-de-la-nueva-edicion-de-Clases-Estado-y-nacion-en-el-Peru-de-Julio-Cotler

Terra Rodrigues, Cassiano, and Daniel Campos. "Originality and Resistance in Latin American Culture," in *Inter-American Journal of Philosophy*, Vol. I, no. I, 2016. https://ijp.tamu.edu/wp-content/uploads/2016/03/Rodrigues_and_Campos-Originality_and_Resistance_in_Latin_American_Culture.pdf

Ubilluz, Juan Carlos. *La Venganza del Indio: Ensayos de interpretación por lo real en la narrativa indigenista*. Lima: Fondo de Cultura Económica, 2017.

Vallejo, César. *Desde Europa: crónicas y artículos*, edited by Jorge Puccinelli, Ediciones Fuente de Cultura Peruana, 1987.

Vallejo, César. El arte y la revolución. Mosca Azúl Editored, Lima, 1973.

Vallejo, César. "El crepúsculo de las águilas," in *Mundial*, December 17, Lima, 1926.

Vallejo, César. "El espíritu y hecho comunista," in *Mundial*, no. 429, August 31, Lima, 1928.

Vallejo, César. *El Tungsteno*. Lima: Edición Cultura Universitaria, 1932.

Vallejo, César. *Epistolario general*. Madrid: Lectorum Pubns, 1982.

Vallejo, César. "Las lecciones del Marxismo," in *Variedades*, no. 1090, Lima, January 19, 1929.

Vallejo, César. *Letter to José Carlos Mariátegui*, December 10, 1926, my translation. Available at: https://www.marxists.org/espanol/vallejo/cartamar.htm

Vallejo, César. *Rusia en 1931*. Madrid: Lingkua Digital, 2014.

Vallejo, César. *The Complete Poetry: A Bilingual Edition*, edited and translated by Clayton Eschleman. Berkeley & Los Angeles: University of California Press, 2007.

Vargas Llosa, Mario, *Interview in El Mundo*, April 2, 2003. Available at: http://www.salman-psl.com/peruanos-en-madrid/n_11.html

Vargas Llosa, Mario, *Interview with RNW*, November 12 2009. Available at https://www.youtube.com/watch?v=z3G34Ea5c-c

Vargas Llosa, Mario. *La utopía arcaica*. Madrid: Fondo de Cultura Económica, 1997.

Vargas Llosa, Mario. *La utopía arcaica: José María Arguedas y las ficciones del indigenismo*. Alfaguara, 2008.

Vilas, Carlos M., and Richard Stoller. "Lynchings and Political Conflict in the Andes," *Latin American Perspectives*, Vol. 35, no. 5, Riverside, 2008, pp. 103–118.

Williams, Alex, and Srnicek Nick. *Inventing the Future: Postcapitalism and a World Without Work*, Verso, 2015.

Zalamea, Fernando. *Ariel y Arisbe: evolución y evaluación del concepto de América Latina en el siglo XX*. Bogotá: convenio Andrés Bello, 2000.

Žižek, Slavoj. "Beyond Discourse-Analysis," in *Reflections of Our Time*, edited by Ernesto Laclau. New York: Verso, 1990, pp. 249–60.

INDEX

acculturation 12, 123–26, 124n19, 135–36, 147, 164, 170
aesthetics: colonial 33, 39; modernist 68, 80; *modernista* 77–79; social realist 33–35; of transmutation 87–96
Agamben, Giogio 144n58
agony, agonic 48, 107, 141, 161
Alegría, Ciro 2n9, 4n12, 120n11, 123, 127, 133, 166
Amauta 34, 42, 44n48, 45–46, 53, 56
ancestralism 20, 48, 50, 59, 70–71, 76, 79–80, 120–22, 124n19, 140, 152, 183
Andes 118, 128n25, 142n53, 154n82
anxiety 77, 94, 108, 180–81, 186, 194
Aragón, Luis 56–57
Aréstegui, Narciso 1, 1n2, 1n4
Arguedas, José María: and indigenismo 2n9, 4n12, 19–20, 113–73, 152n79; and socialism 150–51, 160–61; and universalism 113–15, 155–61
Atusparia 15
authoritarian 21, 148, 173, 175–77, 181, 188

Badiou, Alain 6n16, 26n5, 44, 51–52, 60–65, 78–79, 86n16, 86–87, 94–95, 106–8, 173–83
barbarism 8, 30, 134–35, 143–49
Barbusse, Henri 41n40, 41–42, 46, 53
Baudelaire, Charles 75n9, 77
Belaunde, Victor A. 121
Belaunde Terry, Fernando 167n3
Bosteels, Bruno 6, 52, 54n66, 173, 179, 181
Bourdieu, Pierre 50
Brassier, Ray 178n15, 187–88
Bryce Echenique, Alfredo 169
Burneo de la Rocha, Zulema 190

Campos, Daniel 5n14

capitalism 41, 48, 54–61, 71, 85–86, 93, 97–99, 114, 140–60, 162–66, 180–88, 193–95
Castro Arenas, Mario 1n3
Chile 7
civilization 8–10, 27, 42, 57–58, 64, 134, 143–44
Clayton, Michelle 70, 76, 81, 88n20, 99
colonialism 3, 30, 31n17, 33
Colonida 31–32
communism 55, 61, 93, 107, 186–87; agrarian 37, 54, 59; generic 176; poetry 71, 107–8
contradiction: fundamental and principal 60–63; between Indian and mestizo 19, 38; between proletariat and bourgeoise 24, 54
Cornejo Polar, Antonio 2, 7, 125, 125n21, 141n51, 175
Cortázar, Julio 115–18
costumbrismo 9–10
creative antagonism 6, 17, 24–49, 53, 57, 91, 182
creole 2n2
Critchley, Simon 186n22
critique: of ideology 42–43; of liberalism 12–17; of revolutionary politics 21, 165, 175–77; of violence 177–83; of western culture 76
Cuzco 9n21, 11, 14, 78, 98

death: of God 74; of man 76–83, 89
Degregori, Nieto 2n9
destiny: mankind 69, 106–7; national 48; of revolutionary 16, 18, 69, 78, 103; of the rural Indian 18, 25, 31, 71
destruction 61–62, 78, 91–95, 154, 180–83
dialectics 18, 23–25n4, 33, 34, 37, 40, 43–47, 49–52, 59–60, 62–66, 64n77,

72–73, 90–91, 109, 120–21, 129, 141, 179, 180, 184–85
Diez Canseco, José 189
dogmatism 42–45, 63, 71, 90, 93–95, 127, 173–74

economicism 17, 19–20, 37
Eguren, José María 32
eloquence 107, 155, 160
ethics, ethical: cooperativist 122, 146–47, 150, 170; ethical turn 21, 173–83; liberal 29–30, 38–39, 98–99
existential: crisis 19, 36, 69, 74, 79–80, 96; resolution 18, 86, 90

faith: in Arguedas 144; in Mariátegui 37, 39–40, 43, 45, 62–63; in Vallejo 90, 91
fanatism 90, 127, 142, 179
Favre, Henri 152
Feldman, Irina 141n51, 142n52, 144n58, 147n65, 149n71
Ferreira, César 171n8
figuration: of revolutionary subject 63–65, 89, 96, 130, 152, 161
finitude 18, 36, 69, 72–80, 85, 102–12
Flores Galindo, Alberto C. 44–47, 55, 93, 161
Freud, Sigmund 42–44, 51

gamonalismo 36, 38, 54–56, 60, 97, 131, 135, 149
González Prada, Manuel 4, 7–16, 28–33, 98, 182, 191
The Great Uprising of the South 15
Gutierrez Girardot, Rafael 4n12, 68–69

hacendados 30, 143n55
Haya de la Torre, Víctor Raúl 41n40
Hegel, G.W.F 179–80
heresy 18, 40, 72, 74, 83–89, 103, 111, 117
hermeneutics 51, 77, 122n15
hermetism 80–83
Hermuthová, Jana 130, 130n29, 130n30
Hidalgo, Alberto 32
humanism 8, 9, 11–14, 20, 37, 83, 85, 165, 168–77

idealism: in indigenista literature 27, 30, 32–33; in philosophy 176–85
indianismo 5, 25, 37, 49
indigenismo: after Arguedas 163–83; for Arguedas 117–21, 126, 133, 161; definition 1–3; for Mariátegui 24–27,

34–41; for Marquez 49n60, 49–51; *neoindigenismo* 50n60, 166n2; for Vallejo 67–70
indigenous: cooperativism 49, 57, 60, 66, 102, 113, 149, 161; culture 50n60, 114, 118, 120n11, 123, 125–26, 136, 152, 163, 182–84; literature 25–27, 45, 50n60, 51, 64, 66–67; problem of the Indian 5, 12, 30–31, 34–35, 38, 58, 69, 115, 129, 133, 189; world 19, 120n11, 140, 171
intelligence 44n48, 46, 146; active 41–42

Jauja 20, 120n11, 169–77
jaylli 117

Katscher, Leopold 30n13
Killac 9n21, 11
Kommintern 55, 93n28
Koselleck, Reinhart 3

Laclau, Ernesto 183
Land, Nick 155, 183
latifundio 12, 16, 31, 57, 59, 61, 64, 114, 142–43, 149, 163–69, 182–85
Latin America: culture 124; intellectuals 25n4, 114–16, 124n18; Marxism 6–7
Lauer, Mirko 172
Lenin, Vladimir. 23, 55, 87, 90, 93, 175–76
Lima 33, 127, 169
Lima, Lezama 117

magical: and rational conception of the world, for Arguedas 19, 113, 119, 146, 151, 156, 163, 164, 187; realism 50n60
Mariátegui, José Carlos: critique of ancestralism 28–32; critique of liberalism 12–18, 28–33; dialectical philosophy 17, 24, 32–43; on *indigenismo* 2, 5–8, 23–28; on socialism 26, 43
Marquez, Ismael 3n10, 49n60, 50n60, 166, 167n4, 171n8
Martinez de la Torre, Ricardo 44n48
Marx, Karl 41n39, 42, 47, 51, 54n66, 66, 90, 175–76, 180, 186
Marxism 6, 14, 61, 185–88; for Arguedas 185–88; in Mariátegui 18, 40–47, 52, 55; retrospective 6; for Vallejo 88–90
Matto de Turner, Clorinda 1, 7, 9–11, 98
Meillassoux, Quentin 110, 111
Mendoza, Veronika 189

metaphysics 8, 35, 181; metaphysical protest in Vallejo 35, 71–73, 80, 109, 133
modernism, modernist 4n12, 33, 44, 50n60, 69
modernismo 28n9, 77–79, 81
modernity, modern, modernizing: alternative 3, 30, 65, 114, 147, 154, 163, 166, 170, 173, 194; capitalist 20, 29, 32, 48, 59, 98, 119, 142, 153, 155–57, 169–71, 182; and tradition 4
Moreiras, Alberto 155–56
myth, mythos 49; in Arguedas 132, 134–37, 147, 149, 156, 158; in Mariátegui 37, 39–41, 62–64, 70; in Vallejo 89–90, 101

nation, nationalism 16, 46, 88, 99, 115–16, 128, 171, 187, 189
negation, negativity: in Arguedas 143; in Badiou 182; in Mariátegui 46–48, 62–65; in Vallejo 74, 89, 94
Nietzsche, Friedrich 31
nihilism 31, 36, 39, 85, 144, 180–82, 184–85
nostalgia 28, 29, 31n18, 35; of absence 71–79; ancestralist 28, 31, 31n18, 35, 48, 113; for what is to come 78, 80, 81, 106–9

oligarchy: capitalist 156, 163–64; landlord 2, 7–8, 11–13, 16, 20, 30, 55, 97–99, 114, 121, 131–32, 139, 142–46, 163
ontology 103, 110, 174; of democratic materialism 174; of the Indian 27
Ortega, Julio 81–82
Ortiz, Fernando 122

Palma, Ricardo 2, 9
pasadismo 30, 35, 71
peasant 54–59, 64, 121, 185, 185n21
perricholismo 30, 35, 71
Poole, Deborah 151n76
pragmatism, pragmatic 20, 39, 42, 50, 80, 88n20, 114, 130, 142, 143, 146, 148, 172
primitivism 137
production, productivity: cultural 1n1, 2, 24, 27, 33, 49n60, 55, 169; forces and means of 60; intellectual 17, 23, 87, 106, 115; literary 6, 31, 49, 49n60, 114, 166; mode of 21, 24, 28, 42, 58, 140, 149–50, 163–65, 180, 182, 184–87, 194

productivism 21, 59, 114, 153, 165, 184–86, 194–95
proletariat: in Badiou 44, 61–63; and bourgeoisie 24, 54, 55, 60–61; Indian subject 17, 20–21, 39, 42, 55, 56–60, 63–66, 96–101, 108, 112, 121, 143, 161; for Marx 45, 49, 92; revolution 17, 23

rabble of culture 20, 155, 159, 161, 184
race 10, 15, 18, 30n13, 36, 56, 67, 70, 71, 79, 106, 125, 141, 176
Rama, Ángel 2, 19, 25n4, 113, 120n11, 121n12, 122n15, 122–26, 154–55
rational, rationalism 29; and magical conception of the world in Arguedas 19, 20, 113–14, 119, 143, 146–48, 150–51, 153, 158, 161, 164, 169, 187; in Mariátegui 29, 33, 39; in Vallejo 95
realism, realist: for Arguedas 120; critical realism 177; effect of realism 50, 5n15; epistemic antirealism 35; in Mariátegui's dialectical materialism 12, 36–37, 49, 63, 65; relative realism 5; social 9, 25, 173; in Vallejo 81
recollection 102, 124n18
relativism 42, 63
religion, religious: in Arguedas 158; as socialist philosophy in Mariátegui 38, 40, 44; in Vallejo 103, 104
Republic: Aristocratic 31; state 54
restoration 1, 35, 59, 119, 148
resurrection 35, 109, 110
revolution: in Arguedas 114, 127, 130, 132, 134, 137, 140, 141, 148, 151–54, 160–61; artistic 34; Indian 16, 65, 133, 137, 140, 141; in Mariátegui 41, 42, 47, 63; mestizo 15, 16, 65, 170; poetry and art 78, 88, 91, 94; politics 6, 16, 17–18, 23, 25, 29n13, 32–33, 39, 54n66, 55, 66, 93–96, 171, 175, 178, 183; postrevolutionary 20, 164–65, 166–71; priests of the revolution 40; proletariat 17, 23, 57n70, 65, 99; revolutionary subject 3, 5, 19, 21, 31, 32, 38, 39, 43, 45, 61, 65, 71, 89, 94–96, 108, 113, 134, 137, 165, 171–75, 180, 182; socialist and liberal 33; Soviet 88, 91–92; for Vallejo 91, 94–95
Ribeyro, Julio Ramón 167
Rivera Martínez, Edgardo 20, 165–73, 177
Rochabrun, Guillermo 120n10, 152–53
Romero Romaña, Eleodoro 191n30

Rowe, William 85–86, 103, 104, 108, 136, 151, 155, 159
Rumi Maqui 15

Salazar Bondy, Sebastian 152
Sanborn, Cynthia A. 192n33
Schirová, Klára 141
Scorza, Manuel 20, 167–68
secular, secularism: Intelligence 20, 146, 148; in relation to myth, faith, spirituality, and teleology 40, 62, 89, 143, 147, 150, 160
Shining Path, The 165, 167n3, 168, 172, 174, 188
Sicard, Alain 72, 72n5, 73, 74
Sobrevilla, David 39
socialism, socialist: after Arguedas 164, 166, 168–71, 172, 175–78; for Arguedas 113–14, 118, 142, 153, 161; in indigenista literature 4–6, 21, 165, 167, 168–73, 175–78; for Mariátegui 14–16, 18, 23–26, 30–33, 37, 40–50, 52–55, 57–60, 183; Peruvian 5–7, 12, 17, 18, 52–55, 57–60, 165, 183, 184, 185–94; in philosophy 4, 14, 17, 18, 30, 37, 183; for Vallejo 70, 88–97, 101–2, 106, 108, 112
Solitude: in Bryce Echenique 169; in Vallejo 36, 74, 89, 108
Sorel, George 39, 40, 43, 64n77, 89
Spitta, Silvia 123n17
Srnicek, Nick 183
synthesis 28, 94, 122, 123, 141, 149, 150, 171, 175, 195

teleology, teleological 25, 75, 140, 147, 155, 195
telluric 4n12, 68, 114, 134, 183
Terra Rodrigues, Cassiano 5n14
theology, theological, atheological 8, 9, 38, 63, 89
theory: of contradiction 60, 63; and practice 23, 25, 39, 41, 42, 49, 51, 52, 93–95, 100, 103, 104, 108, 183, 184; and revision 40, 52, 91, 194
transculturation 2, 19, 20, 113–14, 122–26, 134, 140–41, 145–46, 151–53, 156, 158–59, 161, 163–66, 169–73, 175, 177, 184–85, 187, 195
transmutation (aesthetics of) 18, 87, 94–96, 102, 194

trauma: in relation to the War of the Pacific 7; in response to subversive violence 165; of the unconscious in psychoanalysis 43

Ubilluz, Juan Carlos 15, 17, 133, 173–74, 179
universality, universalism: after Arguedas 175, 183, 194–95; in Arguedas 19, 113–15, 118, 128–30, 160, 173–74, 175, 184; in Mariátegui 42, 63, 174; and regionalism 4, 4n12, 19, 124n18, 128; and utopia 21, 177, 195; in Vallejo 18, 19, 68–71, 88n20, 89, 92–96, 104, 106, 108, 110, 112
utopia, utopian: anti-utopianism 172, 174–78, 186–87; in *indigenista* literature 3, 9, 16, 17, 24, 25, 65, 102, 141, 154, 154n82, 155, 165, 167, 174, 195; *La utopía arcaica* 4n12, 21; the liberal utopia 178, 179, 194; in socialism 20, 40–42, 110, 165, 167, 168, 171, 174–78, 183, 187–89

Valcarcel, Luis E. 16, 40, 64
Vallejo, César: and existential despair 70, 72, 74–77, 82–87; and *indigenismo* 16, 18–19, 76, 102–4; and Mariátegui 34–37, 40, 42, 49, 67; materialist poetics 80–87; and socialism 69, 70, 87–112; and universalism 68, 69, 71, 103, 106–11
Vargas Llosa, Mario 2, 4n12, 21, 167n4, 175–76, 178
Vasconcelos, José 125
Velasco Alvarado, Juan 153, 163, 167, 169
Vilas, Carlos 168
vitalism 31, 42, 96, 104, 131, 148
voluntarism, voluntarist 43, 44, 63, 107, 182

world: capitalist 187; rural indigenous 2n9, 9, 11, 26, 35, 53, 71, 75, 78, 102, 113–14, 119–20, 140, 166, 171; urban 9, 120n11, 139; worldview 135, 144, 155, 161

yanaconazgo 59

Zalamea, Fernando 4n13
Žižek, Slavoj 21, 173, 178, 185

www.ingramcontent.com/pod-product-compliance
Lightning Source LLC
Chambersburg PA
CBHW021141230426
43667CB00005B/213